Maybe Next Year

MAYBE NEXT YEAR

*Long-Suffering Sports Fans and the
Teams That Never Deliver*

Greg Pearson

McFarland & Company, Inc., Publishers
Jefferson, North Carolina

ISBN (print) 978-1-4766-6679-2
ISBN (ebook) 978-1-4766-2730-4

LIBRARY OF CONGRESS CATALOGUING DATA ARE AVAILABLE

British Library cataloguing data are available

Front cover: Exterior of Wrigley Field
(photograph by Matt Brown)

Manufactured in the United States of America

*McFarland & Company, Inc., Publishers
Box 611, Jefferson, North Carolina 28640
www.mcfarlandpub.com*

To Dee Pearson, who loved her UConn Huskies
To Craig Pearson, who loved every underdog he ever met
To Deedy Pearson Johnson, who loved her daughters

Table of Contents

Acknowledgments

There are many people to thank for this book. Some had a direct role; others provided inspiration, past and present.

My wife, Michele Bannister, listened, edited and offered suggestions. Tom Riggs provided valuable and careful copy editing.

My brother, Jonathan Pearson, as always was supportive and helpful.

The many people I interviewed were generous with their time as they answered questions about painful playoff losses and disappointing seasons. Their reminiscences were poignant, funny, sad, and sentimental, but almost all contained at least a tinge of never-say-die optimism.

A special thanks to Liz Young, who helped with questions on photos.

Others who helped: Melanie Jones at Harry Caray's Restaurant Group; Laura Armstrong of the *Toronto Star*; Jenny Callaghan; Brittany Meckelborg; Kelly's Bleachers in Milwaukee; Field House American Sports Pub in Sacramento; Coaches Sports Bar & Grill in Houston; Wizards Sports Café in Richardson, Texas; Chickie's and Pete's in Philadelphia; Glory Days Grill in Towson, Maryland; Holy Grail Tavern and Grille in Cincinnati; Kings Oak in Philadelphia; the Redmond, Washington, city clerk's office; the Mercer Island, Washington, city clerk's office.

Those who have helped along the way: Charles and Donna Pearson, Phyllis Amato, Warren Johnson and Diane Tribbett, Hana and Tim Lasell and lovely Lucy Kaylana, Julia Johnson-Viola and Mike Viola, the late Vinnie Amato and Bill and Trudy Pearson, and all of the Pearson, Amato, Carlson and Ahlberg clans.

From high school and my hometown of Durham, Connecticut: Wally and Judy Camp, Evelyn Cocores, Don Gates, Bill Wamester, Judy Yeston, Mike Baruschke, Jennie Stevens Marsh, Cyndi Berten Blackwelder, Anne Kerschner Schubert, Bonnie Jean Hill, Janet Ackerman, Don Ackerman, Jack Stahl, Lisa Larsen, Betsy Lyman Bascom, Becca Cook Vines, Sam Gerber, Kerry Monroe, Skip Pearce, Joel Otte.

From college days: Ed Franklin, Manny Faria, Linwood Putney, Ellen Cohane DePalma.

From Manchester, Connecticut: Sue Vaughn Harris and the late, great Tom Vaughn, Doug Bevins, Charlie Maynard and the late Alex Girelli.

From Holyoke, Massachusetts: Bob Unger and Barbara LeBlanc Unger, Bill Zajac, Ronni Gordon, Diane Lederman, Sue Eaton, Bill Eager, Miriam Disman, Barry Werth.

From Milwaukee: Bill Windler, Marybeth Jacobson, Karen Samelson, John Schumacher, Dan Kwas, Bob Helbig, Enrique Rodriguez, Marty Kaiser, Verne McDoniels, Pete Sullivan, Ron Smith, Anne Klemm and John Podsedly, Barbara Zack Quindel, Darren Carroll, Tom Silverstein, Cindy Eggert Johnson, Jim Lynch, Dave Vogel, Bob Friday, Dennis Black, Jen and Ben Steele, Mabel Wong, Kent Lowry, Kathy Schenck, Chris Foran, Louann Schoenberg, Alec Dobson, Amy Rodenburg Maillet and Jeff Maillet, Joanne Weintraub, Tom Kertscher, Tom Tolan, Russ Maki and Amy Rinard, Annysa and Mike Johnson, Georgia Pabst, Jim Higgins, Dave Kallmann, Jan Uebelherr, Dave Umhoefer, Tom Held, Ernie Franzen, Berford Gammon, Sonya Jongsma Knauss, Mark Johnson and Mary-Liz Shaw, Larry Sandler, Mary Louise Schumacher, those Cubs diehards Meg Kissinger and Cary Spivak, and the never-to-be-forgotten Don Walker.

Preface

Most sports fans go through the three stages of devotion. There are the early years when you root with the wild optimism of youth, no matter how bad your team is. The players likely are your heroes, and you can't figure out why a team so good always finishes in next-to-last place.

The late teens and 20s are filled with distractions—girlfriends or boyfriends, high school, college, landing a job, starting a family. You still root hard; it's just more difficult to find the time.

In the third stage, you settle into the true test of fandom. You've lost some of that youthful optimism, and all those next-to-last-place finishes have perhaps made you a tad cynical. Still, there you are—watching the ninth inning in late September when your team is hopelessly out of it; remaining in your seat, hoping a 20-point deficit somehow will disappear in the last 2 minutes of the game.

I've often wondered what it is that keeps fans going through all the bad times. How and why do fans remain devoted after lousy seasons and crushing playoff defeats? I know those feelings well. As a New England native, I started rooting for the Boston Red Sox in 1961 when I was 6. I cheered them on through some terrible seasons; I cheered even louder when they got good but then found inconceivable ways to lose in the post-season. Of course, all those painful moments were worth it when 2004 came around, not to mention 2007 and 2013. Three World Series titles in a decade are more than most fans can imagine.

Teams like the Red Sox and Chicago Cubs have received plenty of publicity for their dry spells, but fans of other teams have suffered, with much less media coverage. Those in this book haven't gotten to experience the elation of a championship in a long time, if ever.

I spent 14 months interviewing more than 100 fans who are waiting for a winner. I wanted to talk to them about how they've hung in there through the lean years and the near misses. One quality struck me again and again. Optimism invariably outweighed negativity.

The guidelines I set are simple. I focused on teams that haven't won a championship in 40 years or more, figuring that covers a couple of generations. I mostly stuck to teams that have been in the same city for that entire time. The notable exception is the Sacramento Kings, a team that moved to the California capital in 1985. I wanted to include the Kings because the fans united to help keep the team in Sacramento.

Of course, by the time you read this, there's a chance one of the teams I've included in this book has broken its championship drought. If so, just remember how deserving those fans are, and how true their words were as they spoke during a time of longing for their own version of sports euphoria.

Interviews were conducted from January 2015 through February 2016. Biographical information—including occupations and ages when mentioned—were current at the time of the subject's interview. Some interviews were done in person; others were done by telephone; a few were conducted via email.

Most fans spoke in great detail about specific plays or games. Many displayed a precise memory of those moments. Descriptions of games or specific plays, as well as team statistics and player statistics, were verified at the following websites: www.hockey-reference.com; www.baseball-reference.com; www.basketball-reference.com; www.pro-football-reference.com; www.sports-reference.com; www.baseball-almanac.com www.laketheposts.com; www.mlb.com; www.nfl.com; www.nhl.com; www.nba.com; and www.youtube.com. In some cases, team or school websites also were consulted for verification.

Other research sources were the *New York Times*, *Milwaukee Journal Sentinel*, *Toronto Star*, *Chicago Tribune*, *Seattle Times*, *Houston Chronicle*, *Vancouver Sun* and fans.clevelandbrowns.com.

Introduction

Let's face it, we all want to be winners. Whether it's fighting for a job promotion, buying a lottery ticket or rooting for our favorite team, we dream of coming out on top.

So what is it that keeps sports fans coming back for more—year after year—when their teams lose? These fans speak of this being the year, of rookie phenoms and veterans putting together career years. But, again and again, the result is the same—another year without a championship.

Sure, some seasons are better than others. There are near misses, such as Scott Norwood's field goal veering wide right, resulting in the first of four straight Super Bowl losses for the Buffalo Bills. Then there are sheer disasters—the Denver Nuggets' 11–71 record in 1997–98, anyone?

Through it all, the fans show their loyalty, shelling out big money for season tickets, hoping this really will be the year. Such devotion can have many roots—family tradition, geographic ties, good old-fashioned stubbornness, a strong sense of pride.

"There's that real badge of honor of sticking with something when it doesn't come easily," said Dr. Edward R. Hirt, a professor of psychology at Indiana University whose research includes investigating the psychological and social aspects of fandom. "How much do you want this? It reflects positively on you. It shows you're truly committed."

Hirt sees the bond among sports fans as something that isn't easily duplicated in today's splintered society. That bond brings fans together to celebrate victories, but it can be just as strong when rooting for a loser.

"There's this perverse feeling that we suffered through it together. We made it. We're such great fans," Hirt said. "It's like going through boot camp together."

That loyalty factor plays a strong role for many, said Dr. Eric A. Zillmer, who has written extensively about sports psychology and is a professor of neuropsychology at Drexel University, where he also serves as athletic director. "It's our need to believe in something or to belong to something. A sports team is easy to access.... That need for group identification isn't easy to give up," he said.

When fans discuss their devotion, they echo the words of Hirt and Zillmer. As Matt Verderame said about his team, the Kansas City Chiefs, "They can't do anything to shake us." Brian Bernardoni, a longtime supporter of the Chicago Cubs, explained it simply: "In life, you've got to stand for something."

Susan Gemmett, a fan of the Buffalo Bills, put it this way: "It's the whole thing about the team—the little engine that could. You hope one day they'll get over the mountain. You want to be there when that happens."

This book takes a look at these fans who keep coming back for more. Their teams—whether it's the Toronto Maple Leafs in hockey, the San Diego Padres in baseball or the Cleveland Browns in football—haven't won a championship in a long time, if ever. Their supporters sit in the stands through the 2–14 seasons, then suffer the heartbreak of a tough postseason loss after a 14–2 season.

These are fans who have had to watch relatively new arrivals—such as a baseball team in Miami and a hockey team in Anaheim—win championships while the wait for their teams' title seasons goes on and on. These are the folks who have St. Jude, the patron saint of lost causes, as their team mascot.

And maybe if he was still alive, Casey Stengel could be their manager. Stengel had great success in baseball, winning a World Series as a player with the New York Giants and seven as the manager of the New York Yankees. But he also knew a little bit about losing, finishing his baseball career as manager of the New York Mets for their first 3½ feeble seasons of existence.

Stengel once offered this thought, a mantra for frustrated fans everywhere: "Without losers, where would the winners be?"

Of Wrigley Field
and Billy Goats

The Chicago Cubs

Brian Bernardoni has a box he keeps sealed tight with silver duct tape. It is marked "Do Not Open." Inside are newspapers with stories from the 2003 baseball playoffs.

The year 2003 is to Cubs fans what 1912 is to the *Titanic*. In the eighth inning of Game 6 of the 2003 National League Championship Series, the Cubs had a 3–0 lead—five outs from the World Series. Mark Prior, a 23-year-old rising star who had gone 18–6 with a 2.43 ERA that season, was on the mound, efficiently dispatching Florida Marlins hitters. Then, after an uncaught foul ball and a crucial error, it all came crashing down. The Marlins scored eight runs in the eighth inning to win. The next day they won again, eliminating the Cubs.

"The stars were lined up. It's hard to talk about. It was ours," Bernardoni said. "Everything that was supposed to happen was lined up. You see it all unravel. It's horrible and it's painful. That probably taught me about foreboding."

It's just one of the moments of pain for a fan base that has been waiting since Teddy Roosevelt was president for a World Series championship—the longest dry spell of any pro team in the United States.

The Cubs dominated in their early days, winning six National League pennants in the last quarter of the 19th century and then appearing in three straight World Series from 1906 to 1908, winning the last two with key contributions from pitchers Orval Overall and Three Finger Brown. Both times they beat Ty Cobb and the Detroit Tigers.

"What are we going to say—yeah, we were great when Thomas Edison was around?" Bernardoni said.

The Cubs did have their moments in the post–Edison years. The 1938 team was in third place on September 4, seven games behind the front-running Pittsburgh Pirates. The Cubs chipped away at the lead and trailed by just one-half game as they met the Pirates at Wrigley Field on September 28.

As they came to bat in the ninth inning, the Cubs were tied with the Pirates. Darkness was settling over the park, meaning there wasn't much time left to win the game in an era long before lights at Wrigley.

After the first two Cubs batters were retired, catcher Gabby Hartnett came to the plate in the dim light and belted a homer into the left-center field seats. The 6–5 win moved the Cubs into first place, a position they wouldn't relinquish the rest of the way. Hartnett's game-winning clout became known as "The Homer in the Gloamin.'"

Including that 1938 team, the Cubs made the World Series seven times from 1910 to 1945. They lost each time—twice to the New York Yankees, Detroit Tigers and Philadelphia Athletics and once to the Boston Red Sox.

"I think any Cubs fan in 1945, if you had said you won't get there again for 70 years, they would have laughed at you," said Al Yellon, a Chicago resident who writes about the Cubs at www.bleedcubbieblue.com.

Yellon and Bernardoni share a similar childhood memory. They both got hooked on the Cubs by watching broadcasts of day games at Wrigley Field on Chicago's WGN.

"At that age, you think everybody could do this," said Yellon, whose pre-teen years coincided with the Cubs getting good in the late 1960s. They were 59–103 in 1966. The next season they went 87–74, the first of six straight winning seasons, with a team fueled by stars Ernie Banks, Ron Santo, Billy Williams and Ferguson Jenkins.

Bernardoni grew up on the southwest side of Chicago, prime territory for the White Sox. His parents were divorced and he lived with his dad, who worked second shift. Bernardoni came home from school to a house that was empty except for the Cubs games that filled the television screen during baseball season.

The team and those broadcasts meant so much to Bernardoni that in 1998 he attended the funeral of Jack Brickhouse, the legendary Cubs announcer, and shared a few words with Brickhouse's widow, Pat.

"I told her, 'Jack babysat me all through my childhood,'" Bernardoni said. Eight years later, Pat Brickhouse gave a toast at Bernardoni's wedding.

Bernardoni is too young to remember 1969, but Yellon was in his prime, youthful rooting years. For much of the season it was a great run for Cubs fans. The team started 11–1 and held first place by a comfortable margin throughout the summer.

It was also the season that got Marcia Colton hooked on the Cubs. She had grown up in a White Sox household, but Wrigley Field proved to be an irresistible draw for the young schoolteacher in the summer of '69. She and a friend, who was also a teacher, had the summer off. They spent many of those days in the right-field bleachers at Wrigley.

The ivy on the outfield walls was in full bloom. The bleacher seats were cheap. The sun was often shining, especially on the Cubs, who stayed hot all summer.

"It's The Friendly Confines. It was just a fun place to be," Colton said.

The starting rotation was solid with two 20-game winners—Jenkins (21–15) and Bill Hands (20–14). They were supported by three other pitchers who hit double figures in wins–Ken Holtzman (17), Phil Regan (12) and Dick Selma (10). The offensive stars were Santo, with 29 home runs and 123 runs batted in; Banks, with 23 home runs and 106 RBI; and sweet-swinging Williams, who batted .293 and drove in 95 runs.

The Cubs led by nine games on August 16. The lead still was five games in early September, but then an eight-game losing streak kicked off an 8–18 finish to the season. In true Cubs fashion, there was even an omen for all of this. On September 9, 1969, a black cat appeared on the field at Shea Stadium, home of the New York Mets, during a game with the Cubs. The cat wandered over near the Cubs dugout, walking past Santo in the on-deck circle.

Whether one believes in the bad luck of black cats or not, one fact is certain: After five months of solid baseball, the September swoon sent the Cubs plummeting into second place. That's where they finished, eight games behind the Mets in the National League East and out of the playoffs in the pre–wild-card era.

"That's my biggest disappointment as a Cubs fan," Colton said.

"The 1969 season is still seared into my memory," Yellon said. "The history of the franchise might have been quite different if they had won."

It's one of the many "if only" thoughts that have echoed on Chicago's North Side for decades. After all, this is the team that inspired the late Steve Goodman to write "A Dying Cub Fan's Last Request," a song that includes the lyrics, "Do they still play the blues in Chicago when baseball season rolls around?"

There is 1984, which saw the Cubs win the National League East, thanks to an MVP season from Ryne Sandberg, who batted .314, scored 114 runs and drove in 84.

In the National League Championship Series, the Cubs won the first two games against the San Diego Padres, then lost the next three to drop the best-of-five series. In the final game, the Padres rallied late for a victory, helped when a ground ball went between the legs of Cubs first baseman Leon Durham.

"Do I hate Steve Garvey? Yes," said Bernardoni, referring to the Padres first baseman who hit .400 with seven RBI in that series.

Five years later, the Cubs lost the National League Championship Series to the San Francisco Giants despite an otherworldly performance by first baseman Mark Grace. In the five games, Grace batted .647 with 11 hits and eight RBI.

Then, of course, there's 2003, the source of Bernardoni's sealed box of unread newspapers. The starting pitching staff was anchored by Prior, Kerry Wood, Matt Clement and Carlos Zambrano, who combined for 59 wins. Sammy Sosa had cooled from his home-run pace of the late 1990s, but he still contributed 40 homers and 103 RBI.

The Cubs ousted the Braves in the first round of the playoffs, thanks to a sterling Game 5 pitching performance by Wood. He limited the Braves to five hits in eight innings as the Cubs won, 5–1, to take the series, 3–2.

In the National League Championship Series, the Cubs held that 3–0 lead in Game 6 over the Florida Marlins, moments away from a trip to the World Series. With one out and a runner on second in the eighth inning, Florida's Luis Castillo lofted a foul fly ball that headed toward the front row of seats along the left-field line. Fan Steve Bartman reached for the ball, which Cubs leftfielder Moises Alou had a chance to catch. The ball glanced off Bartman's hand and fell into the front-row seats.

The non-catch drew huge media attention—a die-hard Cubs fan somehow being involved in a Cubs late-game collapse. Bartman took heat for months—there were even death threats—and the incident lives on today as one of those moments of pain that baseball followers never forget. But most reasonable fans knew Bartman was not a factor in the Cubs loss. "I feel sorry for him," Yellon said. "The whole thing was blown way out of proportion."

Yellon was at Wrigley Field to see it all, including what happened after the Bartman play. There was a crucial error by Cubs shortstop Alex Gonzalez on a probable double-play ball and some ineffective pitching that played a far greater role in the eight-run rally than a fan's attempt to catch a foul ball.

"I remember walking along the street after the game and seeing people with stunned and dazed looks on their faces," Yellon said.

For Colton, it brought back memories of 1969, that first painful season she followed the Cubs. "I was depressed for days," she said of the 2003 loss to the Marlins. "I had been a fan for so long. I thought for sure they were going to the World Series."

Bernardoni has heard many Cubs fans talk about the suffering of the 1969 collapse. He'll bring up 2003, which he thinks is more painful. "I say, 'Dude, five outs away.'"

Cubs fans also are part of a passionate North Side-South Side rivalry with the Chicago White Sox, who won the 2005 World Series, ending an 88-year drought of their own.

Of the White Sox championship, Colton said, "I wasn't happy, but I went along with it. I did watch the games. I was very jealous."

Yellon attended the White Sox's World Series games. "It's Chicago. The World Series is being played in my city. Why wouldn't I go?" Yellon congratulated a friend who is a White Sox fan after the team's championship. "He told me, 'You're a bigger man than I would be.'"

Bernardoni's reaction was a bit different. The night the White Sox won the World Series? "The worst night of my life," he said. "It was horrible because I knew my phone was going to ring."

The rivalry also hit home on a personal level for Bernardoni. He has a teenage daughter whose mother married a White Sox fan. A few years ago, Bernardoni was driving with his daughter when she announced she wanted to switch her support from the Cubs to the White Sox.

This was a girl who had taken her first steps on the Wrigley Field grass. Bernardoni is a Wrigley Field historian and was leading a tour of the ballpark at the time. Adding to the significance of the moment, those first steps were taken near where Bernardoni's grandmother had played second base in an international softball tournament during the 1933 Century of Progress, the second World's Fair hosted by Chicago.

Brian Bernardoni has many fond memories of Wrigley Field. He also has plans for how he will celebrate when the Chicago Cubs win it all (courtesy Brian Bernardoni).

"My daughter said she was going to become a Sox fan," Bernardoni said. "I literally stopped the car and said, 'This is the first adult decision you are going to make. When the Cubs win it all, you won't have that total joy and ecstasy of having stuck with your team.'"

With a century-plus of never winning it all, Cubs fans find joy and ecstasy in other parts of the game. There's Wrigley Field, which, as Bernardoni pointed out, is the only major-league stadium left where Jackie Robinson played. Packed tightly into the Wrigleyville neighborhood, the park has ivy-covered walls and an exterior from another era, complete with the well-known red sign that reads "Wrigley Field Home of Chicago Cubs." Wrigley and Boston's Fenway Park are the only ballparks left from baseball's early years.

There are a bevy of great moments: Banks winning the National League's Most Valuable Player Award in back-to-back seasons (1958 and '59) playing for below-.500 teams, the homer spree in the late 1990s and early 2000s by Sosa, terrific seasons by Grace, Andre Dawson, Hank Sauer, Hack Wilson and Rogers Hornsby.

There's the Ryne Sandberg game. On June 23, 1984, Sandberg helped lead a comeback from a second-inning 7–1 deficit against the St. Louis Cardinals. The Cubs had cut the lead to 9–8 heading into the ninth inning. Sandberg homered off all-star closer Bruce Sutter to tie the score. The Cardinals scored twice in the top of the 10th, but Sandberg homered off Sutter for a second time, this time a two-run shot to again tie the score.

An inning later, the Cubs won, 12–11, when pinch hitter Dave Owen singled in the winning run. Somehow, the game-winning rally didn't involve Sandberg, who finished the day 5 for 6 with seven RBI.

There are the fans who pack Wrigley—the ones who throw back home-run balls hit by opponents. They wear white T-shirts with a bold, blue "W," replicating the flag that is raised above Wrigley after a Cubs win.

These fans sit through the April chill, when the wind is whipping off Lake Michigan, and the September sadness, when the Cubs are often again hopelessly out of it. They tackle their long title drought with a mixture of melancholy and humor. When cement fragments crumbled from the upper deck of Wrigley in 2004, one fan attended the next game wearing a Cubs batting helmet with a piece of cement taped to its top.

A Cubs game is the crowds hanging out on Waveland Avenue and the fans sitting in sun-splashed seats atop nearby apartment buildings that overlook the ballpark.

There are the memories of announcer Harry Caray leading the singing of "Take Me Out to the Ball Game" during the seventh-inning stretch, and of Banks, a Cubs lifer who died in 2015 and was known for his optimistic approach to baseball and life.

"He transcended the Cubs and the City of Chicago," said Yellon. Bernardoni, a father of four daughters, said he seldom cries, but he did the day Banks died. "That was really hard. I have pictures of Ernie holding my kids."

There are the joys of childhood, converted to our adult lives. Yellon recalls running into Williams at an airport several years ago. "Here I was a 50-year-old man, and I was tongue-tied because he was my childhood hero."

Those joys are tempered by a team that has found incredible ways to lose. No one game might spotlight those crazy losses more than May 17, 1979. With the wind blowing out at Wrigley, the Philadelphia Phillies scored seven runs in the first. The Cubs scored six. The Phillies scored eight in the third to build their lead to 15–6, and they kept scoring. So did the Cubs, piling up 13 runs from the fourth to the sixth inning to cut the Phillies' lead to 21–19.

A three-run rally by the Cubs tied the score at 22 in the eighth inning. The craziness ended in the 10th inning when Philadelphia third baseman Mike Schmidt hit a home run. Final score: Philadelphia 23, Chicago 22. The Cubs got seven RBI from Bill Buckner and six from Dave Kingman, who hit three home runs, and *lost*.

The Cubs carry the Curse of the Billy Goat, a hex allegedly placed on the team in 1945 when local tavern owner Billy Sianis brought his pet goat to a World Series game for luck. Sianis and his goat were asked to leave, apparently because the goat didn't pass the smell test for fans sitting nearby.

True fans don't buy the goat hex. Yellon called it "utter nonsense," while Bernardoni said, "There's no way a farm animal can cause a team to suffer."

Billy goat curse or not, the fans' devotion lives on.

Colton, a season-ticket holder for a number of years, has retired from teaching after 30 years in the Des Plaines, Illinois, and Chicago school systems. She still gets to Wrigley Field for games, though not as often as that glorious summer of 1969.

She has plenty of memories. There are the good ones, such as May 19, 2007, when one of her favorite Cubs, Derrek Lee, came off the bench to pinch hit and belted a grand slam against the White Sox. It was the key blow in a six-run eighth inning that led the Cubs to an 11–6 victory over their crosstown rivals.

There are the painful memories. She still holds on to two souvenirs—
unused tickets to Wrigley Field for Game 4 of the 2007 World Series and
Game 5 of the 2008 World Series. In both seasons, the Cubs were swept
away in the first round of the playoffs.

Colton loves the nachos with cheese at Wrigley and she stays till the
end because she doesn't want to miss a chance to sing "Go Cubs Go"—
another Goodman song—with the rest of the fans after a victory.

When she's not at Wrigley, she's following the Cubs at home. "I watch
every night unless I have something more important to do. But what could
be more important?"

She and her husband get to spring training in Arizona every year.
Once the season starts, she's keeping close tabs, memorizing the player's

**Marcia Colton tries out the media room at the Chicago Cubs' spring training
facility in Mesa, Arizona. She started following the team in the summer of 1969,
a season that ended painfully for the Cubs' faithful (photograph by Steve Colton).**

statistics and watching every pitch. "My husband says I could be the manager."

She dreams of celebrating a World Series championship with family and friends, and she knows she'll keep watching even when there might be something better to do.

"I just have an addiction to them," she said. "There's something about it. I guess maybe I wanted to be a professional baseball player."

Bernardoni, who is a lobbyist for the Illinois Association of Realtors in Chicago, has a man cave in his basement that includes a dozen Wrigley Field seats, two seats from the locker room and part of the original backstop at Wrigley. He has instructed his beloved ones that his ashes one day be scattered at Wrigley Field. Not all of his ashes, though. Some are to be set aside and brought to the game on the night the Cubs finally do win the World Series.

And if that World Series win comes while he is still alive, Bernardoni is prepared. "My God, I can finally get that tattoo," he said. "If I died on the spot, the look on my face wouldn't be one of pain. It would be a smile."

The 2015 season gave Bernardoni and all Cubs fans hope. A group of highly touted prospects proved to be worth all the attention they had been getting. The pitching staff was led by Jake Arrieta, who won 22 games, while the offense was powered by a blast of youth from Anthony Rizzo, Kris Bryant and Kyle Schwarber.

The Cubs won 97 games, a 24-game improvement over the previous season. In the playoffs, they beat their most hated division rival, the St. Louis Cardinals, with Jorge Soler, Javier Baez and Schwarber all hitting .500 or better. The turnaround season came to a screeching halt in the next series, in which the New York Mets, bolstered by their youthful crop of power-armed pitchers, swept the Cubs.

"The best part of the season for me was beating the Cardinals," Bernardoni said. "Boy, oh boy, there's nothing better for me than watching dejected Cardinals fans leaving Wrigley Field."

While losing to the Mets was disappointing, the season was one that brought a pile of optimism to the North Side. This Cubs team, and its youthful core, lived up to the hype. In fact, most felt the team got to the playoffs a year or two earlier than was projected.

"When they met those expectations, there was a sense of relief. They are legit," Bernardoni said of the prospects. He was speaking soon after the season had ended. "If there's a level of frustration, it's that it's not opening day already."

He was pleased the Cubs saw the benefits of a rebuilding effort that required fans to sit through five losing seasons, including a painful 61–101 record in 2012. The Cubs finished that season a mere 36 games behind the first-place Cincinnati Reds in the National League Central division.

"It's the first time in my memory the Cubs stuck with the program. It's nothing but positive," Bernardoni said.

A Halloween junkie, he stretched the 2015 season by dressing up as Cubs manager Joe Maddon for the holiday. "It was great—just the positive reaction—but more importantly, everyone knows who the Cubs manager is," he said.

Bernardoni loved Maddon's work in his first season in Chicago. "Joe Maddon did a great job of managing Chicago—not the team, but the city. He said a goat doesn't matter. He said a black cat doesn't matter."

The success of the young players and the entire season only enhanced Bernardoni's feeling that he's not giving up on his Cubs. "It's all I know. When you find out there's no Santa Claus, it's a painful experience because where else are you going to go? This is an adult version of that.

"In life, you've got to stand for something. The Cubs have never left me. I don't want to break up with somebody that's a constant."

0 for 4

The Buffalo Bills

A little thing like not winning a championship since 1965 isn't going to stop Buffalo Bills fans from enjoying a good time. Just ask Mike Dmowski, Jr.

On game days at Ralph Wilson Stadium, he and his buddies line up in an RV outside the parking lot at 1 a.m. on Saturday. That's right, Saturday morning—a good 36 hours before kickoff. They'll leave Monday morning, after a weekend of camaraderie that centers around their beloved Bills.

"It's like a vacation every weekend when we play a home game," Dmowski said.

All this for a team that last won a title on December 26, 1965, when the Bills blanked the San Diego Chargers, 23–0, to win the championship of the old American Football League. Pete Gogolak kicked three field goals, Jack Kemp threw a touchdown pass to Ernie Warlick, and Butch Byrd returned a punt 74 yards for a score.

It was the second title in a row for those Bills, who featured a defense that allowed only four rushing touchdowns. Since then, there have been four consecutive Super Bowl defeats, the "Music City Miracle" and enough losing seasons to discourage the most ardent of fans.

What keeps Dmowski and his fellow Buffalo diehards coming back for more?

"It is a way of life," he said. "This being a small town—it's not New York City, it's not L.A.—this team is what you grew up with. Everywhere you go you see Bills fans."

Del Reid grew up in a Buffalo-area household so devoted to the football team that he said, "I'm 39. I tell people I've been a Bills fan for 40 years. It's in my DNA."

His parents, Bud and Colleen, were fans, and they let it show. "You know how some people have a framed photo of the pope in their home? We had one of O.J. Simpson," Reid said.

Simpson was a star running back in the 1970s, rushing for 10,183 yards—including a then-record 2,003 in 1973–in nine seasons in Buffalo. (The photo in the Reid home came down in 1994 after Simpson was charged in the murder of his ex-wife, Nicole, and her friend Ronald Goldman. Simpson was acquitted on October 3, 1995, after a televised trial that held the nation's attention for months.)

Reid has carried on the tradition of honoring the Bills. "My kids will say they grew up in a home that had a painting of Jim Kelly in the upstairs hallway."

After his parents taught him all about the Bills, Reid had a revelation in 1988 as he neared his teenage years. In November of that season, he watched the Bills clinch their first AFC East title in eight years. Fred Smerlas blocked a late field goal by the New York Jets' Pat Leahy, and Scott Norwood kicked a field goal in overtime to give the Bills a hard-fought 9–6 victory. It was the Bills' seventh straight win and gave them an 11–1 record, helping them clinch the division title with four weeks left in the season.

"That was when my parents' team became my team," Reid said. "It was a huge rush." That Bills team would beat the Houston Oilers in the playoffs but lose the American Football Conference championship game, 21–10, to the Cincinnati Bengals.

Family ties also played a big role for Liz Young in her love of the Bills. She lives in Hoboken, New Jersey, where she owns a web-based software development firm, but she remembers her younger days in South Buffalo, a tight-knit neighborhood so close you could stand between two houses and with arms outstretched almost touch both of them at once.

Her grandmother and two aunts also lived in the neighborhood. All those who lived in between were called "aunt" and "uncle," even though they weren't related.

On Sundays during Bills season, her aunts and grandmother—and cousins and neighbors and siblings and friends—would gather to watch the game. In nice weather, the television set was dragged outside, and there would be a barbecue to capture the feel of a true Buffalo tailgate.

At halftime, most everyone took part in a game of two-hand touch football in the street, interrupted only when a driver had the audacity to navigate a car through the middle of the playing field. But, when the Bills game was on, there were no distractions. "It was the best day of the week during football season," Young said.

Liz Young and John Wojcik, the man behind the mask, hang out before a Buffalo Bills game. Young now lives in New Jersey, but she has fond memories of growing up in a tight-knit South Buffalo neighborhood (photograph by Jennifer Young).

She attended her first game when she was 5 with her father, Clyde, who went by "Ike." It was the mid–1980s, and the Bills weren't very good. But, by early in the next decade, they were really good, making it to four straight Super Bowls, led by quarterback Kelly, defensive end Bruce Smith and running back Thurman Thomas.

Young remembers being dressed head to toe in Bills gear, including Bills earrings and Bills temporary tattoos, for the team's first Super Bowl appearance. Despite her fashion efforts, the Bills lost to the New York Giants, 20–19, when Norwood's last-second 47-yard field-goal attempt slid wide right.

Snow in October? Big deal. It's not stopping these Buffalo Bills fans. Left to right are Jennifer Young, Kelley Wojcik, Joelle Woelfel-Hibbs and Liz Young (courtesy Liz Young).

"I remember just bawling when Scott Norwood missed," Young said. "I was so little; I just remember thinking this was the worst day of my life."

Her Bills-loving family members told her she shouldn't cry because there was another season ahead. The team would rebound, they said. It's an optimistic spirit that she has carried on, despite the three consecutive Super Bowl losses that followed the Norwood miss. Those defeats included a 52–17 pounding by the Dallas Cowboys in 1993.

"The Super Bowls were crushing—just crushing—but those seasons were awesome. I'd love to be able to feel that again," Young said.

She flies from New Jersey to Buffalo for three Bills games a year, always attending the home opener with a group of friends. She also usually makes it to a game in October and another near Christmas. Her Aunt Tudy of South Buffalo remains her first choice to take to a game.

Aunt Tudy was part of a group of family and friends who joined Young for a trip to London in late October 2015 to see the Bills play the Jacksonville Jaguars. When Young found out the Bills would be playing in London, her first text was to her aunt.

When the Buffalo Bills traveled to London to play the Jacksonville Jaguars on
October 25, 2015, Liz Young was there with friends and family. Left to right are
wife Jennifer Young, mom Betty Weber, aunt Tudy Young, Liz Young and Michelle
Leonardo. The Bills lost that day at Wembley Stadium, 34–31 (courtesy Liz Young).

"When she responded, it was all excited: 'Are you serious!'" Young
said. "There was no turning back at that point." Their trip included a visit
to Paris as well as going to the game at Wembley Stadium, which the
Jaguars won, 34–31. The crowd included other Bills fans, but many in the
stands had no allegiance to either team.

Some weren't quite sure how this game of football even works. "People around me were asking, 'Why are they kicking? Why are they giving
the ball back to the other team?'" Young said. "We lost to one of the worst
teams in the NFL, but the trip was worth it."

When Young attends the season opener with friends, the talk is
always the same. "We're going to be great, so-and-so is going to blow up,
the defense is going to be solid," she said.

The near misses of the '90s, as well as the losing of recent seasons,
do not get her down because of the camaraderie involved in all of this. "If
I didn't have the group of friends who go to the home opener, if I didn't
have my family that always watches—it's a community thing."

Buffalo—a city that also has the Sabres, a National Hockey League
team that has never won a Stanley Cup—has to deal with plenty of trash

talking from fans of teams that have won titles. When that starts, Young knows just how to react.

"There's a sense of pride there," she said. "You kind of ruffle your feathers and puff out your chest. You say, 'I'd like to know how much fun you have at your tailgate.'"

Young isn't the only fan who feels this ongoing Bills devotion. Susan Gemmett, a Rochester, New York, resident, explained her love of the team this way: "There's something that ties you to Bills fans—that long-suffering thing is a bond with other people.... It's the whole thing about the team—the little engine that could. You hope one day they'll get over the mountain. You want to be there when that happens."

Gemmett's family moved frequently when she was young, and they spent a year in Buffalo in the early 1970s. She latched onto the Bills and their star running back.

"It was the whole O.J. Simpson excitement—when he was a star for the right reasons," Gemmett said. Many years after O.J., she remains as devoted as ever. "Mondays are a hard day at work anyway, but coming in after a loss—it's so painful."

Dmowski grew up in Cheektowaga, a Buffalo suburb, and now lives in Lockport, New York, about 30 miles northeast of Buffalo. In those early years in Cheektowaga, his dad passed on a love of the Bills. They went to their first game together when Dmowski was about 8.

"There were guys all around us yelling at the ref, yelling at the coaches. I asked my dad if he could get them to stop. He said, 'If you're going to go to these games, this is what you're going to have to deal with.' He defended random Bills fans over me."

Dmowski was a budding fan during the four-year Super Bowl run. "I fed off my dad's love and emotion. You could just feel it throughout the game," he said. He also remembers the Bills troll his dad gave him. "He got it for me for good luck. I grabbed that thing and stroked its hair—anything to help the Bills."

Dmowski was in high school when the Bills added to their pile of famous losses. The Bills met the Tennessee Titans in Nashville on January 8, 2000, in an American Football Conference wild-card playoff game. Buffalo had taken a 16–15 lead with 16 seconds left on Steve Christie's 41-yard field goal.

The ensuing kickoff was fielded by Tennessee's Lorenzo Neal, who handed the ball off to tight end Frank Wycheck. Wycheck then threw it across the field to wide receiver Kevin Dyson, who sprinted 75 yards untouched for the winning touchdown.

Game officials reviewed the play to determine whether the Wycheck toss to Dyson had been an illegal forward pass. After several minutes the officials ruled the play was a touchdown.

The Dyson touchdown became known as the "Music City Miracle," although Buffalo fans have used different adjectives to describe this "miracle." Dmowski said he has watched that play an "infinite number of times." At first, he convinced himself the ruling was correct. Now, he believes it should have been ruled a pass and not a lateral, negating the touchdown. What he does remember most is this: "The next day at school, everybody wore their Bills stuff."

Gemmett recalls watching that game at a friend's house and thinking, "My gosh, really? What else can happen to this poor team?"

Reid said that finish stings more today than it did at the time because the loss was followed by a long string of seasons that saw the Bills miss the playoffs. "We thought we'd be back the next year. It's 15 next years, and we haven't been back," he said. "It seems that wound gets deeper."

Young, then working in New York City, was at a bar in the city that was packed with Bills fans cheering wildly for every Buffalo score in the playoff game against the Titans. "What I remember at the very end of that game was every single person leaving the bar as the saddest person on Earth."

Fans who stay until the last play sometimes have been rewarded for their dedication. On January 3, 1993, Bill Rotach was at his apartment watching with some friends as the Bills played the Houston Oilers in a wild-card playoff game. By early in the second half, Buffalo, playing at home, had fallen behind, 35–3.

Rotach continued to watch as his guests, figuring there was a better way to spend the rest of the day, filed out. "People were laughing at me," said Rotach, a Sterling, New York, resident. He soon was the one laughing. Backup quarterback Frank Reich, filling in for an injured Kelly, threw four touchdown passes, leading a wild comeback that brought the Bills a 41–38 victory in overtime.

Buffalo fans have had to deal with the pain of four straight Super Bowl losses, of the miracle in Nashville, of losing games played in the snows of a Buffalo December. They've also had to watch a bitter division rival, the New England Patriots, and a geographic rival, the New York Giants, win several Super Bowls.

Dmowski is philosophical about those titles won by the Patriots and Giants, painful as they might be. "They're only champions for one year," he said. "We're always curious about the next season; that could be our season. If we win it next year, that's our Super Bowl."

Bill Rotach's man cave provides plenty of clues about which team is his favorite (courtesy Bill Rotach).

He doesn't think about giving up on his team. If the Bills are getting blown out, he might switch the station, but it's only for a short while. "I don't know what it is, I have to go back and watch that team." He knows he owes this all to his dad. "I'm thankful he got me into it. It's a mess, but…"

Reid has a soft spot for the Giants, which grew from watching them beat the Patriots twice in the Super Bowl. In the early years of Tom Brady and the Patriots' glory, he couldn't hate the team. He respected the Patriots for their continued excellence.

Then, at a Patriots-Bills game in Buffalo, he sat near a New England fan who berated him and other Bills followers for 3½ hours. It created a hatred in Reid for all Boston teams, not just the Patriots.

"Now, whenever a Boston team wins, I know that guy is sitting in the stands or sitting on the couch in his living room with a smile on his face. I hate it," Reid said. "When the Giants beat the Patriots, I almost cried. That's sad."

Buffalo is a city that often is the butt of jokes. Set on the eastern edge of Lake Erie, snow can pile up in winter. Many remember it as the place where President William McKinley was assassinated. But it's the city that brought us Buffalo wings, Christine Baranski and Rick James. There's a coolness that goes along with the blue-collar image.

It's a city that takes pride in its sports teams, despite the futility. Residents have created a special bond with Kelly, the star of the Super Bowl years. Kelly has settled in the Buffalo area after a career that saw him throw 237 touchdown passes for the Bills from 1986 to 1996. That total includes a league-leading 33 scoring passes in 1991.

Buffalo's love for Kelly was more than support for a guy who could throw a football well. Kelly's son, Hunter, died at age 8 in 2005 after battling Krabbe disease, a degenerative disorder of the central and peripheral nervous systems.

Kelly himself has had a couple of bouts with cancer. Through all of these health issues, the Buffalo fans have offered lots of support to him and his family.

"He's not from Buffalo originally, but he might as well be," Reid said. "If you show this city some love and acknowledgment, this city will love you back."

These fans aren't going anywhere. They've all shared in the painful losses. Reid remembers talking to a friend after Norwood's missed kick in the Super Bowl. The phone conversation lasted about an hour and mostly consisted of silence and the sighs of the defeated.

"That play has become a part of us—it's our national identity," Reid said of the Norwood miss. "If you can't win an argument with a Bills fan, just say, 'Wide right.' It's fed into that collective consciousness we all have."

He sees that collective consciousness in the "Bills Mafia." That phrase came into being, thanks to Reid, after Bills receiver Stevie Johnson dropped a game-winning touchdown pass against the Pittsburgh Steelers in 2010. After the game, Johnson sent out a tweet to God, "I PRAISE YOU 24/7!!!!!! AND THIS HOW YOU DO ME!!!!!"

Johnson's tweet was later retweeted by an ESPN reporter, a little too late in the eyes of Bills fans, who sent tongue-in-cheek comments to the reporter about the delay in retweeting. The reporter eventually blocked the fans' messages, leading Reid to respond with the hashtag "BillsMafia," as in the fans are so scary, their tweets had to be blocked. Others picked up on the hashtag.

For Reid, it was all in good fun, and "Bills Mafia" stuck. "When I hear ESPN or the NFL Network say 'Bills Mafia,' I can't believe it took off," Reid said. Today, the group has expanded to become a nonprofit organization that raises money for charities, and it still loves its Bills.

Despite all this devotion, there was a fear the Bills might move when the team was up for sale after the death of owner Ralph Wilson. But Terry and Kim Pegula bought the team in 2014 and are promising to stay in Buffalo.

Bills fans praised the Pegulas' devotion to Buffalo. There were grown men choking up on sports talk radio as they called in to celebrate the news that the Bills were staying, Reid said. "To this day, people are still tweeting, 'Thank you, Pegula family.' We are so tied into this team. The team is the city, and the city is the team," he said.

That thought hits home for Reid on a personal level. His two young daughters are Bills fans, but they haven't experienced the excitement of a playoff run by the team. He hopes they can soon enjoy that kind of season.

"When they're good, all is right with the world," Reid said of the Bills. That's why he hopes that he and his children get to see a championship.

"It's the anticipation of how good it is going to feel," he said. "Even if they lose for the next 30 years, I'm going to have that moment."

Gemmett shares those sentiments. "It's a working-paycheck-to-paycheck town," she said. "The teams feel the same way—as if they're never getting anywhere. Man, would a championship be wonderful for everyone's peace of mind."

Brew City Blues

The Milwaukee Brewers

It's a little after 7 on a late February morning in Milwaukee. The temperature is zero with a bit of a breeze to negate any chance of warmth from the sun starting to peek over the horizon.

Andrea Cheney and Franz Michels left their Dousman, Wisconsin, home, 30 miles west of the city, at 4:15 a.m. and have been in line for two hours at Miller Park, home of the Milwaukee Brewers. They're in the concourse, which is unheated, so even with the stadium's roof closed the temperature inside is barely warmer than outdoors. They are bundled in blankets and winter coats and fur-lined hats.

"Get a little frostbite. Have a good time," Cheney said of their morning adventure. "I've got all the blankets right now. We're in it for the long haul."

"It will only be a couple of degrees warmer than this for opening day," Michels said, not entirely joking in a climate that can be cruel in early April.

Cheney and Michels are not alone. There are several hundred fans lined up for the Arctic Tailgate, the first day of single-game ticket sales for the Brewers.

The crowd is dressed in everything from blaze orange hunting gear to the bulkiest winter coats found in America's Dairyland. Hand warmers are essential. Some folks brought folding chairs; many are standing, bouncing from foot to foot in an effort to ward off the morning chill. Free coffee and doughnuts help ease the pain.

In a city filled with summertime festivals and year-round lakefront beauty, this event is a wintertime tradition. It often includes fans camping in line for several days before tickets go on sale. Team officials banned camping this time because of the frigid temperatures.

That stopped Zach Zwadzich and the rest of his group of a half-dozen—sort of. They didn't camp out as they usually do, but they did spend the night outside the stadium in their cars, assuring them the first spots in line on this Saturday morning.

This day is about camaraderie. Fans are getting to know each other in line, swapping stories of past seasons and past Arctic Tailgates.

"You'll be at a game later in the season, and another fan will shout over to you, 'Hey, Arctic Tailgate. Hey, Arctic Tailgate,'" said Zwadzich.

But, more than anything, this day is about a fan base showing its support for a team that hasn't always loved it back. The Brewers came to Milwaukee in 1970, an expansion team that relocated to the Midwest after one hopeless and hapless season as the Seattle Pilots. The Pilots joined the American League in 1969 along with the Kansas City Royals, but poor play and poor attendance doomed the first season in Seattle. The team finished 33 games out of first place with a 64–98 record, and financial troubles led to a quick move to Milwaukee.

That first Brewers team wasn't much better than those Pilots, finishing 65–97. The 1970 Brewers roster included a number of holdovers from Seattle, such as Gene Brabender, Tommy Harper and Marty Pattin. The team also had new faces, such as Max Alvis, who displayed some power as a third baseman with the Cleveland Indians in the 1960s, and outfielder-first baseman Tito Francona, whose son Terry would become a major-league player and World Series-winning manager.

Since that rugged beginning, the Brewers have won just one pennant, capturing the American League title in 1982 before losing the World Series in seven games to the St. Louis Cardinals.

For these fans, it doesn't matter. "You have to support your local team," said Lori Groen, standing a few hundred people back from the start of the line. "When it's good, it's really good. I'd hate to miss something like that."

The South Milwaukee resident has been a fan since the 1970s. Before that, she didn't pay much attention to baseball. "I thought it was boring. I didn't understand it. I thought the games went on forever."

It was in the 1970s that she started dating her future husband, Boyd, a huge baseball fan. "I thought, 'It's either going to be a very, very long summer, or I can join him,'" Groen said.

He showed her the finer points of the game, explained the rules and discussed the nuances that have hooked many baseball fans. She soon became one of them.

"How can you not love being in the sunshine, being in the fresh air, sitting with your feet up for two or three hours?" she said.

In her early years as a Brewers fan, Groen saw some pretty ugly

Boyd and Lori Groen have been attending Milwaukee Brewers games together since the 1970s. Once again in 2016, they traveled to Arizona to catch some spring training contests (photograph by Richard Holmberg).

baseball, but in 1978, the Brewers went from 67 wins to 93. Some veterans sparked the turnaround. Outfielder Larry Hisle smashed 34 homers and drove in 115 runs. Left-hander Mike Caldwell won 22 games and tossed 23 complete games. But the lineup featured a number of young, rising stars—Robin Yount, Paul Molitor and Jim Gantner—who would be the foundation of a baseball revival in Milwaukee for the next several seasons.

Watching those Brewers teams helped make Groen's conversion to baseball complete. She regularly attends spring training, she gets to at least a dozen Brewers games a year, and she has attended games in other cities—even if the Brewers weren't playing—when she has traveled for her job with the United States Postal Service.

She and her husband have a collection of about three dozen autographed baseballs, some signed by the greats of the game, including Willie Stargell and Nolan Ryan.

The prized possession, though, is a baseball signed by most of the members of the Brewers' 1982 American League championship team. As a gift to her husband, either for Christmas or for his birthday, she has sent the ball to a member of that team whose name was missing. The ball has always been returned with the signature added.

Groen's love of baseball even has a touch of activism. She attended rallies to support a new stadium in Milwaukee before the Brewers built Miller Park, which opened in 2001 after a rugged political battle over funding for the structure.

She backed the new stadium, not only for her love of the game, but because of what she believes are the benefits for the city and its surrounding communities. A team gives the city a national image as well as providing a social outlet for residents who tailgate before games throughout the summer, she said. "I don't want us to be Des Moines."

The park opened in the midst of 15 straight non-winning seasons for the Brewers, including a hideous 56–106 record in 2002. That didn't stop Groen from coming to the ballpark. "You always want your team to win. You anticipate they are going to win. You don't go thinking you're going to lose."

Zwadzich, who lives in Madison, Wisconsin, 90 miles west of Milwaukee, shares Groen's approach to rooting for the Brewers, even though he was born a few years after that 1982 pennant-winning season, and grew up with mostly losing teams in the 1990s.

As a youngster he rooted for several teams based on such youthful reasons as uniform color or a favorite player. But, he said, "Every time, I'd turn the radio on to Uecker."

That would be Bob Uecker, who has handled Brewers radio broadcasts since 1971, all the while cracking jokes and poking fun at his career as a backup catcher in the big leagues. He played from 1962 to 1967 with four teams, finishing with an even .200 batting average.

But Uecker is about more than baseball. He played Harry Doyle, the wisecracking broadcaster in the *Major League* movies, was sportswriter George Owens on the ABC series *Mr. Belvedere*, and made many appearances on *The Tonight Show* with Johnny Carson. With all that Hollywood fame as well as his beloved connection with Milwaukee baseball fans, Uecker became the face of the Brewers, appearing on media guide covers and in television commercials.

The joy of Uecker was one factor in Zwadzich's devotion to the Brewers. So was the pride of watching his state team, even through its darker days.

"You know that somewhere in the future, you can look back and say, 'I stuck with them.' They're my team," Zwadzich said. "You stick with them through the good years and the bad years. I'll have stories to tell about both."

One of those good years was 2008. Two young stars, Prince Fielder and Ryan Braun, each drove in more than 100 runs. A starting rotation led by Ben Sheets got a huge boost in July when the Brewers traded with the Cleveland Indians for left-hander CC Sabathia. All he did was go 11–2 with a 1.65 ERA in his three months in Milwaukee.

Zwadzich was at Miller Park for the last game of the season when Braun's two-out, two-run homer in the eighth inning beat the Chicago Cubs, 3–1, clinching a National League wild-card berth for the Brewers. (The team switched from the American to the National League in 1998.)

The Braun homer sent Miller Park into a frenzy, the crowd celebrating the team's first postseason berth since that 1982 World Series.

"I thought, 'This is what I've been a fan for,'" Zwadzich said. The joy didn't last long in the postseason. The Brewers were knocked out in the first round by the Philadelphia Phillies, a team that would go on to win the World Series.

The Brewers returned to the playoffs three years later, winning a first-round series against the Arizona Diamondbacks. The deciding Game 5 at Miller Park went 10 innings before Nyjer Morgan slapped a one-out single to center field to score Carlos Gomez and win the series.

Marlene Buechel, a retired schoolteacher from Verona, Wisconsin, was there with her grandson's girlfriend. "I just remember hugging her and jumping up and down," she said.

In the next round, the Brewers met an old nemesis, the St. Louis Cardinals, who knocked them out in six games. The Brewers won Game 4 to even the series at two games each, but they were undone by ineffective pitching and a combined seven errors in Games 5 and 6.

"To watch St. Louis beat us was awful," Buechel said. "It just fell apart before your eyes."

It was a poignant moment for Buechel, who has been watching baseball in Milwaukee since 1953, the year the Braves moved to Milwaukee from Boston. She went to her first game that season with her future husband, Pat. They were in high school.

She was a farm girl from New Glarus, Wisconsin. He was from the nearby, rival town. "You were really not supposed to look at a guy from Monticello. Somehow I broke the rules," she said.

They married a few years later, and Pat joined the Army. He was stationed at Fort Sill in Oklahoma in 1957. That was a big year back in Milwaukee, where the Braves were winning the city's only World Series title.

Marlene Buechel got to meet Hank the Dog in 2014. The dog became a Brewers mascot/good luck charm after wandering onto the Brewers' spring training site in Arizona earlier that year (courtesy Marlene Buechel).

Right-hander Lew Burdette won three times in the Series to defeat the New York Yankees in seven games.

"We were way down in Lawton, Oklahoma, with a little black-and-white TV in the corner of our apartment," Buechel said. "When they won the World Series, we put the roof down on our convertible and drove around, beeping our horn. I'm sure people didn't have a clue why those people from Wisconsin were so excited."

The Braves spent a dozen years in Milwaukee before moving to Atlanta after the 1965 season. What did she do when the Braves left? "Pout and sputter and grumble to anyone who would listen."

The Brewers' arrival five years later helped ease some of the pain of the Braves' departure. Buechel and her husband were on board from the start with the new team and were rewarded in 1982 when the Brewers won the American League pennant.

That team had Pete Vuckovich, who went 18–6 and won the American League's Cy Young Award. Yount was the American League most valuable player with a sturdy .331 batting average, along with 29 home runs and 114 RBI. His bat was the biggest one in a lineup full of them, including those of Cecil Cooper, Molitor, Gorman Thomas, Ted Simmons and Ben Oglivie.

They became known as "Harvey's Wallbangers," after manager Harvey Kuenn, a Milwaukee-area native who replaced Buck Rodgers after the Brewers got off to a 23–24 start. The nickname was well-deserved. The team mashed 216 homers and scored 891 runs.

The Brewers entered the final weekend needing just one win in Baltimore over the second-place Orioles to clinch the American League East title. The Orioles won the first three games to move into a tie with the Brewers. On the final day of the season, with a disastrous collapse looming, Yount homered twice and Cooper drove in three runs as the Brewers pounded Jim Palmer and the bullpen for a 10–2 victory.

The Brewers then met the California Angels in the American League Championship Series. Milwaukee pitchers couldn't contain Angels centerfielder Fred Lynn, who hit .611 for the series. The Brewers' offense was a bit more balanced, led by Charlie Moore hitting .462 and Molitor driving in five runs. Even though Lynn was named the series' most valuable player, it was the Brewers who prevailed, winning the deciding Game 5 in Milwaukee.

The victory over the Angels set up the "Suds Series," a World Series matchup between two cities known for brewing beer—Milwaukee and St. Louis. Yount and Molitor combined for 19 hits in the first five games, and the Brewers got two solid starts from Caldwell to build a 3–2 lead.

"I really thought we had it made," Buechel said, recalling how she felt as the Series headed to Game 6 in St. Louis.

Game 6 was one of those unmitigated disasters for Milwaukee. With a chance to clinch a championship, the Brewers couldn't do anything right. They collected just four hits, matching the number of errors they made. Starter Don Sutton gave up seven runs in less than five innings. It all added up to a 13–1 shellacking by the Cardinals.

In Game 7, the Cardinals pounded out 15 hits, scoring three runs in the sixth inning and two more in the eighth to erase a Brewers lead and win, 6–3. The Cardinals won the Series with a balanced offensive attack that saw five players drive in at least five runs.

Five years later, the Buechels cheered along when the Brewers started the 1987 season winning 13 straight games. The most dramatic win was Game 12 on Easter Sunday. The Brewers trailed the Texas Rangers, 4–1, in the bottom of the ninth inning. Rob Deer tied the game with a three-run homer, and Dale Sveum won it with a two-run blast.

Despite the hot start, that Brewers soon lost 12 in a row and finished the season 91–71, only good enough for third place in the American League East.

Pat Buechel died in 1993. Without him, Marlene just couldn't renew their Brewers season tickets. She was disgusted the next season when a labor dispute ended the season early, but she soon was back in her seats at County Stadium.

She sat through that 106-loss season in 2002. "I guess you keep hoping next year will be better," she said. She celebrated the playoff seasons of 2008 and 2011.

Best of all, her children and grandchildren are fans. She's waiting for the day her great-grandson is old enough to go to a game with her. There are still a few bumps to deal with, however. Her granddaughter is dating a Chicago Cubs fan. "How could this be?" she asked. "We're learning to be tolerant."

Buechel is the kind of fan who leaves Brewers-related messages on her telephone answering machine. Those messages change throughout the season—and off-season. "My friends roll their eyes and say, 'She has too much time on her hands.'"

She has a license plate that reads LV BRWRZ, although someone once told her he thought it meant "Love Bratwurst." She knows the workers at Miller Park by name, from Kent, the beer vendor, to Ashley, the popcorn wagon lady.

She ventured to Cooperstown for the Hall of Fame inductions of Yount and Molitor. She recalls one of the remarks Yount made: "The game of life can be too short, so play with everything you've got." Those words so inspired her that she wants them to be part of her memorial service. "Anyone who shows up will be encouraged to wear Brewers gear," she said.

She has been to 37 major-league stadiums, and in 2010 made it to the one major-league city she hadn't visited, Denver and Coors Field, home of the Colorado Rockies. She loves Milwaukee's Miller Park, but Pittsburgh's PNC Park is her favorite.

She has a partial season-ticket package, so she still makes the hour and a half drive from Verona to Milwaukee for baseball. It's a journey she's been making for more than 60 years.

Sometimes, it's a painful trip. "My son says baseball will break your heart. How many times can they break my heart? It happens too many times." But there's a flip side to all those hard times for her. "How do you get through the tough times in other parts of life? You just keep clinging to hope," she said. "Yes, it breaks your heart, but the joys outweigh the sorrows."

Butch Foeckler has seen plenty of joys and sorrows while rooting for the Brewers since their first opening day in Milwaukee.

When Foeckler's youngest daughter, Laura, asked him recently what was on his bucket list, he realized it was something he'd never thought much about.

After some reflection, he came up with two entries for his list: He wanted to see his four grandchildren get married, and he wanted to see his Brewers win the World Series.

"Don't ask me which one is at the top of the list," said Foeckler, a resident of the Milwaukee suburb of West Allis who is retired after working three decades at engine manufacturer Briggs & Stratton.

Like Foeckler, many Brewers fans are just a bit too young to remember the Braves' World Series title. He is old enough to remember the Braves' final seasons in Milwaukee—sitting in the County Stadium bleachers and enjoying the showmanship of Rico Carty and the wizardry of Hank Aaron.

"When the Braves left, it was heartbreaking," Foeckler said. "The last season for the Braves in Milwaukee was traumatic." Everyone knew the team was leaving town, and attendance plummeted to 555,584 in that last year. The team had ranked first in attendance in the National League during its first six seasons in Milwaukee.

When he wasn't at County Stadium, Foeckler was studying box scores to keep up with the game's best players. His love of the game came early. He and his neighborhood buddies would gather at a place they called "The Dump," a patch of land at 96th and Lapham streets that had a home plate and a backstop but little else.

"My sister would come get me for lunch, then we'd go back out and play some more," he said.

These days, he's no longer playing ball with the guys from the neighborhood, but he still pores over the morning box scores and follows the Brewers.

He was at County Stadium for Game 5 of the 1982 American League Championship Series against the California Angels. He was watching as Cooper made a downward motion with both hands as he ran to first, urging the ball he'd just sliced to left field to find the grass. It did, scoring two runs and sending the Brewers to the World Series.

"That was probably the most enjoyable time for me at County Stadium," Foeckler said.

Butch and Karen Foeckler are ready to take in a Brewers game at Milwaukee's Miller Park with their four grandchildren (left to right), Jonathon, Brionna, Samantha and Hannah. When asked about his bucket list, Butch had his grandchildren and his Brewers right at the top of the list (photograph by Brenda Banovich).

That win set off a celebration along downtown's Wisconsin Avenue, similar to the spontaneous bursts of joy that followed the Braves' World Series victory in 1957 and Marquette University's national basketball championship in 1977.

The trip to the World Series ended with the loss to the Cardinals in seven games. Foeckler was working second shift at the time, so he recorded all the World Series games. He watched them, win or lose. "That's part of being a fan," he said.

That World Series loss might be his worst moment as a Brewers fan. "We may never get there again—you never know. As you get older you realize that more and more. Our seasons are limited."

He's seen the good—that 1982 American League title and being at County Stadium on Sept. 9, 1992, for Yount's 3,000th hit. He's seen the bad—losing to the Cardinals in the 2011 National League Championship Series and watching the Brewers blow a divisional lead in September 2014.

"That collapse? Oh, that hurt," Foeckler said of 2014, which saw the Brewers finish 9–22 after leading the National League Central in late August.

There's no doubt he's sticking with the Brewers.

"It's part of being a loyal fan. It's like a marriage. You deal with all the ups and downs."

Honolulu Blue,
Sweat and Tears

The Detroit Lions

Mention Honolulu Blue to Jeremy Reisman, and he's got a quick response. "It's the color of my blood," he said.

The Detroit Lions' team color is just one of the factors that generates a sense of pride for Reisman and a group of fans still waiting more than 58 years for another championship.

Reisman, who grew up in the Detroit suburb of Northville and now lives in Los Angeles, has been alive for only about half of that Lions drought, but he knows the pain. His family owned season tickets for decades. He has suffered through one losing year after another, including the first 0–16 season in National Football League history.

The 2008 Lions started their winless run against the Atlanta Falcons and allowed a 62-yard touchdown on the first NFL pass thrown by quarterback Matt Ryan. "That pretty much encapsulated the Lions' entire season," said Reisman. "They couldn't stop anybody from passing the ball that year."

A few weeks later the Lions lost, 12–10, to the Minnesota Vikings. Minnesota scored two of its points when Detroit quarterback Dan Orlovsky stepped out of the back of the end zone. The Associated Press' game story read: "It's been that kind of season—that kind of existence, really—for one of the most hapless franchises in professional sports."

Those 0–16 2008 Lions finished last among the NFL's 32 teams in two key defensive categories—yards allowed (404.4 per game) and points allowed (32.3 per game).

None of this stopped Reisman. He watched every game that season. "I feel I'd be doing some kind of disservice if I wasn't watching. It was a helpless feeling. It was this disaster happening, and I couldn't look away."

Even crazier, he plans to sit down and watch all of the 2008 season again on video. "I feel it would be a little cathartic to exorcise some of those demons and to see how far the team has come since then."

Sean Yuille, an Ann Arbor, Michigan, resident, has similar bad memories of 2008. There was some hope after the Lions went 7–9 in 2007, an improvement over the previous year's 3–13. Matt Millen, who was widely regarded as an ineffective executive, had left the team.

"There was no reason not to be optimistic," Yuille said. Then it all came tumbling down with 16 losses in a season. "Nationally, the Lions were a punch line. That was nothing new," he said. "Locally, the focus was

Sean Yuille's stance on his favorite football squad is simple: "For better or worse—which is usually the case with the Lions—they're my team" (courtesy Sean Yuille).

on, can they get that one win?" The next season wasn't much better. "In 2009, the whole thing was to get a win," Yuille said. "They got two of them."

Yuille inherited his love of the Lions from his father, Bruce, who grew up in the 1950s, a decade that saw Detroit rule the NFL, winning three championships (1952, '53 and '57).

Those are three of the four titles won by the team. The first came in 1935, when the NFL had teams such as the Brooklyn Dodgers and Pittsburgh Pirates. In the 1935 championship game against the New York Giants, the Lions rushed for 246 yards and got scoring runs from Dutch Clark, Ace Gutowsky, Ernie Caddel and Buddy Parker to win, 26–7.

There were some dark years between the 1935 title and the glory years of the 1950s. The 1942 team needed two coaches to average 3.5 points per game and end up with no wins. In 1946, the Lions went 1–10, throwing 11 touchdown passes and a resounding 33 interceptions. The 1948 team was a bit of an improvement, going 2–10, but it couldn't stop anyone on defense. The Lions allowed 33.9 points a game, and they were outscored by an average of 17.2 points a game.

Detroit's championship run in the 1950s featured a boatload of memorable NFL names—quarterback Bobby Layne, running back Doak Walker, linebacker Joe Schmidt, safety/punter Yale Lary and ends Cloyce

Box and Leon Hart. The 1953 team intercepted 38 passes, with defensive back Jack Christiansen leading the league with 12.

The Lions didn't just win their 1957 title, they seized it, crushing the Cleveland Browns, 59–14. Quarterback Tobin Rote, filling in for the injured Layne, threw four touchdown passes. Lions fans have been waiting for another championship ever since.

As with many floundering teams, that title drought comes with the tale of a curse. Layne broke his leg in the seventh game of 1957 and was traded after the season to the Pittsburgh Steelers. Legend has Layne placing a curse on the Lions because of that trade.

"The curse he put on the Lions was supposed to last 50 years, and we're well beyond that point," Yuille said.

Whether the curse is real or not, there's evidence to support a long, dark time for Detroit. The Lions went decades after 1957 with only one playoff win, a 38–6 victory over the Dallas Cowboys on Jan. 5, 1992. The Lions and the Cleveland Browns are the only teams in existence at the start of the Super Bowl era that have never appeared in that game.

Layne's alleged curse took an interesting twist in 2009 when the Lions used the first pick in that year's NFL draft to select Georgia quarterback Matthew Stafford, who attended the same high school as Layne—Highland Park High in Dallas. In November 2013, Stafford broke Layne's record for career passing yards with the Lions.

Stafford, receiver Calvin Johnson and a tougher defense got Detroit back to the playoffs in the 2011 and 2014 seasons. They helped snap an 11-season run from 2000 to 2010 that saw the Lions average more than 12 losses a season.

Those playoff appearances in 2011 and 2014 both ended in first-round defeats, but they accentuated the support from Lions diehards. Detroit's loss to Dallas in a playoff game after the 2014 season included a crucial pass interference call against the Cowboys that was waved off by the officials. Yuille said the aftermath of that game led to the biggest day for www.prideofdetroit.com, the Lions website where he worked. There were more than 2 million hits. Many were Lions fans who needed to vent, but others had different messages to put forth.

"That shows how fans hate the Cowboys, but even more, they don't want bad officiating deciding playoff games," Yuille said.

Despite all these failings, fans such as Yuille and Reisman stick with it. They have seen three teams that started in the 1990s—the Baltimore Ravens, Jacksonville Jaguars and Carolina Panthers—all have more recent playoff success than the Lions.

"It's amazing that one year it didn't all come together for the Lions," Yuille said.

The fans have dealt with the Ford family's management of the team, which hasn't always been stellar. "They've never shown signs of not caring. They're just not particularly good at running a franchise," Reisman said.

Reisman, who now is the managing editor of the www.prideofdetroit. com website, finds joy in any hints of success for the Lions. "I feel like it's a party every time they make the playoffs."

Reisman's father, Ken, got him hooked on the team. "There came a point where my fandom passed his," Jeremy said. "I went farther down the rabbit hole."

Now retired in Florida, Ken Reisman, a Detroit native, has been a fan long enough that he remembers freezing at more than a few home games before the Lions moved into a domed stadium in 1975. He admitted there have been times he has thought about dropping out of the Lions fan club. "You feel each year, 'Am I going to join this stupid thing every year even though I know they're not going to win?' Then I succumb.

"At one point I said, 'Enough's enough. What team could I pick to root for instead?' But I just couldn't do it. It's like it's in my DNA. Obviously it's not, but it feels that way."

Besides, Lions football has always been a time for family unity. As Jeremy said, "We attempted to go to temple one Sunday. We realized we liked football better. We ended that tradition real quick."

And Ken marvels at the continuity in his family of backing the Lions. Ken's father was a fan, and so were his siblings and aunts and uncles. Now he gets to watch his son rooting for the same team that his father did decades earlier. "The whole idea of carrying on that tradition is kind of fun."

With son now in Los Angeles and father retired in Boynton Beach, Florida, they still find a way to enjoy their Lions together. Jeremy traveled to Florida for Christmas in 2010, and the two were able to see back-to-back Lions games, one in Tampa Bay and the other the next week in Miami.

The Lions provided a pre–Christmas miracle, beating the Buccaneers, 23–20, in overtime. Dave Rayner tied the score with a 28-yard field goal as time expired in regulation, then kicked the game-winner in overtime. The victory halted a 26-game road losing streak.

"I remember walking in the concourse at Tampa Bay after the Lions won, celebrating and exchanging high-fives with other Lions fans," Jeremy said. "It was kind of bizarre for fans of a 3–10 team to be so ecstatic, but that's where the state of the team was at that time."

The Lions went and won the next week, too, beating the Dolphins, 34–27, on the day after Christmas. Linebacker DeAndre Levy won that game with a late touchdown on a 30-yard interception return. It was one of three turnovers forced by the Lions.

As with that Florida venture, there have been some joyful moments despite the overall lack of success. Lions fans have been able to watch great players such as receiver Calvin Johnson and defensive back Lem Barney. They got to enjoy seeing Barry Sanders spin and sprint for 15,269 yards during his 10 NFL seasons.

The running back was Jeremy's boyhood sports hero. Even these days, long after Sanders left the game in 1998, Jeremy will turn to YouTube to watch Sanders' highlights.

"He was miraculous to watch," he said. "It was something that made it worthwhile watching the Lions. Whether you won or not, you knew you'd see something amazing from Barry at least once a game."

Even though they now both live far from Michigan, Ken Reisman and his son Jeremy have maintained a tight bond when it comes to the Detroit Lions. In 2012, they got together not for a game, but for a visit to the Los Angeles County Museum of Art in Jeremy's new home state (photograph by Debbie Reisman).

There is also that most Detroit of traditions, the annual Thanksgiving Day game hosted by the Lions.

"That's the tradition I miss the most. It was definitely a bonding time with my dad," said Jeremy, who now has to watch that game from his California home instead of being there in person. He remembers there always being a warm, energetic feeling in the stadium, whether the Lions were 2–7 or 7–2. It was an opportunity to show off for the entire country, or as Jeremy said of the down years, "It was at least a chance to get sympathy from a national audience."

After the game, Thanksgiving dinner was waiting at home. "I was probably too young—and too distracted by football—to notice all the effort my mom put into dinner." The worst part for his mom and all the guests "was us usually coming home miserable."

Al Marino and Phil Cavill have had Lions season tickets together for more than 25 years. They look forward each year to the Thanksgiving Day game.

"I love the tradition of Thanksgiving," Marino said. "Detroit needs that. Detroit is a blue-collar city. There is a lot of stuff wrong with Detroit. That's one of the good things."

Even that tradition comes with some pain. Cavill remembers Thanksgiving Day 1980, a few years before he started getting season tickets for Lions games. He was watching the Lions and the Chicago Bears at his aunt's house as everyone was about to sit down for the holiday feast. No one else was much interested in the game, so he told them to start eating without him as the game neared its conclusion.

The Lions led the Chicago Bears, 17–10, when Chicago quarterback Vince Evans engineered a long drive that he finished with a game-tying touchdown run as the fourth quarter ended.

The calls for Cavill to join the dinner table continued, but he asked for a few more minutes to watch the overtime. It wouldn't even take that long. Chicago's Dave Williams caught the overtime kickoff at the 5-yard line, broke a tackle at his own 20 and sprinted untouched the rest of the way for a game-winning score.

"After that, I couldn't eat. I couldn't eat Thanksgiving dinner," Cavill said.

Since then, he and Marino have experienced many Lions memories. Other friends of theirs have no interest in football, so this is something Marino, who is chief of operations for a string of pizza restaurants, and Cavill, who runs a Goodyear dealership, share.

The two of them have a rat-a-tat, back-and-forth style when they talk about their Lions. Marino likes Stafford, the Lions quarterback. Cavill is always blaming him. Marino is the calm one who will watch with his arms folded, analyzing pass patterns and studying the game. Cavill is the guy loudly exhorting the Lions to dig a little deeper.

"Phil is a screamer and a yeller," Marino said. "One time he said, 'We're not winning because you're not yelling.'"

"The whole stadium is screaming, and Al is sitting there like a bump on a log," Cavill said.

"I used to scream, and I'd go home with a headache," Marino said. "Until they show me something, I ain't screaming."

Cavill had season tickets first. He invited Marino to join him at a game. Marino had only been to a Lions game once before, in the 1970s. The Lions weren't very good, and the Pontiac Silverdome was empty, he recalls. "It was boring."

This time with Cavill, he got to see Sanders' first home game. "After I went to that game and saw Barry Sanders run, I said, 'Oh my god.'" Marino has missed just one home game since then, and that was because Cavill needed extra tickets for visiting relatives.

The two host a tailgate before home games that can attract more than 50 people. The menu usually includes lamb chops, steaks, shrimp and sausages with peppers and onions. They get to the parking lot about three hours before game time.

"Within 15 minutes, I'm cooking," Marino said. He's pretty good at it. "There is never anything left."

Cavill is old enough to remember the Lions' last championship, but he wasn't paying much attention back then. He didn't really get interested in football until he started playing in high school. Marino tells a similar tale, adding, "I went out for football because that's where the cheerleaders were."

On this day, they are discussing the horrid start to the Lions 2015 season in which the Lions lost seven of their first eight games. The terrible start led to such commentary as this Facebook post by a Detroit fan: "Lions bye week. Bye favored by 14." (The Lions did improve as the season progressed, finishing 7–9.)

The season included a call that went against the Lions, leading to a loss in Seattle. Johnson fumbled late in the game, inches from scoring the go-ahead touchdown. As the ball bounced in the end zone, Seahawks linebacker K.J. Wright clearly batted the ball out of the end zone.

It should have been a penalty that would have allowed Detroit to keep the ball with a chance for a game-winning score. No call was made, and the NFL later admitted the game officials made a mistake.

In their decades of following the Detroit Lions, Phil Cavill (left) and Al Marino have seen some crazy losses (courtesy Phil Cavill).

"You feel so helpless. You're just screaming at the TV," Cavill said. With calls like this one, and the one in the playoff game with the Cowboys in 2015, it feeds into Marino's theory: "They don't want us to win. It's as if the refs get together and say, 'If it's a crucial play, call it against the Lions.'"

Lions fans would get handed another inexplicable loss two months after the Seattle game when Detroit, playing at home, led the Green Bay Packers, 23–21, in the final seconds. The game appeared to be over when a Packers play with a couple of laterals fell far short of succeeding as Detroit's Devin Taylor tackled Packers quarterback Aaron Rodgers. But Taylor was called for grabbing Rodgers' face mask, a call the Lions disputed, giving the Packers one more chance.

On that last play, Rodgers threw a 61-yard Hail Mary pass that was caught by tight end Richard Rodgers—somehow unguarded at the goal line—for the winning score. Lions fans sat stunned, no doubt thinking to themselves: "Only the Lions."

Marino and Cavill have had plenty of those "only the Lions"

moments, from the team's ownership to bad play to Millen. They even scoff at the name of the Lions mascot, Roary. "What do we have—a team of 10-year-olds?" Cavill said.

They watched the 0–16 season. "There were only two things we thought about: One, who's going to get fired? And two, who will we get with our draft picks?" Cavill said.

Even with the memories of all those losses, Marino and Cavill keep cheering. "The odds are if we give up our tickets, the next year they're going to win," Marino said. "We're boaters in the summertime and we snowmobile in the winter. In the fall, it's Lions football. It's camaraderie between Phil and I. It's our misery. We have to see this to the end. We are hundreds of thousands of dollars into this."

Jeremy Reisman is right there with them. He has no thoughts of changing teams, even in his new West Coast home. "It's something I couldn't imagine being without. It's like family. To lose my Lions fandom would be losing part of my identity."

Yuille echoed those words. "For better or worse—which is usually the case with the Lions—they're my team."

Frozen Passion

The Toronto Maple Leafs

Here's how much Jennifer Rogers and Scott Protomanni love their hockey team. Their wedding in March 2015 was held on the ice at Air Canada Centre several hours before a Toronto Maple Leafs game.

She wore a white Maple Leafs jersey. He wore a blue one. Floral displays were in the team colors. The numbers on the jerseys of the wedding party showed the date of the ceremony: 3–19–15.

When that night's game started, the newlyweds and their wedding guests—about 60 in all—got to watch from an arena suite. The couple's names and images were everywhere that night—on the Jumbotron during the Kiss Cam, in the game program, on the arena's ticker board.

"It was a fantastic experience," said Rogers, a first-grade teacher and resident of the Scarborough section of Toronto.

The wedding on ice contest sought die-hard fans, and Rogers and Protomanni qualify. Their home is a tribute to the Maple Leafs. There are lamp shades and bar stools, night lights and light switches, all with a team theme. They own a Stanley Cup–shaped popcorn maker. The garage door is covered with Maple Leafs logos.

In winter, blowup snowmen on the front lawn are dressed as players for the Leafs and their hated rivals, the Montreal Canadiens.

"We've had quite the traffic jams," said Rogers. Some families have stopped to pose for pictures to be used on their Christmas cards.

The love of the team dates from Rogers' childhood. Her grandmother had season tickets for years. Rogers' Christmas stocking often would contain a couple of tickets. "I wondered how Santa Claus knew I wanted to go to the games," she said.

"It's just our mentality that we bleed blue," Rogers said. "Even as a teenager, I understood Saturday nights were spent at home watching the game. It was family time."

Rogers' mother, Leslie, is a passionate fan. Like mother, like daughter. Rogers once confronted some people on the subway who were, as she put it, "bashing the boys." It turned out they were Canadiens fans.

"It was a heated exchange," Rogers said. "I find it my duty to remind people that everybody has a season."

She said there's nothing quite like the postseason in her city. "Playoff hockey in Toronto is a buzz. People who don't like hockey are willing to get a beer with you and watch the game because it's the Toronto thing to do."

The Maple Leafs were once a force in the National Hockey League, but in recent decades they have played the role of the also-ran. The franchise began in 1917 and won a championship that season, when it was known as the Toronto Arenas. Corb Denneny scored the game-winning goal in the decisive Game 5 of the finals, a 2–1 Toronto victory.

Since then, Toronto has won 12 more Stanley Cups, the most celebrated of all sports' trophies. But the last season that ended with the Leafs holding the Cup aloft was 1966–67. So what is it that keeps Leafs fans passionate after all those decades?

"They are part of the city. They're part of the fabric," said Lance Hornby, hockey columnist for the Toronto Sun.

For many years, there was lots of success for the Maple Leafs. "They were like the New York Yankees. Played in a beautiful arena that was well-kept. People got dressed up," Hornby said.

Radio broadcasts from the team's old arena, Maple Leaf Gardens, blasted across Canada, with Foster Hewitt at the microphone. It helped build a loyal fan base, as well as a nationwide image of the Gardens as "this magical place," Hornby said.

When television took over for radio, Toronto's team had a prominent role in "Hockey Night in Canada" broadcasts. As Hornby put it, "The Maple Leafs are perfect Canadian theater."

In winning their last Stanley Cup in 1967, the Maple Leafs beat the Canadiens. It was the year of Canada's centennial celebration. "That really cemented the Maple Leafs," Hornby said.

Like any Leafs fan, Rogers knows the painful history since 1967. As a younger follower, her memories focus on more recent events. One of the toughest for her was the 2013 playoff series against the Boston Bruins.

After falling behind three games to one, Toronto won Games 5 and 6 by 2–1 scores behind the goaltending of James Reimer. The Maple Leafs led, 4–1, midway through the third period of Game 7, closing in on victory in their first playoff appearance since 2004. The Bruins then scored three times, including twice in the last 82 seconds. Boston's Patrice Bergeron tallied in overtime for the victory.

"I can't ever remember being that mad," Rogers said. "I had to walk out of the house. I was standing on the porch swearing. When people talk about Game 7, I have to cover my ears."

After such devastating losses, or a 2014–15 season that saw the Leafs fall apart after being three points out of first place in mid–December, Rogers looks back on all that is good about being a Leafs fan—those tickets in her Christmas stocking, Saturday nights spent at home with her family, that unforgettable wedding ceremony. Her allegiance isn't swayed by a little losing.

"Our house is a shrine to the team. We really don't have any options," she said.

Toronto makes a great first impression. When snow isn't covering the ground, its downtown features patches of green parkland spread below the gleam of the financial district. The CN Tower stands tall, overlooking Lake Ontario. Within walking distance are the Air Canada Centre, home of the Maple Leafs and the National Basketball Association's Toronto Raptors; the Rogers Centre, used by baseball's Blue Jays; and BMO Field, home for pro soccer and the Argonauts of the Canadian Football League.

It's a city with a steady buzz that seems hip and comforting at the same time. A big part of that buzz is the love of all things Maple Leafs.

Vlad Zubac picked up on that love at an early age. His parents were from Croatia and moved to Toronto from Germany in 1973. He was 3 months old. It wasn't long before he was playing street hockey in the fall and ice hockey in the winter.

He remembers that as a boy he would get his haircut, and the barber would be talking about the Maple Leafs. Toronto didn't yet have its basketball Raptors, and its baseball Blue Jays were still in their formative years. The football Argonauts were popular but no match for the guys on skates.

"It was a point of conversation," Zubac said of the Maple Leafs. His father became a hockey fan, and they would hear from longtime fans about the strong teams of the past.

There were the Maple Leafs that won three straight Stanley Cups from 1947 to 1949. Those teams were coached by Hap Day and featured the scoring of Syl Apps and Ted Kennedy and the goaltending of Turk Broda. The 1948–49 team finished below .500, winning only 22 games, with 25 losses and 13 ties. But in the playoffs, the Maple Leafs won eight of nine games in beating the Boston Bruins and then the Detroit Red Wings to take the title.

From 1962 to 1964, the Maple Leafs again won three straight championships. Their coach was Punch Imlach. Their scoring punch came from Frank
Mahovlich, George Armstrong, Bob Pulford, Red Kelly and Dave Keon.

Hearing about those champions may have helped ease the pain of
the mediocre teams that Zubac watched as a youth. The Maple Leafs did
not have a winning season in the 1980s before finally hitting the .500 mark
(38–38–4) in 1989–90.

"Throughout the '80s, there were painful years. We just didn't have

**Vlad Zubac moved to Toronto at age three months. It didn't take him long to
discover the city's devotion to the Maple Leafs (photograph by Tedy Gordon).**

the talent," Zubac said. The team soon made a key move, though, acquiring goal-scorer Doug Gilmour as part of a 10-player trade with the Calgary Flames on January 2, 1992.

"Watching the Leafs being resurrected with Gilmour as the key player on the ice, that's what I remember," Zubac said. "He brought life back to the team."

Zubac, who works for IBM, has been rooting for a team that hasn't come close to reclaiming the Cup in his lifetime. The Maple Leafs did get to the conference finals four times from 1993 to 2002, but all four of those series ended in defeat. Those frustrations haven't stopped him from showing his love of the Leafs.

"Obviously, I can't support any other Canadian team," Zubac said. "Regardless of how bad they are, regardless of how dysfunctional ownership has been, regardless of how expensive things are, I'm still going to watch it."

It's a common theme on the streets of Toronto. These fans are watching and waiting, filling the Air Canada Centre night after night to show their support for the Leafs.

"People say, 'Can you imagine what it will be like when they win again?' This place will go crazy," said Toronto native Mike Wilson.

Growing up in Toronto, "there was no other team to watch," he said. "You were born and bred to watch [the Maple Leafs]." Wilson saw his first game in the old Maple Leaf Gardens in 1962 with his father, Ernie.

"It seemed so surreal," Wilson said. "My heart was beating so fast just watching it."

Thirty-seven years later, on February 13, 1999, Wilson took his dad to the last game the Leafs played in the Gardens. The Chicago Blackhawks beat Toronto, just as they had in the first game played in the arena in 1931. Despite the loss, it was a night for father and son to savor.

"As I walked out after the game, I thought, 'It's time.' But there were a lot of memories walking out," Wilson said. "Now I look back fondly about how great it was. All those memories stick with you."

Wilson knows a thing or two about memories. His basement is a museum-quality tribute to his team. Glass cases hold dozens of Maple Leafs sweaters. There are autographed hockey sticks and photos on display. There are seats and turnstiles from Maple Leaf Gardens. There's even a locker from the old Maple Leafs locker room.

Wilson's collection started when he was 7 with a hockey stick autographed by Maple Leafs defenseman Carl Brewer. As Wilson grew older he added to his trove of hockey treasures because, he said, "I wanted to

Mike Wilson's home includes a museum-like tribute to hockey and his favorite team, the Maple Leafs. His collection started when he received a hockey stick autographed by defenseman Carl Brewer at age seven (photograph by Joel Nadel from Event Imaging).

have some stuff and have a few buddies over to watch the game." He hasn't stopped collecting.

Wilson was just entering his teen years when the Maple Leafs won their last Stanley Cup in 1967. They beat the Chicago Blackhawks in the first round in six games, and then won the Stanley Cup Final against the Montreal Canadiens, also in six games.

Wilson remembers being in bed and listening to the clinching game, a 3–1 victory over the Canadiens. Jim Pappin, Ron Ellis and Armstrong scored for Toronto, and goalie Terry Sawchuk shut down Montreal.

Wilson's calm reaction reflected the fact that it was the fourth championship in six seasons for Toronto. "I thought, 'Oh, we won, good. Just go out and try to win another one.'" He and all other Maple Leafs fans are still waiting.

"But I tell you, I'm running out of years," he said. "The little fan clock is ticking. I'm thinking, 'Give me one more shot.'"

It's that hope that keeps Wilson going as a fan. As if he hasn't seen enough hard times with his hockey team, he also roots for football's Buffalo Bills, losers of four straight Super Bowls in the 1990s.

The collection of hockey memorabilia in Mike Wilson's home has attracted some big names in the sport. There aren't many bigger than Wayne Gretzky (left) (photograph by Joel Nadel from Event Imaging).

"I hate the term there's always next year, but they're your team. If it's bred in you and they're your team, you just stick with it. It's my team. I've been with them since I was a kid."

Sticking with it is a daily ritual for Maple Leafs backers. It may be hard to find a more passionate fan base. Games at Maple Leaf Gardens were sold out for decades. That support has continued at the Air Canada Centre, which opened in 1999.

At a game in November 2014, the microphone cut out on singer Michelle Madeira during her rendition of "The Star-Spangled Banner." Toronto fans enthusiastically stepped right in, finished the song and, without missing a beat, moved right on to "O Canada."

Wilson recalls his parents telling him about going to the homes of friends to watch the Maple Leafs on Saturday nights. This wasn't just a social get-together to watch a game, it was an event.

His two children now are fans, as the Maple Leafs baton gets passed to another generation.

"There's that kind of mantra we have as fans. There's that element of hope and the history and the stories mixed in," Wilson said.

Mike Wilson doesn't need a giant picture of Frank Mahovlich (right). He got to meet him when the ex–Toronto Maple Leafs great visited Wilson's display of hockey memorabilia (photograph by Joel Nadel from Event Imaging).

When it comes to picking up the Maple Leafs mantra, it may be hard to top the unique circumstances of Michael Scalzo's conversion to the team. It started when he was isolated for two weeks in a hospital wing.

The Rochester, New York, resident took part in a flu study done by the University of Rochester in 1993. He was part of a group of about 30 guys in their 20s who couldn't leave the hospital during the two-week period.

With that many young men gathered together with nowhere to go, video games and sports viewing became staples of the daily schedule. One of the prime viewing events was the National Hockey League's Campbell Conference finals—the Maple Leafs vs. the Los Angeles Kings.

"We were kind of a captive audience," Scalzo said. The Kings had the Great One on their side, and Scalzo couldn't help but notice.

"It was all Wayne Gretzky," Scalzo said. "Being a brand new fan, it was cool to watch him work, but at the same time, I was rooting for the Leafs."

The Maple Leafs led the series, three games to two, but trailed, 4–1, in Game 6 before Wendel Clark led a rally to send the game to overtime. In the extra period, Gretzky clipped Gilmour in the face with a high stick. There was no penalty, and Gretzky scored the game-winning goal a few minutes later to beat the Maple Leafs.

The Kings then won Game 7, also 5–4, to move on to the Stanley Cup Final, where they lost to the Canadiens.

"I kind of fell in love with that crew—Felix Potvin, Wendel Clark, Doug Gilmour," Scalzo said. "They were real scrappers—a real blue-collar team. After that series, that was it. My love for the Leafs just grew."

His father is a Canadiens fan. "Of all the teams I could have picked, that's the worst I could have chosen from a father-son relationship," he said.

Over the years, he's made the trip from Rochester to see the Maple Leafs in Toronto a handful of times. Those trips made an impression.

"You hear the stereotype that the Canadian kids are born with skates on their feet. It's not just a diversion or a passion. It's a way of life.

"It seemed like the city kind of shut down, and all eyes were on the Leafs. Everyone would say, 'Oh, there's a game tonight.' That seemed to be all that mattered."

In 1999, he traveled to Toronto because he thought a friend had tickets to the team's final game at Maple Leaf Gardens.

As they walked to the arena, Scalzo's friend veered toward a nearby bar. "I asked him, 'Aren't we going to the game?' He said, 'Are you kidding me? You can't get tickets for that game.'"

Since Scalzo became a fan, the Maple Leafs have been a mix of bad—four seasons with just 30 wins—and pretty good—a half-dozen losses in the conference finals or semifinals. The 2003–04 team won 45 games and set a franchise record with 103 points.

"I thought that could be our year," Scalzo said, but the Maple Leafs lost in the Eastern Conference semifinals to the Philadelphia Flyers.

All of these recent failures make the image of the Maple Leafs hoisting the Stanley Cup again seem like a far-off fantasy.

Scalzo is well-versed in heartbreak, though. Long before he became a fan of the Maple Leafs, he started rooting for baseball's Boston Red Sox, a trait he inherited from his father, Dave.

He watched with his father when the ground ball went between Bill Buckner's legs in Game 6 of the 1986 World Series. The New York Mets won the game on that play and went on to win the Series. There were more Red Sox playoff losses in the '80s and '90s.

His Red Sox's suffering haunted him as he watched the Maple Leafs lose that 1993 series to the Great Gretzky and his Kings. "It was like, 'Oh great, I picked another good team. First the Sox, then these guys.'"

The Red Sox have come through for him, winning their first World Series in 86 years in 2004 and then winning it again a couple more times. He's still waiting on his Maple Leafs.

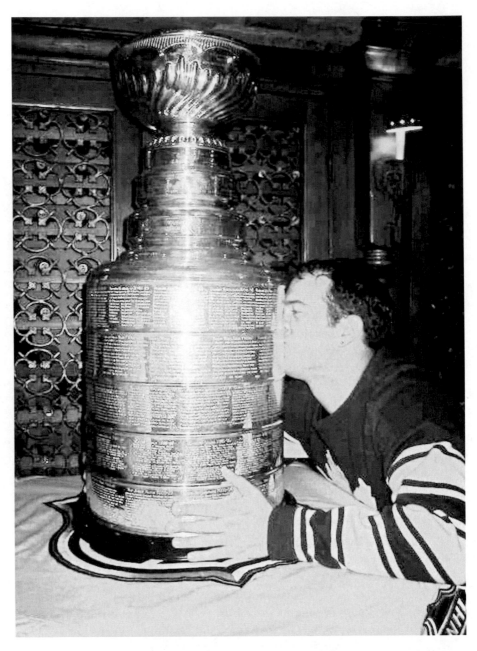

Michael Scalzo was living in California in 2007 when the Anaheim Ducks won the Stanley Cup. The Cup visited a bar while he was there, and Scalzo paid tribute while showing his true colors—wearing a vintage Toronto Maple Leafs sweater (courtesy Michael Scalzo).

"It's been tough, but I don't give up easily. I don't give up at all. Once I assign my allegiance to something, I stick with it."

Just how much does he stick with it? Check out this message he texted in early 2015: "NHL Network is airing Game 6 of the 1993 Campbell Conference series. Leafs vs. Kings. And here I thought I had put it behind me. Painful."

In the Valley of the Suns

The Phoenix Suns

Phoenix is a city of transplants and sunshine, not exactly the perfect formula for a passionate fan base.

Residents have come from elsewhere, often bringing their sports allegiances with them from the chilly north. With sunshine abounding and the nearby desert beckoning, it can be hard to keep fans inside to watch sports.

Not a passionate fan base? Don't tell that to Tom Pomeroy and Jim Rhodeos. The longtime friends live and die with their Phoenix Suns.

They've both held season tickets for more than 30 years. They can rattle off the names of great players and great moments, of painful losses and bad breaks. They can talk about the cleverness of Steve Nash, the coolness of Paul Westphal, the well-roundedness of Shawn Marion.

The Suns started as a National Basketball Association expansion team in 1968 with the usual results for a first-year team. They finished 16–66.

But, the next year saw the Suns make the playoffs and take the Los Angeles Lakers to seven games before losing a first-round series. Since then, it's been mostly successful seasons as well as rosters filled with great players, from Nash to Charles Barkley, from Alvan Adams to Walter Davis.

All that success and all those stars have never brought an NBA title, though. In fact, the Suns have the best all-time winning percentage of any team that has never won an NBA championship.

"I once told friends, the Suns will win before I start collecting Social Security," said Rhodeos. "I've got three and a half more years. It's just so hard to win."

Pomeroy and Rhodeos can list the reasons that the Suns have come close but never won. First, of course, is the coin flip. The Suns and the Milwaukee Bucks, another expansion team, were in line for the top pick in the 1969 NBA draft. A coin toss would decide who got the first choice, which that season was a huge prize, UCLA's Kareem Abdul-Jabbar, then known as Lew Alcindor, a dominant college player who would become one of the NBA's all-time greats.

The Suns got to call the toss, and they went with heads because that's what fans voted for in a newspaper poll. The coin came up tails, and Milwaukee went on to select Abdul-Jabbar. Phoenix had to settle for Neal Walk, a star center at the University of Florida who would become a decent but undistinguished NBA player.

Through the years, there have been near misses in the playoffs along with a few badly timed injuries. "It's like the Suns are a snake-bit team," Pomeroy said.

Rhodeos jumped on the Suns early, drawn by the excitement of watching Connie Hawkins. Hawkins, who played in Phoenix from 1969 to 1973, was a graceful forward known for his midair artistry, finding new and creative ways to score. He was Julius Erving before there was a Dr. J; Michael Jordan before there was an MJ.

"His hand engulfed the ball. He just glided and dunked. Once I saw him, I just got hooked on the Suns," Rhodeos said.

It was Rhodeos who got Pomeroy interested in the team. One night, Rhodeos invited Pomeroy and his wife over. At the time, Pomeroy wasn't into sports, but Rhodeos convinced the couple to watch the Suns game on television with him.

"I remember asking him, 'Why do you like this stuff so much?'" Pomeroy said.

That night, they watched the Suns overcome a double-digit deficit late in regulation against the Seattle SuperSonics. Phoenix ended up winning in overtime.

"They started screaming as much as I did," Rhodeos said. "It was probably the most noise that apartment complex ever had."

The two admit they are opposites when it comes to rooting. Pomeroy is the optimist; Rhodeos tends to see the darker side. Their diverse approaches were never more apparent than during the 1976 NBA Finals, when Phoenix met the Boston Celtics.

The Suns lost the first two games in Boston.

"I remember my die-hard attitude. I said, 'Don't worry, we're going to win the next two games,'" Pomeroy said. That's just what the Suns did, setting up a Game 5 that just might be the greatest playoff game in NBA history.

The Suns and Celtics battled deep into the night in Boston, tied after regulation and a first overtime. Trailing 112–110 with one second to go in a second overtime, Phoenix inbounded the ball near midcourt. Gar Heard caught the pass to the right of the foul line, turned and tossed up a high-arcing shot that swished through the net, sending the game to a third overtime.

Rhodeos never saw the shot. While watching at home, he made one of those crucial mistakes that devoted fans sometimes make. It happened shortly before Heard's basket.

"I was so frustrated. I said, 'I can't watch them lose.'" He hopped in his car with his basketball, planning on shooting some hoops to burn off his nervous energy. While driving, he heard Heard's game-tying shot on the car radio.

"I turned that car around so fast and almost got into three accidents. I raced home and told my mom to turn the TV back on."

It turned out he did end up seeing Phoenix lose, 128–126, in the third overtime as Boston got a late spurt from reserve Glenn McDonald, easily the biggest moment in his three-year NBA career.

"I just hate him, hate him," Rhodeos said of McDonald.

"The Suns came back to Phoenix, and it was just like they were spent," Pomeroy said. After all the excitement of Game 5, Boston won Game 6 and the NBA title, 87–80.

The Suns would get back to the NBA Finals in 1993 with a team led by Barkley, Kevin Johnson and Dan Majerle, with help from key contributors Danny Ainge, Cedric Ceballos, Tom Chambers and rookie Richard Dumas.

During that run to the Finals, Pomeroy and a friend painted a 60-foot-long "Go Phoenix Suns" sign outside Pomeroy's insurance office. The sign still stands, with touch-up work helping to keep fresh the bold team colors of orange and purple.

The Suns dropped the first two games at home to the Chicago Bulls in the 1993 Finals, but Pomeroy again showed his optimistic side. For Game 3, he flew to Chicago, where he figured he was one of about a dozen Suns fans in the crowd.

"Michael Jordan is shooting free throws, and I'm heckling him. I had 11,000 eyes watching me, wanting to wring my neck," he said.

Led by Majerle's 28 points, the Suns won Game 3, another triple-overtime contest, 129–121. But Jordan and the Bulls won the series in six games for their third straight title.

Troy Tauscher is too young to have seen some of the key moments in Suns history, including that 1993 series against the Bulls, but that doesn't make the Arizona State University student any less passionate.

His Suns roots date back to his grandmother, Roberta Plunkett, who was among the first to buy season tickets after the Suns arrived in 1968. Those tickets were passed on to Tauscher's mom, Tracy, and someday they will be his. "That's my one family heirloom," he said.

Even though he wasn't around, Tauscher is aware of the impact of those tough times in team history. "We all collectively have a bitterness about the coin flip and Game 6 of the '93 Finals, but we all feel that's far enough away that it's time to get over it."

In that Game 6 of the '93 Finals, the Chicago Bulls, who led the series three games to two, went cold, and the Suns rallied to grab a 98–96 lead with 14 seconds left. Up to that point, the Bulls had scored just nine points in the fourth quarter, all by Jordan.

On their final possession, Jordan brought the ball upcourt, and the Bulls worked the ball to Horace Grant, who was about five feet from the basket to the left of the foul lane. As the Suns' defense shifted toward Grant, he fired a pass back out to a wide-open John Paxson, who drained a three-pointer. A series that appeared headed for a Game 7 in Phoenix was over.

Don Benner attended that game, and he was confident the Suns would dethrone the two-time champion Bulls in the series. "Charles [Barkley] was playing out of his shoes," he said.

When Paxson nailed the three-pointer, "You could literally have heard a pin drop," said Benner, an executive vice president with a Phoenix-area commercial printer. "Everyone stood there for several minutes with their mouths open. Nobody moved. Dead silent. That was a sad moment. That was our shot."

Tauscher said, "Some fans still argue about who should have guarded Paxson. We all collectively realize that we don't know."

The next two seasons saw the Suns lose conference semifinal series to Hakeem Olajuwon and the Houston Rockets, both in seven games. The Rockets went on to win championships both years.

"For me, that's the lowest point in Suns' history. We just couldn't get by them," Rhodeos said.

Then there was San Antonio's Robert Horry hip-checking Nash in Game 4 of the Western Conference semifinal series in the 2007 playoffs. The hit sent Nash to the floor, sprawled against the scorer's table, and teammates Amar'e Stoudemire and Boris Diaw came off the bench in Nash's defense. The Suns won that Game 4, 104–98, to even the series, but leaving the bench led to one-game suspensions for Stoudemire and Diaw, a factor that helped swing the series in San Antonio's favor.

Nash had 19 points and 12 assists in Game 5 in Phoenix, but it wasn't enough as the Spurs won, 88–85. Back at home in San Antonio, the Spurs got a combined 87 points from Manu Ginobili, Tony Parker and Tim Duncan to win Game 6, 114–106, and close out the series.

"That was the could of, would of, should of season for sure," Dave King, managing editor of a Phoenix Suns website, said of that 2007 playoff loss.

Those "could of" moments are all part of the challenge for even a younger fan like Tauscher. With a grandmother with season tickets and parents who enjoy sports, he said he never consciously chose the Suns. "I just grew up with it."

He has stuck with it, enjoying the star players and great games, even if playoff appearances have been scarce in recent years. One of his favorite moments was Goran Dragic's performance in Game 3 of the 2010 Western Conference semifinals against the San Antonio Spurs.

Dragic had scored three points heading into the fourth quarter. Then he went wild, pouring in 23 points in the final period, hitting nine of 11 shots, including all four of the three-pointers he took. Those are the moments that fans like Tauscher live for and don't soon forget.

Tauscher also is influenced by his father, Karl, who grew up in Pennsylvania and has maintained his devotion to the Pittsburgh Steelers. Like father, like son when it comes to dedication to a team. Of his burning love of the Suns, Tauscher said, "It's the loyalty to the place I've called home for 20 years."

He remembers at an early age how the team's fast-paced offense enhanced his interest in basketball. He grew up with the "Seven Seconds or Less Suns," a team coached by Mike D'Antoni and led by Nash, the nonpareil point guard.

The frenetic offense aimed to score as quickly as possible. "For a young child like me with a short attention span, it was perfect," Tauscher said. "I said, 'I'm in on this.' Everything was fast and chaotic, but there was an organization to the chaos."

The system worked, at least to a certain point. From 2005 through 2010, the Suns led the league in scoring five of six seasons. However, in the playoffs, where defense often rules, the Suns couldn't get past the Western Conference finals.

It was a period that fit in well with the Suns' past. Throughout their history, the Suns have been a flashy, entertaining team, just one that's not been quite good enough to win a title.

"The '80s, we couldn't get by the Lakers. The '90s, we couldn't get by

Houston. Y2K, we couldn't get by San Antonio. There's always that one team that's stopped us," Rhodeos said. He hasn't given up hope of seeing a Suns championship, though.

"I made a promise. I told some friends, and they said they'll hold me to it," he said. "I'm getting that tattoo. You cannot believe how happy I will be if the Suns win."

Don't doubt him on that tattoo plan. Rhodeos isn't shy about showing his Suns pride. In 1980, he had a ring made with the Suns' logo. "It's been on my finger longer than my wedding band," he said. His license plate? SNS4LFE.

Asked why he is still a fan after all the heartbreak, Pomeroy's answer is simple: "I'm still alive." He continued, "Every year there's a hope. They're a fun team. You get endeared to them."

Benner was 10 when his family moved to Phoenix from Michigan in 1976, and kids at school were talking about the Suns. "You want to be in on the in thing, so I started watching. I just fell in love with it."

That feeling has remained true through the years. "I just love the Suns," he said in the middle of a dreadful 2015–16 season. "Things go good, bad and ugly. You just have to stick with it."

In his role with www.brightsideofthesun.com, King has seen and written about the best and worst moments of the Suns. King, who also works for the state of Arizona, started as a Suns blogger because he couldn't get enough to read about his favorite team. He found he wasn't alone.

Left: Don Benner moved to Arizona when he was 10. After hearing the other kids in school talking about the Phoenix Suns, he decided to check the team out (courtesy Don Benner). *Right:* When Dave King couldn't get enough to read about the Phoenix Suns, he started his own blog (courtesy Dave King).

"There are a lot of people who are so invested in the team, they'll read about it all day and night," he said. King remembers the throngs that turned out for a parade in 1993 when the Suns lost the NBA Finals to Chicago, beaten by Jordan and that late jump shot from Paxson. "The whole town was painted purple," King said.

He moved to Phoenix from Erie, Pennsylvania, in 1983. Back then, the Suns and whatever sport was in season at Arizona State were the only games in town. Now, Phoenix has four major sports teams. It's given fans in the city more options, but the Suns maintain a strong following.

Since his arrival in the Valley of the Sun, King has seen plenty of joy and heartbreak. There was the amazing 2006 playoff run that featured a last-second three-pointer by Tim Thomas to force overtime against the Los Angeles Lakers in Game 6 of the first round and the last-second three-pointer by Raja Bell to force a second overtime against the Los Angeles Clippers in the Western Conference semifinals.

"Those kinds of shots are what make me love the NBA," King said.

Those 2006 Suns rallied from a 3–1 deficit against the Lakers and also beat the Clippers in seven games before losing the Western Conference finals to the Dallas Mavericks.

There were the 1996–97 Suns, who started the season 0–13. That's right—13 games, 13 losses. The first win of the season came on November 27, a 99–77 thumping of the New Jersey Nets. That win sparked a 40–29 finish to the season, and somehow, some way, the Suns made the playoffs, which led to a special moment for King.

In Game 4 of a first-round series against the Seattle SuperSonics, Rex Chapman hit a three-pointer at the buzzer to tie the score at 107, sending the game to overtime. A YouTube video simply labels the play, "Rex Chapman—The Shot!"

Looking every bit like a National Football League wide receiver, Chapman made an over-the-shoulder catch of a cross-court inbounds pass, then turned, leaped and heaved the ball at the basket just before stumbling out of bounds.

King was visiting his in-laws and was the only one still awake in the house when Chapman took his shot.

"I was ready for the game to be over," King said. "I was thinking, 'All right, it's time to go to bed.' After that shot, I was jumping all over the living room, trying not to wake anyone up."

Unfortunately for the Suns, the SuperSonics rallied to win Game 4 in overtime, 122–115. Seattle then won the series two nights later, thumping the Suns, 116–92.

While there was the joy of Chapman's shot, King's reaction was just the opposite during the 2008 playoffs. The Suns had acquired Shaquille O'Neal in midseason from the Miami Heat, and Phoenix fans were thinking this might be that championship season.

The Suns finished with a 55–27 record, but in the competitive Western Conference those 55 wins earned them just a number six seed and a first-round matchup with the defending champion Spurs.

In Game 1 of the first-round playoff series, San Antonio's Michael Finley hit a three-pointer with 15 seconds left to send the game to overtime. With San Antonio trailing by three late in the first overtime, Duncan hit a three-pointer—his first of the season—with 3 seconds left to keep the Spurs alive. In the second overtime, Ginobili made a late layup to give the Spurs a 117–115 victory.

"I remember not moving or speaking or doing anything on the couch for 30 minutes. Life felt like it was over at that moment," King said.

The series was pretty much over for the Suns. After the draining Game 1 loss, they dropped the next two games. They got 27 points from Bell to win Game 4 at home, 105–86, but San Antonio closed out the series in Game 5, winning at home, 92–87, with Duncan and Parker combining for 60 points.

Despite such tough losses, King has gotten to see many thrilling moments, including the great point-guard play of Nash.

"You just can't be an average point guard on the Suns anymore," King said. "Fans are saying, 'Why don't these passes look so good? Why don't these players look so good after getting these passes?' We're going to look back 20 years from now remembering those passes Nash made."

King recalls the joy of covering the 2013–14 Suns, who finished with a 48–34 record. They missed the playoffs by a game, but it was 23 more victories than they had the previous year.

He remembers swingman P.J. Tucker describing the team by saying, "We're just playing stupid." It was a team that just went out and played hard, not worrying about what might happen.

"That was a great, fun team. I love seasons like that," King said. It's a key part of his philosophy as a Suns fan. "What really keeps me going is I want to see the team grow, and I want to see the team get better. I'm not a pessimist. There's always a chance that next year will be so much better than this one."

J-E-T-S

The New York Jets

When it comes to football teams with long dry spells, perhaps no squad gets as much attention as the New York Jets. ESPN morning host Mike Greenberg loves talking about his Jets. So do comedians Ray Romano and Kevin James. Then there's young Kevin Arnold, played by Fred Savage in television's "The Wonder Years," wandering his suburban subdivision in his Jets jacket.

When the National Football League draft is held, there's no question which team's fans will take center stage. The green and white jerseys burst from the crowd, just as loud as the J-E-T-S cheers. Of course, there's also the booing, an annual tradition whenever the Jets make a selection that doesn't please the fans in the stands.

"I love Jets fans during the draft. They're hilarious," said Keith Meeney, a New York City resident and longtime Jets follower.

The Jets fanatics have been as much a part of draft day as discussions of 40-yard-dash times and players' "intangibles." There are online video montages of Jets supporters and their draft-day rowdiness. As one fan put it in a video interview, "We're great at booing because we have nothing to look forward to."

The franchise started in 1960 as the Titans in the newly formed American Football League, a challenger to the well-established National Football League. The Titans' start was as mediocre as could be, two straight 7–7 seasons. Their most productive players were two wide receivers, Don Maynard and Art Powell.

The name change to the Jets came in 1963, the season before the team moved to the newly built Shea Stadium, located near LaGuardia Airport. In 1965, the Jets made another bold move, using the first overall pick in the draft to select quarterback Joe Namath from the University of Alabama.

With Namath leading the team, the Jets crafted one of the biggest upsets in Super Bowl history in 1969. But, since then, there have been a whole lot of broken hearts. That doesn't keep Jets fans from rooting with all their heart.

Take Ken Filete of Windsor, Connecticut, a Jets fan for more than four decades, who was up late watching as the Jets were losing, 30–7, to the Miami Dolphins on a Monday night in 2000.

New York's quarterback, Vinny Testaverde, threw four touchdown passes in the final 14 minutes, the last one a 3-yarder to Jumbo Elliott with 42 seconds remaining to tie the score at 37. For Elliott, an offensive tackle who lined up as an eligible receiver on the play, it was the only touchdown of his 14-year NFL career. The Jets then won in overtime on John Hall's 40-yard field goal.

"I stayed up to watch the whole game and kept screaming into the couch pillow throughout the fourth quarter as to not wake the kids or my wife," Filete said. "I remember when I finally came to bed my heart was still pounding so hard that I woke up my wife while simply lying in bed."

For Meeney, who grew up in Metuchen, New Jersey, and now is the director of a private art studio in New York, his Jets love was inherited. His mother was a Jets fan from the first day the team joined the American Football League. His father was a fan of all New York teams, but it was his Uncle Bob who helped get him hooked, bringing Meeney and his brother to Jets games.

While most of the kids in the neighborhood pulled for the New York Giants, Meeney approached it a little differently.

"I always wanted to cheer for the underdog, so clearly around here that was the New York Jets," he said. "By the time I reached high school in the mid '90s, my best friend and I decided we were going all in. Die-hard fans. We became a little obsessed."

Compared to Meeney, it took Filete a while to buy into the Jets. He was born in Queens and grew up in Peekskill, New York, about 50 miles north of the city. His first exposure to the Jets was when he was about 8, and his father took him to the squad's training camp, which was then held in Peekskill. It was an interesting team, led by Namath, the flashy, young quarterback who would soon be predicting that the Jets would pull a huge upset in Super Bowl III. They did, beating the Baltimore Colts, 16–7, on January 12, 1969, in the Orange Bowl. Namath threw for 206 yards, and Matt Snell rushed for 121 yards and the Jets' only touchdown. It was the defense that led the way, though, intercepting four passes. It remains the Jets' only championship.

But Filete, despite that training camp visit, hadn't quite caught the Jets bug, even as Namath and company won the Super Bowl.

"That leaves me even more frustrated," he said. "I was on this planet Earth and I wasn't paying that much attention yet."

A few years later, though, he was paying attention, becoming a huge Jets fan, even though most of his pals also followed the Giants. Those friends would tease him when the Jets faltered.

"It started training me for life. When I was younger, I would be devastated when they lost. I learned to take it in stride and move on," he said.

That philosophy has helped him today. Working in Connecticut as a director of direct mail marketing, he is surrounded by fans of the successful New England Patriots.

"A lot of time I'll get defined that way. It will come up at a meeting that I'm a Jets fan," he said. The ribbing continues, much as it did in his youthful days. Like most Jets fans, Filete has gotten used to the suffering.

In 1989, he had season tickets for Jets home games. Somehow, he didn't see them win once. The Jets went 4–12 that season, and three of the victories were on the road. Their lone win at home was in late November against the Atlanta Falcons. Filete and his friends boycotted that game to protest the Jets' miserable performance under coach Joe Walton, who would be fired at the end of the season. Walton wasn't helped much by the "Joe Must Go" chants that echoed through the stands that season or the fact that more than 55,000 fans didn't even bother to show up for the final home game.

There were the Rich Kotite years. Kotite coached the Jets for just two seasons, 1995 and '96, and managed a 4–28 record. The worst of those two teams—the 1996 Jets, who went 1–15—had some talent on offense. Adrian Murrell rushed for 1,249 yards. Wayne Chrebet, a local favorite from nearby Hofstra University, caught 84 passes and was helped out by fellow receiver Keyshawn Johnson, who had 63 receptions. But the Jets defense couldn't stop anyone. It allowed 454 points to rank 29th in the league and gave up 2,200 yards rushing.

"We hoped for the best and prayed that it didn't get worse, but every week it got worse and worse," said Filete.

Things would improve soon. Kotite's firing led to the hiring of Bill Parcells, who had taken the New England Patriots to the Super Bowl the previous season.

It was a bold move by the Jets because Parcells was most closely associated with the Giants, the team with whom the Jets shared a stadium. Under Parcells' reign from 1983 to 1990, the Giants won two Super Bowls.

Parcells had an immediate impact. The Jets went from 1–15 to 9–7 in his first season, 1997. The improved defense, under new coordinator Bill Belichick, allowed 287 points, the sixth-best mark in the league and 167 points fewer than the Jets had given up a season earlier. Belichick, of course, would make his mark later as head coach of the New England Patriots.

The following year, the Jets improved to 12–4, winning the American Football Conference's East division. Testaverde threw for 3,256 yards and 29 touchdowns while having only seven passes intercepted. Running back Curtis Martin piled up 1,652 total yards, and Chrebet and Johnson combined to catch 158 passes and score 18 touchdowns.

With Martin rushing for 124 yards, the Jets won a first-round playoff matchup with the Jacksonville Jaguars, 34–24. They fell the next week in the conference championship game to the Denver Broncos, 23–10. Although Testaverde threw for 356 yards, his two interceptions were among six Jets turnovers that day.

A few seasons later, the Jets' and Patriots' history would take an interesting turn. In a September 23, 2001, game at New England, Jets linebacker Mo Lewis clobbered New England's starting quarterback, Drew Bledsoe, knocking him out of bounds and out of the game. Usually, taking out the other team's starting quarterback is a good thing. But, in a case of typical Jets luck, that play brought Tom Brady into the game to replace Bledsoe.

The Jets would win that day, 10–3, but Brady led the Patriots to a Super Bowl title that year, followed by season after season of success. In fact, the Patriots would win the AFC East 13 of the next 15 seasons, through 2015. As Meeney said of the Lewis play, "It crushed my hopes and dreams for the next decade."

The Jets would have their moments as well. They made the playoffs six times from 2001 to 2010 and reached the conference finals in consecutive years, losing to the Indianapolis Colts after the 2009 season and to the Pittsburgh Steelers the next year.

But the 2015 season brought its own special kind of pain. In the next-to-last game of the season, the Jets upset the first-place Patriots in overtime, 26–20, with quarterback Ryan Fitzpatrick throwing three touchdown passes.

That victory gave the Jets a 10–5 record and put them in control of a wild-card playoff spot in the American Football Conference. All they had to do was go to Buffalo and beat the 7–8 Bills and former Jets coach Rex Ryan in the last game of the season to clinch a playoff spot. Fitzpatrick, who had been solid all season for the Jets, threw three interceptions, and the Bills won, 22–17. That meant the Steelers, and not the Jets, were playoff-bound.

Filete took the loss in stride. He knew there was plenty at stake in that game, including beating Ryan and pushing first-year Jets coach Todd Bowles into the playoffs. Still, he was able to see the bright side of the 2015 season.

"I'm an optimistic Jets fan," Filete said. "Ten and six was not something I expected. It was a good season of success. I'd like to see how they can build on it."

Like Filete, Meeney isn't too discouraged by the losses and down times. "The Jets are my team. That's it," he said. "Even when I hate the decisions they've made over the years, I will always root for them. If you change teams every couple of years, you're not really a fan, are you?"

Filete echoes those sentiments.

"You can't let a sports team define you as a person," he said. But, he added, "I've always stayed with the Jets, no matter what." For both Meeney and Filete, their dedication has paid off in some good times.

Meeney spent several years in California and was at the Jets' playoff game in San Diego on January 17, 2010. He was tailgating with about a dozen folks before the game, wearing the jersey of Jim Leonhard, a scrappy defensive back who played with the Jets from 2009 to 2011.

While manning the grill, Meeney heard a voice from behind asking, "Hey, you're a Jim Leonhard fan?"

"I said, without turning my head, 'You know it, and if you are, you're welcome to eat here with us.'" Turns out it was Leonhard's family, many also wearing his jersey. They stayed for skirt steaks, sausage and peppers, and pork chops with grilled onions.

The game turned out to be even better than the tailgate. Shonn Greene's 53-yard touchdown run midway through the fourth quarter led the Jets to a 17–14 victory.

"We went ballistic," Meeney said. "That might have been the happiest I've ever been in the realm of fandom."

Another moment of Jets joy was the playoff game in January 2011 at New England. A month earlier, the Patriots had crushed the Jets, 45–3. Few people gave New York any chance in the playoff rematch, but Mark Sanchez threw three touchdown passes, and the Jets knocked off the Patriots, 28–21.

Meeney said, "Let's put it this way.... I didn't go to work the next day I was so happy," he said. "We were at a bar in Manhattan Beach all night doing Jets chants like lunatic 15-year-olds."

Of that playoff victory over New England, Filete said, "It was awesome. For all the years I was a fan, it was retribution. It was so relishing to have that experience; to be able to proudly wear my Jets colors in this area was very, very nice."

Filete's love of the Jets has worn off on his mother-in-law, Sandra Scribner of Chicopee, Massachusetts. Living 90 miles west of Boston, her family is made up of Patriots fans. Scribner has always loved football, but she never felt a strong allegiance to the Patriots or any other NFL team. Filete changed that.

"He was so enthusiastic and so proud of his team," she said. "I had not heard that kind of emotion."

The two ventured to a Jets game at New England's Gillette Stadium on a Monday night in December 2010. It was a memorable trip, but for all the wrong reasons. It was the game the Patriots won, 45–3, and it was frigid, with a game-time windchill of 15 degrees. The cold didn't bother Scribner. "Me, it's just bundle me up—a hat and mittens, and I'm good."

Sandra Scribner had no rooting interest in the National Football League until she saw the passion of her son-in-law, Ken Filete, for the New York Jets (courtesy Ken Filete).

They went incognito, not wearing Jets apparel, but the surrounding fans soon sniffed out that they weren't cheering at every good deed done by the Patriots. At one point, a woman in front of them confronted Filete.

"In a very wicked Boston accent, she turned and used a profanity-laced tirade. Then she punched me in the chest," Filete said. "I turned to my mother-in-law and said, 'This is the abuse you take.'" Such abuse is just part of his job as a Jets fan.

"This team has ripped my guts out many times over but has also provided some of the most thrilling sports moments that I remember," he said. "The Jets for me are what Forrest Gump's quote was: They're like a box of chocolates, you never know what you're going to get.

"There's something about this team," he said. "I have so much emotional investment in this team, I couldn't change. It has helped define me."

Scribner shares those thoughts. "They haven't always been the best, but they play hard, and I'm not switching."

She also has one other mission ahead. A couple of young members of the family have become Jets fans. She's interested in converting a few more relatives to a New York state of mind.

"I'm working hard on that. I retired in December. It can be my full-time job now."

Jets fever isn't confined to the northeastern United States. David Wyatt was born in the United Kingdom and lives in Acle, England, a small village outside of Norwich. He's been a Norwich City soccer fan for decades, but the Jets caught his eye years ago. It happened late one night.

"I was a young chap who didn't want to go to school the next day. In my infinite, youthful wisdom, I thought that by staying awake I was putting school off for the longest time possible. So there I was flicking through the channels when I stumbled across the NFL."

The Jets and Patriots were playing in that 1997 contest. New York won, 24–19, on a fourth-quarter touchdown pass from Glenn Foley to Lorenzo Neal, but the play Wyatt remembers best was a 45-yard interception return by Jets defensive back Jerome Henderson.

"I can't remember why I took to the Jets more than the Patriots, but it was instant. I liked the Jets' style, and from that moment on, I never missed an opportunity to read about them, watch them or just talk about them to anyone who would listen," he said.

The Internet and improved NFL television packages make it much easier to follow the sport in England today than in 1997. Wyatt has been able to connect with other Jets fans in the United Kingdom, although they live too far apart to gather for watching games together.

Social media helps unite them. It also has its downside, especially when a rival team like the Patriots or Giants wins a Super Bowl.

"Years ago, if one of them won a title, you could turn the TV off, ignore the newspapers, and it would be old news relatively quickly," he said. "Now, you have to deal with very obnoxious fans on Twitter and Facebook, and the hype around the victory lasts a lot longer."

Wyatt loved the 2010 playoff win on the road against the Patriots. "Their fans were very loud before the game, and very quiet after the game. It was just one of those memorable nights that I'll remember for the rest of my life."

He hated a first-round playoff loss on January 15, 2005, against the Pittsburgh Steelers. Playing in the January cold and breeze at Pittsburgh's Heinz Field, the Jets battled to a 17–17 tie late in the fourth quarter. With just over 2 minutes to go, Jets kicker Doug Brien lined up for a 47-yard field goal … and missed. The Jets got the ball back on the next play when cornerback David Barrett intercepted a Ben Roethlisberger pass.

Five plays later, Brien tried another field goal, this one from 43 yards. He missed again. The game went to overtime, and Pittsburgh won on a 33-yard field goal by Jeff Reed.

"The name Doug Brien still makes me shake my head," Wyatt said. "The 2004 team was another very talented unit who looked to be going all the way until Doug Brien met the elements coming off the Ohio River."

Wyatt knows that Jets fans soon need a repeat of the Namath magic from 1969.

"That victory was a long time ago, and many fans weren't even alive at that point. You should never ignore or forget history, but it's important to treat it as such. It's time to start making some history instead of constantly reliving it." He plans to stick with the Jets so he can watch that happen.

"I've put in nearly 20 years of fanship, and many fans have put in considerably more," he said. "We may not get success every single year, but when it does come—and the law of averages suggests it will at some point—boy, is it going to be sweet.

"Have I ever contemplated giving up? Absolutely not, and I never will because that's not what being a fan is all about. If you can't be loyal during the championship drought, you don't deserve the bounty that comes with championship success."

Rocky Mountain
Not-So-High

The Denver Nuggets

There's something special about the city of Denver. Modern buildings are interspersed with surroundings that still have a tinge of the pioneer days. And in the background, always in view, the Rocky Mountains tower above all else, providing scenery that will take your breath away.

Then there are the Denver Nuggets, the National Basketball Association team that has historically scored a ton and played at a brisk tempo meant to take the opponents' breath away in the mile-high atmosphere.

"The Nuggets have a beautiful history. It's just never translated to postseason success," said Andrew Feinstein, a fifth-generation Denverite who has been going to Nuggets games since he was a boy.

Denver's team is one of only a handful to never make an appearance in the NBA Finals. There has been plenty of fun along the way, but a title seems a long way away these days for Nuggets fans.

"We're Denver. We're not L.A., we're not Chicago, we're not New York," said longtime fan Eric Meyer. "We can never get that superstar you have to have to win a championship. Denver is a flyover city for the NBA."

The pain on this topic for Feinstein, Meyer and other Nuggets fans is fresh. Carmelo Anthony, one of the NBA's top scorers, spent seven and a half seasons in Denver before being traded to the New York Knicks in 2011.

The Nuggets made the playoffs each of Anthony's first seven seasons. But they lost in the first round every year except 2009, when they made a memorable run to the Western Conference finals before losing to the Los Angeles Lakers.

Anthony's Denver years were a bumpy ride, with rumors sometimes surfacing that he wanted to leave. When he married disc jockey/actress

Andrew Feinstein, a fifth-generation Denver resident, meets point guard Emmanuel Mudiay, who began playing with the Nuggets in 2015 (courtesy Andrew Feinstein).

La La Vazquez, speculation grew that he would want a hotter media market than Denver, and he found it in his 2011 move to the Big Apple.

Without Anthony, the Nuggets won 57 games in 2012–13, but two seasons later that win total dipped to 30.

"In the NBA, unless you get *the* guy, and he wants to stay, it's very hard to win," said Feinstein. All of this has altered the perspective for those who back the Nuggets, Feinstein said.

"Historically, it's been a history of low expectations," he said. "Denver fans have always realized we're on the second or third tier in the NBA. I can't fathom a scenario where we win an NBA championship in my lifetime."

Or, as he put it in his best *Game of Thrones* reference, "With Denver basketball, winter is coming and we're heading for a long winter." That approach, though, isn't quite as dark as it seems.

"My take with the Nuggets is just make the damn playoffs and play entertaining basketball," Feinstein said. Of course, this is from a self-described "basketball degenerate." Feinstein said, "I'll watch the [Sacramento] Kings play the [Minnesota] Timberwolves on a Wednesday night. We all have our vices. Some people like opera. Some people go to concerts. I like going to basketball games."

The Nuggets have often rewarded their fans with an exciting, fast-paced style of play. It's a team with its roots in the old American Basketball Association, a league so colorful that Will Ferrell used it as the basis for his 2008 basketball farce *Semi-Pro*.

It was the league of the red, white and blue ball, the sky-walking dunks and the list of stars that included George McGinnis, Julius Erving, Artis Gilmore and Moses Malone.

The ABA's last season in 1975–76 saw the Nuggets, led by David Thompson and Dan Issel, win 60 games and advance to the league championship series against Erving and the New York Nets.

In Game 6, Thompson scored 42 points, but it wasn't enough. The Nets won, 112–106, to take the series. Erving scored 31 for the winners, but it was a strong performance by John Williamson, who had 28 points, that made the difference.

"We should have won that game," said Kevin Thurston, a Parker, Colorado, resident and fan of the Nuggets since the team's early days. "John Williamson was the guy who turned that game around." When discussing the loss some four decades later, Thurston said, "That gets more and more painful each year because that's as close as we got to a championship."

The following season, the ABA disbanded and four of its teams—the Nuggets, New York Nets, Indiana Pacers and San Antonio Spurs—joined the more-established National Basketball Association. The Nuggets fit right in, finishing their first season in the NBA with a 50–32 record, as Thompson and Issel each averaged more than 22 points per game.

A few more successful seasons under coach Larry Brown were

Andrew Feinstein and fiancée Amy Whiteside Schaeffer get to spend some time with Rocky, the Denver Nuggets mascot. Feinstein has been a fan since he was a boy and Doug Moe was the Denver coach (courtesy Andrew Feinstein).

followed by a downturn in the early 1980s with Donnie Walsh as head coach. Halfway through the 1980–81 season, the Nuggets replaced Walsh with Doug Moe. It was the start of an era that still makes Denver fans smile.

Shy these teams were not. Moe's philosophy was to get the ball and shoot it. In his first full season as head coach, Moe's Nuggets allowed 126.0 points per game. No problem. They scored 126.5, finishing with a 46–36 record.

Feinstein was a youngster during the Moe era. His family had good seats near the Nuggets bench.

"I learned every bad word I've ever known from Doug Moe," Feinstein said. When he met Moe years later, Feinstein told the former coach about those early vocabulary lessons. Moe's response? "He said, 'You wouldn't believe how many people tell me that.'"

Moe's fast-paced style worked. Playing a mile above sea level, the Nuggets wore down visiting teams that were still adjusting to the thinner air. During Moe's nine full seasons as coach, the Nuggets averaged 44½ wins per season.

Alex English, Calvin Natt and Fat Lever led the 1984–85 Nuggets to 52 wins and postseason victories over the San Antonio Spurs and Utah Jazz, setting up a meeting with the Los Angeles Lakers in the Western Conference finals. Throughout the playoffs, English was superb, averaging 30 points a game. He scored 40 in a Game 2 victory over the Lakers, a game the Nuggets won, 136–114, with Issel adding 22 points, Natt contributing 18 and Elston Turner just missing a triple-double with 18 points, 11 rebounds and eight assists. But Denver's defense couldn't stop the Lakers, who averaged 132.4 points a game in breezing past the Nuggets, 4–1. Game 5 was especially painful. The Lakers won at home, 153–109, with Magic Johnson providing 17 points and 19 assists as seven Lakers scored in double figures.

There was no shame in losing to the Lakers, who would beat the Boston Celtics in the next round to win the second of their four NBA championships in the 1980s.

A few seasons later, with Michael Adams and Danny Schayes added to the roster, the Nuggets won 54 games. For the season, six Nuggets players averaged in double figures, and Natt at 9.6 points per game almost made it seven. All that firepower didn't go far in the playoffs, though. The Nuggets fell in the second round to the Dallas Mavericks.

Despite those playoff failings, Moe's victories and style won the hearts of many fans.

"Doug Moe was just a lot of fun," Thurston said. "He was a guy who was never full of himself. He preserved the idea of we're here to have fun."

Feinstein has honored Moe by naming his website about the Nuggets the Denver Stiffs. Moe used the term "stiffs" to describe the scrappier players on his team who perhaps didn't have the most talent in the league.

"It's an homage to what Nuggets basketball is all about," Feinstein said. "We play really, really hard, but in the end we're not that good."

From the ABA days to the Doug Moe era to the present, the Nuggets have won over fans by sprinting hard.

Thurston was a tall kid in junior high school, but he got cut from his seventh- and eighth-grade teams. His freshman coach advised him to watch more basketball to learn about the game, and Thurston gravitated to his local team.

He also spent plenty of time in the driveway playing basketball with a friend. Thurston pretended he was Spencer Haywood, a budding star during his one season with the Nuggets before he bolted for the NBA. The friend played the role of Connie Hawkins, another ABA standout. "The

If Kevin Thurston isn't watching the Denver Nuggets, he just might be hanging out with his pet cockatoos (photograph by Mike Barry).

irony of two white kids wanting to be black guys—that never occurred to us," Thurston said.

Watching the Nuggets and playing in the driveway paid off for Thurston, who eventually made the varsity at Heritage High School in Littleton, Colorado.

Meyer's introduction to the Nuggets took place while he was growing up 700 miles to the northeast in Mound, Minnesota, a town to the west of Minneapolis-St. Paul.

As a boy, he would sneak a television into his room to watch NBA games. It was an era when sometimes the only way to see the NBA was late at night on tape delay. It also was the era of Thompson, Issel and Bobby Jones in Denver.

"I fell in love with the Nuggets," Meyer said. "They scored and they ran. I watched them and said, 'Wow, that's how I want to play basketball.'"

During his high school years, Meyer moved to the Denver area when his father was transferred there. Moving during high school is seldom easy, but Meyer had one factor that eased his pain. He was moving into Nuggets territory.

He got to see the Moe years up close and later would witness one of the great moments in Nuggets history. With Issel back in Denver as head coach, the Nuggets completed the 1993–94 season with a 42–40 record, good for the eighth seed in the Western Conference. They faced a first-round playoff matchup against the top-seeded Seattle SuperSonics, who finished the season 63–19 with a powerful lineup that included Gary Payton, Shawn Kemp and Detlef Schrempf.

As expected, the SuperSonics handily won the first two games in the best-of-five series. Then, something funny happened. Back in Denver, the Nuggets got 31 points from Reggie Williams to breeze to a Game 3 victory, 110–93. In Game 4, LaPhonso Ellis led the way to a Nuggets victory with 27 points and 17 rebounds.

The deciding Game 5 shifted back to Seattle, where most of the world figured the SuperSonics would regain their mojo and take the series. It didn't happen. Ellis had 19 points, Dikembe Mutombo grabbed 15 rebounds, and the Nuggets got huge help from their bench, especially Robert Pack [23 points] and Bison Dele, then known as Brian Williams [17 points, 19 rebounds].

Denver won, 98–94, becoming the first eighth-seeded team to win an NBA playoff series. A lasting NBA image followed moments after the game ended—Mutombo stretched out on the court, holding the basketball and crying.

"I was crying, too, quite frankly," Meyer said.

For Feinstein, it was the payoff of being a fan. "Talk about sticking with them and anything can happen," he said.

The magic of that first-round upset didn't last long. The Nuggets were knocked out in the next round by the Utah Jazz. Then, Ellis was injured and played only six games the following season.

"That '94 team could have been a contender for years to come, and he was the glue," Feinstein said of Ellis.

By the 1997–98 season, the Nuggets had hit rock bottom. They lost their first 12 games before finally beating Minnesota, 95–84, on November 28. After three more losses they won again and then went winless from December 9 to January 23, a stretch of 23 straight defeats that put their record at 2–38. Another 16-game losing streak soon followed before the Nuggets won three of four games in mid–March and two of their last six. They finished the season 11–71.

"I don't know who put that roster together, but I think it was a 2-year-old with a dart board," Meyer said. The late-season semi-flurry of wins disappointed him in a way that only die-hard fans can understand. "They screwed up my dream of having the worst team in NBA history." (The 1972–73 Philadelphia 76ers went 9–73; the 2011–12 Charlotte Bobcats were 7–59 in a shortened season.)

A string of coaching changes and roster shifts didn't bring much success. Then the 2003 NBA draft arrived. It was a draft class loaded with big names, topped by LeBron James, who was a certain choice for the team selecting first, the Cleveland Cavaliers. The Detroit Pistons picked second, just before the Nuggets, and chose Darko Milicic, a star in Serbia.

Meyer recalls watching Detroit's selection while at the Denver airport, where he was picking up his stepdaughter.

"I was screaming and jumping around like an idiot because I knew the Nuggets had to pick Carmelo," he said of his reaction to Detroit's choice. Denver did just that, and so began the Carmelo Anthony marriage with Denver, a rocky one with some highs and a disappointing ending.

Anthony immediately returned the Nuggets to the playoffs. The Nuggets got an added boost in 2004–05, when George Karl was hired as coach at midseason for a team that was 17–25 at the time. Karl led the Nuggets to a 32–8 finish and another playoff berth. Like so many of the Nuggets' seasons in the 2000s, that one ended with a first-round playoff loss, but Denver broke out of its rut in 2009.

The Nuggets blew past the New Orleans Hornets and Dallas Mavericks in the first two rounds with Anthony leading the offense, averaging

24 points a game against the Hornets and 30 per game in the Dallas series. Next up was another Western Conference finals matchup with the Lakers.

Anthony scored 27.5 points per game against the Lakers and got help from old pro Chauncey Billups, who averaged 18.2 points and six assists. But Kobe Bryant was ferocious throughout the series, pouring in 34 points a game and leading the Lakers to a 4–2 series victory.

"He crushed us. That was just brutal," Feinstein said. Once again, as in 1985, the Lakers went on to win the NBA title after beating the Nuggets in the Western Conference finals.

For Meyer, it was another painful loss in a career full of them as a fan. He also roots for Colorado's baseball team and has kept close to his Minnesota upbringing by pulling for the National Football League's Vikings.

"When the Nuggets or Vikings or Colorado Rockies lose, I say it takes another year off my life. I'm lucky to still be alive at the age of 50," he said.

The NBA cycle has turned down again for the Nuggets, but their fans find a way to keep hope alive.

Meyer: "I started liking them at such a young age that it became ingrained in me. They became part of my fabric as a sports fan and as a person. There's been enough success that there's always a light at the end of the tunnel."

Thurston: "I still have that same thing I had when I was a kid. I'm a basketball guy. If I'm going to follow basketball, I have to root for the local team. For good or for bad, these are my guys. This is my team."

Feinstein: "I'm 40 years old. I've devoted my entire life to supporting them. I'm not going to give up now, even though it's against my better judgment of how I spend my time and money."

The final word on the team has to go to Vicki Ray, better known as the Denver Nuggets Sign Lady.

When Vicki and her husband, Russell, arrived in Denver in 1993, she was homesick, calling relatives back in Virginia several times a day. One day, Russell asked whether she wanted to go see the Nuggets.

Her reaction was direct. "I said, 'I don't want to go to no damn bas-

Opposite top: When Denver Nuggets players arrive at the arena for home games, they are greeted by the team's sign lady, Vicki Ray (photograph by Russell Ray). *Bottom:* Vicki Ray's signs aren't just to support the home team. She shows some love for the game officials, many of whom have autographed her sign (photograph by Russell Ray).

ketball game.'" But go they did, and Vicki was hooked. She said she has missed two games since 1993, and that was when her mother died in 2005.

Soon after they started going to Nuggets games, she made her first sign, a tribute to Bryant Stith, who had played at the University of Virginia and was then a young guard for the Nuggets.

Playing off the "Virginia is for Lovers" slogan, the sign read, "Virginia is for Nuggets Lovers." The sign caught Stith's attention, and he autographed a picture for her at the next game.

The signs haven't stopped since. She eventually made signs for every player and started showing up at the arena hours before game time to greet the Nuggets as they arrived.

"It did not matter the weather, I was out there every game day, before and after the game," said Vicki, who has quit jobs that couldn't accommodate her Nuggets viewing habits. When former Nuggets players or coaches return to Denver with their new teams, she dusts off their old signs and brings them to the arena.

Soon after Russell and Vicki Ray arrived in Denver in 1993, he suggested they go to a Nuggets game. She wasn't very interested but she decided to give it a try. Now, she rarely misses a game (courtesy Russell Ray).

It doesn't matter the weather, when the Denver Nuggets are home, Vicki Ray is there to greet the players when they arrive at the arena (photograph by Russell Ray).

Vicki regularly makes candy bags for players—gummy bears are the most requested item—and has a Christmas card list full of former Nuggets. Her house is a shrine to both the team—autographed shoes, hats, jerseys, etc.—and the league—she even has autographs from referees.

During the 11–71 season in 1997–98, she held up a sign that said, "Nuggets, Your Real Fans Always Love You." It's the essence of her fandom.

"The Nuggets' past, present and future players will always be like family to me. I enjoy going to every game whether they win or lose, though I prefer that they win," Vicki said. "I don't give up on them, no matter what, even when they seem to give up on themselves. Win or lose, I will be there for them."

Pain on Ice

The Vancouver Canucks

Comedian Ian Bagg knows that rooting for the Vancouver Canucks is serious business.

As a native Canadian, he understands the code of the game: "You win with grace. You lose with grace. People ask, 'How do you lose with grace?' At the end of the game you line up and shake hands. But, holy shit, as a fan it's draining."

Growing up in Terrace, British Columbia, about 850 miles northwest of Vancouver, Bagg was exposed to hockey at an early age. "We played road hockey, street hockey, basement hockey," he said. A neighbor had an outdoor rink in the yard where Bagg and his friends would play until it got dark. Then an outdoor light was turned on, and they played some more.

"I'm sure it's got something to do now with my eyesight," he said.

He recalls anxiously awaiting the release each September of the new season's Canucks calendar put out by Shoppers Drug Mart, a huge pharmacy chain in Canada. Those calendars got him hooked on the team to the south.

He's been watching ever since, through three Stanley Cup Final losses and a few forgettable seasons, such as 1998–99's 23–47–12 affair.

The Canucks came into the National Hockey League as an expansion team in 1970. The early years provided the struggles you would expect for a young team. The Canucks' first pick in the expansion draft was Gary Doak, a defenseman who played the previous season with the Stanley Cup champion Boston Bruins. He had just two goals and 11 assists in Vancouver before being dealt to the New York Rangers in November 1971. The Canucks' first four seasons all ended with losing records.

After that sluggish start, the Canucks improved, making the playoffs five times in seven seasons from 1975 to 1981. Then came a stunning turn— a trip to the Stanley Cup Final. The Canucks, who had never even won a playoff series, finished the 1981–82 season with a losing record, 30–33–7. It still was good enough to make the postseason, and they battled through playoff victories over the Calgary Flames, Los Angeles Kings and Chicago Blackhawks before meeting the New York Islanders in the finals.

In Game 1, the Canucks got a goal from Jim Nill late in the third period to take a 5–4 lead. But these were the Islanders, a powerhouse in the midst of winning four straight Stanley Cups. Mike Bossy scored in regulation and again in overtime to give the Islanders a 6–5 win. Bossy scored seven goals in the Islanders' four-game sweep, and he won the Conn Smythe Trophy, given to the most valuable player in the Stanley Cup Final.

The result was expected. Even so, it was still painful at the time for young followers of the Canucks.

"I remember being heartbroken," Bagg said. But the experience was one of those great ones for fans—a heavy underdog that got on a roll and almost pulled off a miracle. As Bagg put it, "It was like you didn't expect to get to the dance, and then a beautiful girl asks you. You didn't get to kiss her, but you're at the dance."

It was the season that really turned Sean Zandberg, a Smithers, British Columbia, resident, into a Canucks fan.

"The 1982 Canucks were a hard-working, physical team that really had no chance against the powerful Islanders," Zandberg said. "I still cried when they lost Game 4."

A dozen years later, the Canucks had a dramatic first-round playoff series with Calgary. The Canucks trailed in the series, 3–1, before winning Games 5 and 6, both in overtime. Bagg recalls performing his standup act in Winnipeg during the Calgary series, expecting the worst.

"I was on stage being mad about the Canucks losing ... and they won," he said.

It was a memorable victory. Game 7 also went to overtime, and Calgary appeared ready to win when Robert Reichel fired at an open net. But Vancouver goaltender Kirk McLean went sprawling feet first across the goal line, kicking the shot away at the last possible instant. Canucks fans refer to the play as "The Save."

The Canucks won, 4–3, in the second overtime on Pavel Bure's goal. They then breezed past the Dallas Stars and Toronto Maple Leafs to get to a second Stanley Cup Final. Again, they met a team from New York, this time the Rangers, who had last won a Stanley Cup in 1940.

Playing in Madison Square Garden, the Canucks won Game 1 thanks to 52 saves by McLean and an overtime goal by Greg Adams. The Rangers, though, won the next three games.

The Canucks bounced back, winning the next two to force a Game 7. Despite two goals by Vancouver's Trevor Linden, the Rangers won the Cup with a 3–2 victory.

"That team had so much heart and soul," Mark Ramos, a Vancouver native, said of that Canucks squad.

"The Canucks-Rangers series in 1994 is the best I have ever seen," Zandberg said. "That loss hurts more than any of the others; it was so damn close. I still watch that Game 7 once a year. Phenomenal hockey. I am so proud of what that group accomplished."

Bagg's memories of a roster filled with players from Bure to Dave Babych are just as fond. "I just remember thinking, 'How great is this team?' Suddenly, we had talent. We'd never really had talent. And we had tough guys and workhorses."

The Canucks also had Pat Quinn, who coached the team. He had built the foundation for that squad while serving as the team's general manager.

"Pat Quinn just reeked of hockey," Bagg said. "He knew how to play, he knew how to manage a team, he knew how to coach a team."

Bagg did a courageous thing soon after that Canucks-Rangers series. He moved to New York. "The Canucks had lost, and I move to the devil's spot," he said. He took some razzing from Rangers fans, but there was a real plus side to the move. He grew up in Terrace, many, many miles from any NHL arena. "Now I could see the Canucks play on Long Island or in New Jersey or in Madison Square Garden."

After that Stanley Cup Final loss to the Rangers, the Canucks were in a time of transition by the late 1990s. Linden was traded in 1998 to the Islanders for Todd Bertuzzi, Bryan McCabe and a draft pick; Bure was dealt the following year to the Florida Panthers in a massive trade that involved seven players and two draft choices. The Canucks also made another trade to acquire one of the stars of that 1994 Rangers team, Mark Messier, a winner of six Stanley Cups in his career. The move didn't take. In Messier's three years in Vancouver, the Canucks averaged 26 wins a season.

On the positive side, the Canucks drafted brothers Henrik and Daniel Sedin in 1999. It was a major step in rebuilding the franchise.

The Canucks rebounded and returned to the Stanley Cup Final, a memorable visit in 2011. Vancouver had piled up 117 points to win the franchise's first Presidents' Trophy, awarded to the NHL team with the best regular-season record. They had Roberto Luongo, who allowed just 2.1 goals per game, and the Sedin brothers, who combined for 60 goals and 138 assists.

Comedian Ian Bagg knows a thing or two about hockey. It's no surprise. He is from Terrace, British Columbia, and started playing the sport at an early age (photograph by Dan Dion).

The first challenge of that postseason was meeting up with the Chicago Blackhawks. This was no small task. The Blackhawks were the defending Stanley Cup champions. All they had done to the Canucks the previous two seasons was knock them out of the playoffs. It was a grudge match that captured the city of Vancouver.

It even grabbed the attention of Shilpi Rao. She had moved to Canada from India six years earlier. At that time, she didn't even know what ice hockey was. She knew field hockey, a major sport in India, and she was a big fan of cricket, which is *the* sport in India. But ice hockey was a mystery, and she paid little attention to it during her first years in Vancouver. The playoff rematch with Chicago, though, changed that. The whole city wanted revenge after losing two straight years in the postseason to the Blackhawks.

"Everyone at work would talk about hockey all the time," Rao said. "Finally I was like, OK, let's see what this is all about."

She picked a good time to jump on board. The Canucks won the first three games of the series, but the Blackhawks came back to pound the Canucks in Games 4 and 5, and Chicago won again in overtime in Game 6. It set up a deciding Game 7 in Vancouver's Rogers Arena.

Rao met friends from work to watch the deciding match on television. It would be the first NHL game she had ever seen. She would not be disappointed.

Alex Burrows scored 2 minutes and 43 seconds into the game, and the Canucks held onto that 1–0 lead through the rest of the first period, the entire second period and most of the third. Luongo, who had struggled in goal during the series, was superb for the Canucks.

Then, with less than 2 minutes to go and the Blackhawks playing a man down because of a penalty, Chicago's Jonathan Toews scored a short-handed goal to tie the game. It was the kind of goal that had most of Vancouver swallowing hard, wondering whether that knot in the stomach would ever disappear. It was the ultimate here-we-go-again moment.

But after a little more than 5 minutes of overtime play, Burrows intercepted a clearing attempt and sent a slapshot over the right shoulder of Chicago goaltender Corey Crawford. Final score: Vancouver 2 (and redemption), Chicago 1 (and finally defeated).

"That game—you could define the franchise in that game," Ramos said. "There was so much hope, and then it looked like we were going to lose."

The new fan, Rao, was impressed. "I was on the edge of my seat for the whole game." She also was captivated by the spirit of the city during the 2011 playoffs. "Everything in Vancouver was all about the Canucks. You couldn't help but become a fan."

The Canucks then ousted the Nashville Predators and the San Jose Sharks, setting up a Stanley Cup Final matchup with the Boston Bruins.

Bagg said he had a bad feeling before the series against the Bruins started. He remembers seeing a video montage at the start of the series set to Adele's hit song, "Rolling in the Deep." The familiar refrain? "We could have had it all."

"It was a foreshadow. I knew we were going to lose," Bagg said.

Lose, they did, in a crushing manner. The Canucks won Game 1, 1–0, on a Raffi Torres goal, and Game 2, 3–2, on an overtime goal by Burrows. After winning those first two games at home, the Canucks traveled to Boston and got smoked, 8–1. The teams split the next two games before Boston won Game 6, 5–2, setting up a Game 7 in Vancouver.

In the deciding game, Boston goalie Tim Thomas made 37 saves, and the Canucks were shut out at home, falling, 4–0. It was an odd series, with the Canucks winning the first three games in Vancouver, all by one goal, but getting outscored, 17–3, in the three games in Boston.

"It was just so close. I'm mad still," Bagg said of the series.

Zandberg was a bit harsher. "The sting of the 2011 choke job still resonates with me. How could they suck so badly in Boston? It's as though they were intimidated playing in that rink. It was embarrassing to watch."

The Game 7 pain was all consuming. "After they [the Bruins] made it 2–0, I stopped watching and sat outside in the sun with a rum and Coke—or 10—being consumed," Zandberg said. "When the final buzzer sounded, I smashed my glass in disgust and anger. So much for home ice advantage in a Game 7. Yeesh."

Even as a newcomer to hockey, Rao shared in the collective pain of the city. "I was a fan for just a month. I can just imagine what the others were going through."

Ramos thought that 2011 team was the one to get it done for Vancouver. "It seemed like all the stars were aligned." Of the loss to Boston, he said, "That was brutal." The best way I can describe it is you just broke up with your high school sweetheart. It was that devastating."

Ramos got a close look at all of the city's emotions through that playoff run. He went to several games. When he wasn't at Rogers Arena, he was downtown with tens of thousands of others, watching the games on a giant outdoor screen.

"The energy was electric. It was hard not to be engulfed in it," he said. People skipped work. There were downtown traffic jams at 2 in the morning.

But, much of that joy emptied out when the Bruins won. The pressure and anxiety of watching a tense, taut series led to rioting in Vancouver after Game 7, though Ramos is convinced it wasn't the true hockey fans who started the mischief. "To think we're destroying property over a freakin' hockey game, it blows my mind," he said.

For Vancouver fans, the loss to the Bruins continued a long drought, although the city can claim one Stanley Cup. It was won by the Vancouver Millionaires, playing in the Pacific Coast Hockey Association. Of course, it was 1915, two years before the National Hockey League was even born. "It was a little bit before my time," Bagg said.

The Millionaires clobbered the Ottawa Senators of the National Hockey Association to win hockey's crown. That title run got some publicity in 2015, the 100th anniversary of their championship.

The Stanley Cup series was an odd event, according to a March 16, 2015, story by John Mackie of *The Vancouver Sun*. The leagues had different rules, so one league's rules were used one game; the other league's in the next contest. Ottawa's league played with seven men; Vancouver's used six. Ottawa's league also did not allow forward passes.

The players on the winning team got $300. Ticket prices at Vancouver's Denman Arena ranged from 50 cents to $1.25.

Vancouver's roster had several future Hall of Famers, including Fred "Cyclone" Taylor and Barney Stanley, who scored four goals in the decisive Game 3, a 12–3 pounding of the Senators.

While hockey has grown in the United States in recent years, it still is—and always will be—Canada's sport. For Canadians, there has been the pain of a two decade-plus gap since a team from Canada, the 1993 Montreal Canadiens, won the Stanley Cup. There has been the odd sight of fans celebrating in such warm-weather places as Tampa Bay, Raleigh, North Carolina, and Anaheim, where teams won the Cup in consecutive seasons from 2005 to 2007.

Bagg recalls his reaction when the Tampa Bay Lightning won in 2005. "I remember thinking hell has frozen over. What? In Florida? Are you serious?"

Canadians take pride in their passion for the sport, and the teams they care about the most. "You want them to win one Cup at least before you die," Zandberg said of the Canucks.

Ramos attended the University of Arizona, where, he said, "I was probably the only guy on campus wearing a Canucks jersey in the winter." His pride in the team hasn't wavered since his college days. "They're pretty much the heart of Vancouver. It's everything to us."

Rao may be new to the sport, but she isn't a shy fan. On the website weareallcanucks.com, she posted a picture of herself in a Canucks T-shirt sitting on a clear skydeck, hundreds of feet off the ground, with the city's landscape in the background. The city? Chicago, home of those pesky Blackhawks. Her comment on the photo: "Being a Canucks fan always feels like being on Cloud #9." She admitted she was a little nervous wearing a Canucks shirt in Chicago, but that didn't stop her.

She did contemplate packing away her Canucks gear near the end of a recent disappointing season. Her friend Ramos dissuaded her. "He said, 'You know, this is the time to wear your jersey.'"

Ramos is not shy about displaying his Canucks pride. His wardrobe includes a pair of shoes that are green, white and blue—the team colors.

Bagg's career has taken him to Los Angeles and appearances in movies, on HBO and Comedy Central and *Late Night with Conan O'Brien*. Through it all, he's never lost touch with the sport he loves.

"I've put somebody's kid through college with all the Canucks stuff I've bought. I wear it on my sleeve." And it's not just Canucks gear. "I'm a hockey fan," he said. "I'll show up on stage with a Philadelphia Flyers shirt, for no apparent reason. Or a Minnesota North Stars shirt."

When he's on the road, he'll check out the schedule for the local hockey team. If his touring schedule allows, he'll be at the rink.

"I go to other hockey games, but I don't rush like I do when I'm going to see the Canucks."

The Wildside

The Northwestern Wildcats

When ESPN's Darren Rovell did play by play for the college radio station during his days at Northwestern, his friends would give him a list of 10 words or phrases. These were to be used in case of emergency—the all-too-often occurrence of the Wildcats being blown out by their opponent.

So, during a landslide loss in football to Michigan, Rovell told his listeners, "Michigan coach Lloyd Carr looks as content as America was during the presidency of Calvin Coolidge."

Rovell's color analyst pointed out that he wasn't so sure the United States was all that content under Coolidge. No matter. The key point was "Calvin Coolidge" was one of the 10 phrases on the list for that game, and Rovell had worked it into the broadcast.

So it goes for Northwestern fans. There are the blowouts. There are the heartbreakers. There are the less-than-successful seasons. The loyal supporters try to make the best of it, while offering a little humor along the way.

They pull for the men's basketball team, which has provided Northwestern with the ignominious distinction of being one of only five original Division I schools never to make the NCAA Tournament, first held in 1939. And the other four schools with that level of frustration—Army, William & Mary, The Citadel and St. Francis (N.Y.)—play in smaller—or non-power—conferences that usually just get one bid to the tournament while the Big Ten often gets six or seven.

Let the jokes begin.

"Ah, March Madness. Or as the Northwestern basketball fan knows it, March," tweeted Seth Meyers, former *Saturday Night Live* star and host of *Late Night with Seth Meyers* on NBC.

"I'm a Northwestern basketball fan, which is like being a Cubs fan, only lonelier," wrote Benoit Denizet-Lewis on Deadspin.

And those are comments from the alumni. Northwestern fans take it all in stride.

"I never take it personally. For us, it's almost a sense of pride," said Brian Silverstein (Northwestern Class of 1999), a pharmaceutical representative in Dallas, Texas.

"There is a certain bond to the shared sense of futility," said Ray Daudani (Class of 1999), digital content director at WWBT television in Richmond, Virginia. "Having a good laugh about it—I think it's good."

"We're talking about sports events, not war and peace," said William "Willie" Weinbaum (Class of 1982), a producer and reporter for ESPN and ESPN.com. "Gotta enjoy what you have and not fret about what you don't. So when you hear things like the only colleges Northwestern can beat are the Electoral College and the College of Cardinals, or if NU played William & Mary, it could beat Mary, but not William, or you see someone write 'Northwestern 0' on the lower part of the Interstate sign for Illinois 294, or you hear about the guy calling the ticket office on game day morning and asking, 'What time does the game start?' and getting the reply, 'What

Darren Rovell, left, and William "Willie" Weinbaum are ESPN employees who know something about sports pain. They graduated from Northwestern and have cheered on the Wildcats during some lean years (courtesy Willie Weinbaum).

time can you get here?' you laugh, you add it to your repertoire and you go on with your life better for sharing a common cause with fellow NU alums and rooting for presumably earnest kids who want like hell to win and are likely to win later in life."

In other words, Northwestern fans have developed some thick skin. They have to, especially with a basketball team that always seems to pull off a huge upset but follows it with a series of heartbreaking losses.

"Northwestern finds ways you have never thought about to lose games," Silverstein said. "If it hasn't been done, they'll invent it. If you don't laugh about it, you'd cry. Ultimately, it's another kick to the groin."

"Believe me," said Weinbaum, "there were and are many times when you share head-shaking, muttering, 'I can't believe how the Cats lost that one.'"

It wasn't always so. There was that 1930–31 season when the Wildcats' basketball team, coached by Arthur Lonborg, finished 16–1. This was in the days before postseason tournaments, and Northwestern was retroactively declared the national champion by the Helms Athletic Foundation and the Premo-Porretta Power Poll.

The Wildcats had some more good years under Lonborg, who coached from 1927 to 1950, but the decades following World War II included few winning seasons. It took until 1983 for the Wildcats to get their first postseason bid, and it was to the lesser National Invitation Tournament. There were two more NIT bids in the 1990s before a run of four straight from 2009 to 2012 under coach Bill Carmody. Never, though, has there been a bid to the true prize for college basketball teams, the NCAA Tournament.

The reasons for that lack of success have been plentiful—outdated facilities, high academic standards, an inability to recruit from Chicago's rich high school basketball programs, a lack of past success that hinders recruiting top players.

Northwestern's athletic traditions can be dwarfed by other Big Ten schools. So is its enrollment. Northwestern, which is in Evanston, Illinois, just north of Chicago, has fewer than 10,000 undergraduates; Ohio State has more than 40,000. Such factors can lead to an atmosphere at games that sometimes is a little less than scintillating.

"I remember going to a game my freshman year and thinking, 'Gosh, where is everybody?'" Daudani said. "It just looked like you were at a high school gym."

Many students don't know much about Northwestern athletics until they arrive on campus. Aaron Ament (Class of 2003) is an exception. He grew up in the college basketball hotbed of Louisville, Kentucky. "I've been a huge college sports fan since the first day I could talk."

His father and uncle both attended Northwestern. "I'm one of the rare ones who shot hoops in the backyard dreaming of playing for Northwestern and taking them to the NCAA Tournament," said Ament, chief of staff to the general counsel for the U.S. Department of Education.

That tournament dream seemed a long way away in his freshman year. The Wildcats finished 5–25, 0–16 in the Big Ten.

Gram Bowsher (Class of 2015) is one of those trying to change the

Aaron Ament and his father, Mark, take in a Northwestern–Ohio State football game in Evanston, Illinois, in 2013. They are both Northwestern graduates (courtesy Aaron Ament).

game-day atmosphere, having served as president of the student section, "The Wildside," for two years.

He worked with the athletic department and coaches to boost attendance and spirit at games. Promotions ranged from T-shirt giveaways ("College students love free things," he said) to head basketball coach Chris Collins and his staff serving food for a couple of hours at the student union.

"They embraced the idea that the program is more than the players and coaches. It's a team beyond the team," Bowsher said.

Northwestern's smaller student base and its tough academic standards help bring the student body and the athletes together.

"Here I think there's a greater sense that the players are people you go to school with," said Bowsher, who is working as an analyst for a Chicago market research company.

"You take it very, very personally," Silverstein said of the school's sporting events. "You feel like you have to be there. These are our boys, win or lose."

A friend of Silverstein's, Jason Ross, was a benchwarmer on the football team. When Ross made a tackle late in one game, the television coverage cut to Silverstein, wearing a Ross jersey.

"I went absolutely nuts," he said. "You felt like you were making that tackle." Ross' graduation gift to Silverstein was two photos in one frame. One side showed Ross' tackle; the other was a freeze-frame shot from television of Silverstein cheering wildly.

So, while there may not be a ton of them, the Northwestern die-hard rooters are a stick-with-it bunch. Sometimes they are rewarded.

On January 27, 1979, Magic Johnson and his Michigan State Spartans basketball team came to Northwestern. They were huge favorites over the Wildcats, who were 4–12 and had lost their first seven Big Ten games.

Michigan State would go on to win the national title, beating Larry Bird and Indiana State a few months later to finish a memorable NCAA Tournament. On this day, though, the Spartans were no match for Northwestern. Guard Rod Roberson scored 20 points, and forward Mike Campbell added 16 to lead the Wildcats to an 83–65 victory. It was one of just six wins for Northwestern that season.

"It's a game that any Northwestern fan who was alive then will tell you about," Bowsher said.

The 2011–12 Northwestern team provided a glimpse of how the other half lives in college basketball. On January 12, 2012, Michigan State—sixth-ranked in the country and winners of 15 straight games—came to Northwestern and fell to the Wildcats, 81–74. Northwestern's leading scorer that season, John Shurna, provided his usual offense with 22 points and got help from Drew Crawford (20) and Davide Curletti (17).

"Rushing the court after that was one of the more exciting things I've been a part of," Bowsher said.

The win boosted Northwestern's record to 12–5, and there was plenty of buzz that maybe, just maybe, this would be the team to break the NCAA Tournament drought.

"It gave us hope we'd get a few more résumé-building wins that the [NCAA Tournament] selection committee would notice," Bowsher said.

Turns out it wasn't meant to happen. The Wildcats lost three conference games in overtime and another four by five points or fewer. In the end, their 18–13 regular-season record wasn't quite good enough for a tournament bid.

It is seasons such as that one that help Northwestern fans embrace their futility and show their pride.

William "Willie" Weinbaum gets ready for a Northwestern basketball game at Rutgers in late 2014. Despite some tough seasons, he sees the bright side. "Adversity yields appreciation. I wouldn't trade my experiences for anything" (courtesy Willie Weinbaum).

"There's always that hope," Daudani said. "At the start of the season, there's that inkling that this could be our year."

He mentioned the Lovable Losers label carried by another area team that longs for success—the Chicago Cubs. We may lose, we may get laughed at, but we can deal with it.

"I feel like Northwestern fans have that same sort of affinity," he said. "It's like someday we'll graduate, and we'll buy a basketball team, and it will be fine."

When that elusive NCAA Tournament bid comes, Northwestern fans are ready.

"When we make the tournament, unless I'm having another kid, I'll be there," said Rovell (Class of 2000), already a father of three.

"I have money set aside," Bowsher said. "Wherever that first NCAA Tournament game is, I'm going."

"Forget about winning—just get into the play-in game," Daudani said. "That would be fantastic." But he also fears that a tournament bid would wipe out Northwestern's unique status. "If it does pan out, we're then just one of those teams that made the tournament. That's not nearly as interesting as the current narrative."

These fans show their love in all sorts of ways.

Weinbaum was a graduate student at Northwestern in 1983 when the basketball team was in contention for an NIT bid.

"The day of the announcements, when most people everywhere were, of course, focused on NCAA tourney bids, I listened to news radio, for what seemed like a long time, to get the news on whether the Cats got the [NIT] bid," he said.

They did, and Weinbaum was in the stands for the first NIT game, played at nearby Rosemont Horizon. Northwestern was matched up against the Notre Dame Fighting Irish, coached by Digger Phelps, on, of all days, St. Patrick's Day.

"I can still see the green carnation on Phelps' lapel," said Weinbaum, whose dedication was rewarded. Northwestern cruised to a 71–57 victory over Notre Dame.

Weinbaum's devotion to the Wildcats showed up at home, too. He refused to get high-definition television until his provider added the Big Ten Network.

Silverstein has similar feelings. "It's the curse of cable television. I can watch everything. I'll DVR a game and still watch it, even though we lost by 20 to Indiana. It was almost easier when you couldn't watch."

The hope for the basketball team is inspired by what happened with football in 1995. That team started its season Sept. 2 as 27-point underdogs to Notre Dame, ranked ninth in the country.

Matt Rice and Pat Fitzgerald, who would later become Northwestern's football coach, inspired a staunch defense, and the Wildcats led the Irish, 10–9, at the half.

Silverstein, who would soon be heading to campus for his freshman year, was watching the game at a Dallas restaurant with his father.

"It's the middle of the third quarter, and I'm saying, 'I'm going to be there in a week. We play Air Force in a week. I'm going!'"

The Wildcats held off Notre Dame for a 17–15 victory. They would lose to Miami of Ohio, but the rest of the season was a blaze of glory. Running back Darnell Autry rushed for 1,785 yards and scored 18 touchdowns as the Wildcats went undefeated in the Big Ten to clinch a Rose Bowl berth, Northwestern's first since 1949.

Silverstein was on board from the start. As the season progressed, he cut out every newspaper story he could find about the team and taped it to his dorm wall.

"People would give me articles. I became the shrine guy," he said. The shrine remained until a fire official ordered him to remove it, or it would be removed for him. There also was the threat of a fine. "I thought it over and took it down myself," Silverstein said.

"The campus was awesome for those three months," said Silverstein, who traveled to Pasadena, California, for the Rose Bowl, which the Wildcats lost to the University of Southern California, 41–32.

"The greatest moment of my life—wait, I take that back. I had two kids and got married. One of the top ten moments in my life was waking up and going to the [Rose Bowl] parade and knowing you were going to the game. Even though we lost, there was purple everywhere in that stadium."

The Rose Bowl high continued after the game for Silverstein, even if he couldn't afford a hotel room: "That was a good sleep on an airport bench in the terminal."

What made the Rose Bowl visit so significant was what had come before. Northwestern had lost 34 games in a row from 1979 to 1982. The 0–11 team in 1981 might have been the most futile of all the futile teams in college football history. In five consecutive weeks of Big Ten play, Northwestern lost to Purdue, Michigan, Wisconsin, Michigan State and Ohio State by a combined score of 256–20.

In Weinbaum's four years as an undergraduate, Northwestern football went 1-42-1. He recalls the victory over Wyoming as being less-than-great football. He missed the tie.

Even the turnaround in football had its bumps. The Rose Bowl was the first of nine bowl appearances in 17 seasons. Northwestern lost each one. The streak was snapped on January 1, 2013, with a 34–20 victory over Mississippi State in the Gator Bowl.

Through long droughts in football and basketball, these are fans who have been tested. They've sat in half-empty arenas watching the Wildcats get thumped. They've broadcast games that were decided in the first quarter. "Anyone can fill time when your team is good. It's a lot harder when your team stinks," Rovell said.

Still, their pride shows through.

Silverstein has passed his passion on to his son, Ethan, perhaps the most devoted pre-teen Northwestern fan in all of greater Dallas.

"If it's Saturday, he wants to watch the Northwestern football game. If I tape it and start watching without him, he gets mad."

Rovell, who is a sports business reporter at ESPN, takes pride in the determination of Northwestern basketball fans.

"People who root for Kentucky have no idea how draining it is to root for a team with so few rewards," he said. "When we beat Michigan in the regular season, I'm on my knees pounding the floor. I often feel I'm blessed being a Northwestern fan. When we win, I really, really appreciate it."

Weinbaum even worked his Northwestern devotion into his wedding day on May 5, 1996, just a few months after the Wildcats' trip to the Rose Bowl. He wrote a letter that then-football coach Gary Barnett signed. It said Weinbaum had vowed he wouldn't get married until Northwestern made the Rose Bowl. It also stated that ever since Weinbaum got engaged, the Wildcats became regular winners on the football field, meaning his wife-to-be, Joy, was obviously the good-luck charm.

"I read it during the toast at our wedding ceremony and had given, unbeknownst to my bride, who is not an NU alum, the music for 'Go U Northwestern' to play at that time. A special moment."

One of Silverstein's special moments came when he traveled with the basketball team to Bloomington, Indiana, to help with the game broadcast for the student radio station.

The Wildcats suffered a tough loss to the Hoosiers, and Silverstein was on board as the team was taking a bus to the airport in an ice storm. Coach Kevin O'Neill was known for being a little, shall we say, grumpy after an emotional defeat.

"You know as the radio guys, you look down and don't say a word," Silverstein said. When the bus arrived at the airport, he did look up long enough to see that O'Neill had approached the plane. O'Neill banged on the side of the plane and then announced, in colorful language, that the Wildcats would not be flying out in such crappy weather.

They headed back to Indiana University, which made Silverstein nervous since he had a final exam the next day. When they got back to the Bloomington campus, Indiana coach Bob Knight welcomed them with a huge spread of food.

"I can't tell you what final I missed and had to retake, but I'll never forget that 24-hour stay in Bloomington," Silverstein said.

As a former leader of the student section, recent graduate Bowsher was always annoyed by non-students and alumni who sat throughout the game. Now that he's an alum, he'll be standing and doing all he can to boost the energy level.

"They can be as mad at me as they want. I don't really care," he said.

It's typical of how the Northwestern diehards keep at it as they wait for basketball glory.

"There's the hope of euphoria when we finally do it, and how damn good that feeling is," Rovell said. "I know it well because we did it in football."

"The deep bond of family and friends—who are also fans—helps get us through," Ament said.

"Have never thought of giving up," Weinbaum said. "You appreciate when there is quality, you lament the losses and the lack of rewards for all of the efforts of dedicated people, but you appreciate the way things are done and you cherish the hard-earned accomplishments. It was wonderful to be at the Rose Bowl in 1996. The loss to USC was a downer, but no way it overshadowed the experience…. Adversity yields appreciation. I wouldn't trade my experiences for anything."

Silverstein's view is this: "With my sports teams, with my kids, with my marriage, with my job, I'm a loyal person. Nothing gets my heart rate going like a Northwestern game in the last two minutes. That's 20 years of sports heartbreaks that I'm living with."

Fly Eagles Fly

The Philadelphia Eagles

When it comes to cities with big personalities, Philadelphia is at the top of the list.

There's Betsy Ross and Ben Franklin. The Liberty Bell and Independence Hall. Cheesesteaks and Cheez Whiz at either Geno's or Pat's. William Penn towering over the city, Rocky Balboa running the steps, and the Flyers raising the Cup. Big Five basketball at the Palestra. South Street and Southwest Schuylkill. Philly soul, Patti LaBelle and Harold Melvin & the Blue Notes.

It's been home for Will Smith and Kevin Hart, Jack Klugman and Grace Kelly, Joan Jett and Bradley Cooper. It's also home to a passionate fan base known for its bravado and brashness. Among those fans, one team usually is at the top of the list.

Philadelphia loves its baseball Phillies and its hockey Flyers. It has even tolerated its basketball 76ers during the team's hideous stretch from 2013 to 2016, one of the worst in National Basketball Association history. But when fall arrives, the green jerseys come out of the closet, and Philadelphia turns its attention to its football Eagles. As usual, these folks aren't shy about their rooting interest.

"We probably wear our heart on our sleeve more than any other fans," said Taylor McCormick. "If we don't like it, you're going to hear about it."

Sporting the number 87 jersey of tight end Brent Celek, McCormick is part of a big crowd at Chickie's and Pete's, a restaurant that's just a couple of long field goals from Lincoln Financial Field, home of the Eagles. Fans are gathered on this day to watch their team on the road in a showdown with a division rival, the Washington Redskins.

It's a crowd that will get loud when the Eagles score, show its displeasure when they falter and ultimately go home just a bit more miserable after a last-second loss to Washington.

It's just a typical autumn Sunday in Philadelphia. Eagles fans are known for showing their passion. They cheered when Dallas wide receiver Michael Irvin lay on the field with what turned out to be a career-ending neck injury. They booed Santa Claus and tossed snowballs at him.

It may all sound a little harsh, but Joe Miceli, a lifelong fan who grew up in southwest Philadelphia, has a simple explanation: "We're family here." He was at a game in Philadelphia where a Washington fan showed up in Indian headgear, showing off his pride in the Redskins. "The fans must have thrown every beer and soda they had in their hands at that guy," said Miceli, a maintenance mechanic who now lives in Chadds Ford, Pennsylvania, near the Delaware state line.

Football seems to accentuate that passion.

"Philly is a football town. Turn on a Phillies game. At some point during that game, you will hear an Eagles chant," said Bo Marroletti, a bartender in the city and a third-generation Eagles fan.

Support for the Eagles being passed from one generation to the next is just part of the city's charm. Marroletti's grandfather and uncles were at the 1948 National Football League championship game won by the Eagles. His father and Miceli's were at the 1960 title game, the last championship won by the team.

Early supporters of the Eagles had little to cheer about. The team was founded in 1933 and in its first decade averaged 2.3 wins a season. The first winning season was in 1943 (5–4–1), and that was a team that merged with the Pittsburgh Steelers because of a player shortage caused by World War II.

The post-war years were good ones for the Eagles. They went to three straight NFL championship games, losing the first in 1947 to the Chicago Cardinals, 28–21. Playing at Chicago's Comiskey Park, the Cardinals held the Eagles to 60 yards rushing.

The two teams met again for the title on December 19, 1948, this time at Philadelphia's Shibe Park during a snowstorm. Both teams had to help the ground crew remove the snow-slogged tarp covering the field before the game. Players who were knocked out of bounds ended up plopping into snow banks.

As snow fell heavily throughout the day, the game turned into a defensive struggle. The teams combined to complete five passes for a total of 42 yards. There were six turnovers, three by each side.

Philadelphia proved to be the team capable of running the ball on the snow-covered field. The Eagles gained 225 yards on the ground, compared with 96 for Chicago. Philadelphia running back Steve Van Buren rushed for 98 yards, including a 5-yard touchdown run in the fourth quarter. It was the only score of the game as the Eagles got revenge, beating the Cardinals, 7–0.

In 1949, the Eagles became the only NFL team to have shutouts in back-to-back title games, beating the Los Angeles Rams, 14–0. The Eagles scored on a 31-yard pass from Tommy Thompson to Pete Pihos and a 2-yard blocked punt return by Leo Skladany. It was the NFL's first title game played in California, and a steady rain made the field a swampy mess and limited the crowd to 22,245.

After a mediocre decade, the Eagles returned to the NFL championship game in 1960. Their offense was led by quarterback Norm Van Brocklin and wide receiver Tommy McDonald, who caught 13 touchdown passes. The defense centered around Chuck Bednarik, a tough linebacker nicknamed "Concrete Charlie."

The championship game was played the day after Christmas at Philadelphia's Franklin Field with the Eagles meeting the Green Bay Packers, led by their second-year coach, Vince Lombardi.

One of McCormick's earliest memories as an Eagles fan is watching that game on a small black-and-white television with his father and a room full of relatives and friends. They had all gathered in the town where McCormick grew up, Burlington, New Jersey, just northeast of Philadelphia.

"It captivated me. I've watched them ever since," said McCormick, now a Havertown, Pennsylvania, resident and a retired chief financial officer in health care.

What he saw that day was a tough Eagles team that battled the on-the-rise Packers for 60 minutes. Philadelphia took a 7–6 lead in the second quarter when McDonald caught a 35-yard touchdown pass from Van Brocklin. But, with Jim Taylor churning up yardage, the Packers held a 13–10 lead in the fourth quarter. The Eagles responded with a drive that ended with a 5-yard touchdown run by Ted Dean, giving Philadelphia a 17–13 lead with just under five and a half minutes to go.

The Packers got the ball back and drove deep into Eagles territory. With time running out, Green Bay quarterback Bart Starr flipped a pass to Taylor, who had only Bednarik to beat for the game-winning touchdown. Bednarik dragged Taylor down just inside the 10-yard line, and sat atop him as the final seconds ticked off. Bednarik is then reported to have told Taylor, "You can get up now, Jim. This game is over."

Like the 1948 snowstorm game, the 1960 title is a beloved memory for Eagles fans. Marroletti said guys will come into his bar and still reminisce about being at that game.

Joe Miceli (left) meets Philadelphia Eagles great Steve Van Buren, who scored the only touchdown in the Eagles' 7–0 victory in the 1948 National Football League championship game (courtesy Joe Miceli).

"They take pride in the fact we were the only ones who gave Lombardi a playoff loss," he said. Under Lombardi, the Packers would go on to win five championships in the 1960s, including dominating performances in the first two Super Bowls. Lombardi would win nine playoff games as a head coach. His only postseason loss came on that late December day in Philadelphia.

Most beloved of all from that 1960 team is Bednarik, who died in 2015. He was Pennsylvania born and raised, attended the University of Pennsylvania and spent his entire 14-season career with the Eagles. Bednarik played 60 minutes a game—he was the center on offense—and was one of the toughest guys in a town full of them. A photograph of him with his cocked right arm raised to shoulder level after flattening the New York Giants' Frank Gifford in a November 1960 game is one of the NFL's lasting images. Bednarik said his gesture was a celebration of the fact the Eagles had clinched the game on the play, not that he had injured Gifford, who would miss the rest of the season and all of the following one after the collision.

"He was Philadelphia," Miceli said of Bednarik. "He played the game the way it should be played. He's the king."

As a young boy, Marroletti got to meet Bednarik. The player had been retired for years but still had a souvenir from his NFL days. "The thing I couldn't get over was how disgusting his hands looked," Marroletti said.

Soon after that 1960 championship season, life turned rocky for Eagles fans. There was just one winning season from 1962 to 1977, and the Eagles didn't return to the playoffs until 1978. Two years later, though, a team that featured quarterback Ron Jaworski, wide receiver Harold Carmichael and versatile running back Wilbert Montgomery scrapped its way to a Super Bowl.

"That was a team everybody grabbed hold of," Miceli said. "They were loved."

The trip to the Super Bowl included a victory in the conference championship game over the Dallas Cowboys, a longtime division rival that had tormented the Eagles. Philadelphia fans watched with envy as the Cowboys made five trips to the Super Bowl in the 1970s, winning twice. What was even more painful was the Eagles' performance against the Cowboys from December 1967 through the 1978 season. Dallas won 21 of those 23 games.

The conference title game was held at Philadelphia's Veterans Stadium on a January day with a windchill at game time of 3 below zero. The Eagles came out in their white jerseys instead of the green they usually wear at home. That forced the Cowboys, who preferred to always wear white, into their blue uniforms.

Montgomery broke free for a 42-yard touchdown run in the first quarter, and the Eagles dominated the second half to win, 20–7. With 194 yards rushing and one pass reception for 14 yards, Montgomery outgained Dallas' entire offense.

"Getting over the hump against them was something else. The mood in the city and the neighborhood was unbelievable," said Marroletti, who was in his early teens at the time.

The Super Bowl wasn't as kind to Eagles fans. Oakland contained Montgomery and the Eagles' running game, and Raiders quarterback Jim Plunkett had a superb game, leading his team to a 27–10 win.

"I definitely remember it being really, really rough for a couple of days afterward," Marroletti said. "There were all the what-ifs. You tend to be more of a Monday morning quarterback as a 13-year-old."

The Eagles lost in the first round of the playoffs the next season and then missed the postseason for six straight years. But the Eagles improved to 10–6 in 1988, good enough for a first-round playoff matchup with the Chicago Bears.

Coached by colorful Buddy Ryan, the Eagles brought a defense that featured Reggie White, Andre Waters and Seth Joyner to Chicago for a New Year's Eve playoff game. It turned into one of the more bizarre afternoons in NFL history. Fog off Lake Michigan settled in at Soldier Field during the second quarter, greatly limiting visibility for fans and players, not to mention the millions of television viewers trying to figure out whether a play was a run or a pass. Philadelphia's defense forced four turnovers, but Chicago's offense was able to gain some traction. The Bears' Thomas Sanders rushed for 94 yards, and Dennis McKinnon had four catches for 108 yards, including a first-quarter 64-yard touchdown reception.

Philadelphia quarterback Randall Cunningham did manage to throw for 407 yards in the soup, but the Eagles never scored a touchdown in the 20–12 loss.

"It was really a tough one to lose," Marroletti said. "That team was so loaded on defense. We thought this one could start the run."

After the Fog Bowl, the Eagles had nine more trips to the playoffs before finally returning to the Super Bowl after the 2004 season. Do-everything running back Brian Westbrook, who gained 1,515 yards rushing and receiving, paced the offense along with quarterback Donovan McNabb.

Wide receiver Terrell Owens, who caught 14 of McNabb's 31 touchdown passes, missed the end of the regular season and two playoff games with an ankle injury, but he returned for the Super Bowl. Despite being hobbled, Owens was terrific, catching nine passes for 122 yards. Still, the Eagles trailed the New England Patriots, 24–14, with 5:40 left in the game. McNabb led them on a 13-play touchdown drive, but it ate up almost 4 minutes, time the Eagles didn't have to spare.

"I think I was standing on my chair, screaming at the TV, 'Move it! Move it!'" McCormick said. The Eagles failed to recover an onside kick. They did get the ball back with less than a minute to go but were unable to come close to scoring.

For Ella Plitman, that Super Bowl was her first experience watching the Eagles with a large group of die-hard fans. She was a recent convert—her high school friends had sparked her interest in the team. She was saddened by the Eagles' inability to get a quick touchdown at the end. "We all kind of sat there and said, 'What is going on?'" But she took joy in something she has seen again and again since then—the devotion of Eagles fans.

Of that Super Bowl loss, Miceli said, "I feel like we should have won that one. Part of you dies when it doesn't happen. I'm tired of saying 'next year.'"

Fellow fan Solomon Vincent said, "We thought, 'We can always come back next year.' You know how that turned out."

How it turned out is that Eagles fans still wait for another Super Bowl appearance. Over the years they've had to watch two hated division rivals, the Cowboys and the Giants, win multiple Super Bowls.

"Everybody in this town hates the Cowboys," Marroletti said. "My two favorite football teams are the Eagles and whoever is playing the Cowboys. End of story."

In September of 2015, Plitman took her first trip to Cowboys country to visit a friend. While there, she ventured into a Dallas bar on an NFL Sunday, wearing an Eagles T-shirt. "I was a little nervous, I'm not going to lie," she said of her fashion choice.

At the bar, she got to watch her Eagles beat the New York Jets on the only TV tuned to that game. Most everyone else was watching the hometown Cowboys fall to the Atlanta Falcons.

Despite her wardrobe selection, Plitman received a pleasant surprise. "They were super welcoming," she said of the Dallas fans. "It was pretty cool. I have a newfound respect for them. I never thought I'd say that."

Was it enough to convert her to rooting for the Cowboys? "Never. I don't think I'd have any friends left."

Plitman is a bartender in Philadelphia. There are more than a few Cowboys fans who will venture in to watch with the devoted Eagles followers when the two teams meet. "It's a little more hostile than most games, but it's not as bad as people might think," she said. "Everybody has a good time."

The feelings about the Giants might best be summed up by a DeSean

Ella Plitman discovered a pleasant surprise when she traveled to Dallas in 2015. Fans of the Dallas Cowboys were actually kind of nice (courtesy Ella Plitman).

Jackson punt return on December 19, 2010. Playing at the Giants' home stadium in East Rutherford, New Jersey, the Eagles trailed, 31–10, with seven and a half minutes left in the game. Philadelphia rattled off three quick touchdowns to tie the score, and the Giants were forced to punt with 14 seconds to go.

Jackson, a dangerous Philadelphia returner, stood alone to receive the kick. As the ball arrived, he dropped it at his own 35-yard line, picked it up, retreated a few yards, stutter-stepped, dodged a couple of tackles and then sprinted past the rest of New York's punt coverage team for a touchdown. The loss helped knock the Giants out of the playoffs. Moments after the game ended, New York coach Tom Coughlin was on the field, giving an earful to punter Matt Dodge. Like most of the nation, Coughlin was wondering why Dodge had even given Jackson a chance to return the punt.

"That was sweet. That was absolutely sweet," McCormick said. Vincent, a property manager who lives in Collegeville, Pennsylvania, was watching that game with a group of Giants fans. "I stood up and was running around. They were all upset. It made me feel good."

Marroletti recalls watching the Giants' Super Bowl victories in 2008 and 2012. Both times the Giants beat the New England Patriots. Both times, the Giants got miraculous catches late in the fourth quarter—one by David Tyree, the other by Mario Manningham—that led to game-winning touchdowns.

"Who is watching out for them and screwing us?" Marroletti said.

It isn't always that bad for Eagles fans. Plitman has a favorite memory—a game against the Detroit Lions in December 2013. The weather was not kind as fans had to deal with a snowstorm and a windchill of 20 degrees. Plitman dug into her stash of Eagles clothing—hoodies, hats, socks and scarves—to bundle up for the game. Her usual half-hour drive to the stadium took two hours, but the Eagles rewarded her with a 20-point rally in the fourth quarter to win, 34–20.

"It was brutal," she said. "I couldn't feel anything. As crazy as it sounds, it was worth it. I don't think weather is going to stop anyone here from going to the games."

She usually goes to three games a year, but her bartending duties have recently kept her busy most Sundays. She doesn't mind her Sundays behind the bar when the Eagles are playing. "I'm watching with fans and I'm making money. It's a win-win. If they lose when I'm at the game, I'm broke *and* depressed."

All of this Philadelphia passion has caught the eye of filmmakers.

Mark Wahlberg stars in *Invincible* (2006), which tells the true story, with a few Hollywood flourishes, of Vince Papale, a Philly guy and schoolteacher who earned a tryout with the Eagles and ended up playing three seasons in the National Football League.

In *Silver Linings Playbook* (2012), Robert De Niro plays a fan who has to have everything in its proper place when he sits down to watch the Eagles on television. His sons, played by Bradley Cooper and Shea Whigham, manage to get into a fight in the stadium parking lot before a game. And Jennifer Lawrence shows that, despite her protestations, she knows a thing or two about the Eagles and Philadelphia sports.

So why the Hollywood love for the Eagles? "It has the true underdog feel to it," Vincent said of the team. "People relate to that. It's kind of like 'Rocky.'"

In a tough town that loves

Solomon Vincent remembers the joy of a memorable victory over one of the Eagles' more hated rivals, the New York Giants (photograph by Courtney Johnson).

tough players, these fans have survived all the tough losses. There were the two Super Bowls, the Fog Bowl and, don't forget, Christmas Eve 1978. The Eagles met the Atlanta Falcons in a playoff game and were without kicker Nick Mike-Mayer, who had suffered a late-season rib injury. The Eagles tried using punter Mike Michel to handle the kicking. In the playoff game, Michel missed an extra-point kick and two field-goal attempts, including one in the final seconds. Final score: Atlanta 14, Philadelphia 13.

"Merry Christmas to me," Marroletti said. Despite losses like that, he remains devoted to the cause. After a loss, "I don't look at the newspaper until about Thursday." He even set his wedding date for an Eagles bye week.

The 2015 season ended in disappointment, with the Eagles finishing 7–9, bringing an end to the excitement generated when the team hired Chip Kelly as its coach in 2013. Kelly had the label of offensive genius after coaching at the University of Oregon, leading a team that scored so much it practically made scoreboards explode.

The promise of Kelly never panned out in Philadelphia. He finished 26–21 and was let go with one game left in the 2015 season, amid reports of unhappy players and a tense relationship with the front office.

So what is it that keeps these fans cheering for more, singing the fight song ("Fly Eagles Fly, on the road to victory") even when the Eagles don't always soar?

"Even during the darkest days, you had players who were worth watching," McCormick said. "That keeps you going." Fans can rattle off those names—from Van Buren to Van Brocklin; from Bednarik to White; from defensive back Tom Brookshier to safety Brian Dawkins, a player McCormick said "was pure poetry to watch."

"You keep coming back for more because you love them so much," Marroletti said. "Some people may not be able to understand the relationship."

Miceli thinks about his dad, still going strong in 2015 in his late 90s. His father never booed the team or spoke harshly about the players. He appreciated guys who took a lunch-pail attitude onto the playing field. All of that rubbed off on his son.

"As a kid, I wanted to play sports, and they were my heroes. That was a pretty cool time," said Miceli, who played football at Philadelphia's West Catholic High.

As he's grown into middle age, much of the hero worship has disappeared. He realizes football is a business, and the players are earning a living.

"But," he said, "I still love them."

Number 19

The San Diego Padres

Start talking with a fan of the San Diego Padres and two words are bound to come up early in the conversation: Tony Gwynn.

Perhaps more than any other baseball franchise, there is one—and just one—player linked so closely to the fiber of the team.

"We were fortunate this guy fell in love with this town because this town fell in love with him," said Barry Benintende, who has been a fan of the Padres since their first day of existence.

Gwynn played basketball and baseball at San Diego State and then spent every second of his 20 years in the majors wearing number 19 for the Padres before he retired in 2001.

He led the National League in batting eight times, including hitting .394 in a 1994 season shortened by labor trouble. It's the closest a major-leaguer has come to topping .400 since Boston's Ted Williams hit .406 in 1941.

Gwynn also led the league in hits seven times, won five Gold Gloves for his fielding and was a 15-time all-star.

Brad Beattie is a little too young to remember much of Gwynn's career, but he always thought of him as an underappreciated player. He cited such statistics as Gwynn striking out just 15 times in 577 plate appearances in 1995.

"That stuff amazes me," said Beattie, a student and part-time employee in traffic control with the San Diego Police Department.

Gwynn died of salivary gland cancer in 2014. He was 54. "After his passing, you realize he wasn't underappreciated for his work ethic and his work in the community," Beattie said.

Stevie Vigeveno had a catch in her throat when she started to discuss the late outfielder. "It's pretty hard for a lot of us to talk about him," she said. "His unselfishness and loyalty to the town—he'll never be forgotten."

She mentioned how fans still send cards on Gwynn's birthday and the day of his death to his widow, Alicia.

"He had a lasting impression on me, my children and this town. He was a once-in-a-lifetime kind of person," Vigeveno said.

Gwynn led San Diego to two World Series, one early in his career (1984), the other late (1998). Both times the Padres were matched against teams that might have been the best of each decade. Both times the Padres were beaten soundly—4–1 by the 1984 Detroit Tigers; 4–0 by the 1998 New York Yankees, who were in the midst of winning four titles in five seasons.

It's part of a history that started as a 1969 expansion team. It's a track record that can be discouraging for Padres fans—a few moments of glory that fell short of a title, surrounded by many less-than-stellar seasons. And this in a town where the National Football League Chargers have made just one Super Bowl, losing to the San Francisco 49ers in 1995.

"It's a little tough, but it keeps you coming back for more. You want to see that one championship," Beattie said.

Not that it slows the fans' devotion.

"I bleed chocolate and mustard," Benintende said, referring to the dark brown and yellow uniforms the Padres sported in the 1970s and early '80s. That color scheme still makes an occasional appearance to the delight of the "Bring Back the Brown" crowd—which even has its own website—and the despair of fashion critics.

"I didn't go to the Padres' first game in 1969, but I read about it the next day in the paper. I've been hooked ever since," Benintende said. He was 5 years old at the time.

His early years were spent rooting for a team that lost 100 or more games in four of its first six seasons. The first year saw the Padres finish with an unsightly 52–110 record. That first-season lineup included the good, such as first baseman Nate Colbert (24 home runs, 66 RBI), and the soon to be forgotten, such as second baseman Jose Arcia and shortstop Tommy Dean. The pitching staff included an old Johnny Podres (5–6, 4.31 ERA) and a young Joe Niekro (8–17, 3.70).

To explain those early years, Benintende turned to a passage from *High Fidelity*, written by one of his favorite authors, Nick Hornby. The book's main character, Rob (played by John Cusack in the movie adaptation), is a music fanatic who wonders whether he listens to songs about heartbreak and rejection because he is miserable, or is he miserable because of the music to which he listens.

Benintende converted that to a philosophical baseball query: "Am I loyal to the Padres because I live and breathe with them? Or do I live and breathe to root for the Padres?"

His first game was a Cub Scout trip in 1970. He remembers it was warm, Danny Coombs pitched, there weren't a lot of folks there and Padres outfielder "Downtown" Ollie Brown lived up to his nickname by hitting a home run. "When it hit, you could hear it rattling in the seats," Benintende said.

"Every year, there was one thing worth cheering for," he said. In the mid–1970s, that one thing was Randy Jones, a left-hander with a potent sinker and precise control.

With his bushy head of hair, Jones resembled Harpo Marx, and at times it seemed Jones threw about as hard as Harpo. But Jones improved rapidly from an 8–22 record in 1974 to 20–12 the next year and 22–14 in 1976. That year he led the National League in wins, complete games and innings pitched while also compiling the lowest WHIP (walks and hits allowed per inning). It was good enough for him to win the Cy Young Award, given to the league's best pitcher.

The Padres had their first winning season (84–78) in 1978 with a roster that had some Hall of Fame talent. Young shortstop Ozzie Smith stole 40 bases, while outfielder Dave Winfield batted .308 with 24 home runs and 97 runs batted in. Ageless Gaylord Perry, who turned 40 in September of that season, went 21–6 with a 2.73 ERA.

It took another six seasons for real success. In 1984, the Padres won the National League West with a 92–70 record. It was a season, Benintende said, that "was electric beyond words."

He remembers that team being sparked by the veteran leadership of first baseman Steve Garvey, the intensity of third baseman Graig Nettles and the speed of second baseman Alan Wiggins, who, as Benintende put it, "was stealing every base in sight." Wiggins ended up with 70 stolen bases.

There was Rich "Goose" Gossage marching in from the bullpen for 10 wins and 25 saves, which helped four starters—Eric Show, Tim Lollar, Ed Whitson and Mark Thurmond—reach double figures in victories.

And, of course, there was that man Gwynn. He collected 213 hits, batted .351 and finished with a .410 on-base percentage.

"It finally felt like the skies had opened and manna was falling from heaven," Benintende said. The National League Championship series against the Chicago Cubs only enhanced that feeling.

The Cubs, working on a dry spell of their own since last winning a World Series in 1908, clobbered Show, reliever Greg Harris and the Padres in Game 1, 13–0. The Cubs jumped out to a 3–0 lead in Game 2 and won,

4–2, sending the best-of-five series back to San Diego, where fans were wondering whether the season might end quickly.

Not a chance. Whitson and Gossage combined on a five-hitter in Game 3, and Garvey belted a two-run homer in the bottom of the ninth to give the Padres a 7–5 victory in Game 4.

In the decisive Game 5, the Cubs again burst out to a 3–0 lead off Show, but San Diego's bullpen shut out the Cubs for 7⅔ innings. The Padres rallied for two in the sixth inning and four in the seventh, aided by a crucial error by Chicago first baseman Leon Durham. The 6–3 victory sent the Padres to their first World Series.

"Short of the birth of my three children and getting married, Game 5 is the happiest I've been as a human being," Benintende said. The city was ready for the Series. "I decorated my car with every piece of 'Beat Detroit' paraphernalia I could find," he said.

San Diego got a tough draw in the World Series—a Tigers team that started the season 35–5 and finished with 104 wins. The Tigers had a loaded lineup that included outfielder Kirk Gibson, shortstop Alan Trammell, second baseman Lou Whitaker and catcher Lance Parrish. Their best starter, Jack Morris, won 19 games, and closer Willie Hernandez saved 32.

The World Series turned into a one-sided affair. The Padres won Game 2 to draw even with the Tigers, thanks to a three-run homer by Kurt Bevacqua, who endeared himself to baseball fans everywhere by leaping and spinning as he neared first base, and blowing kisses to the San Diego crowd as he approached home.

That was the Padres' high point. As Benintende put it, "Reality came thunderingly back the next game when Detroit beat us, 5–2. Crestfallen may have been putting it mildly."

His feelings were on target. Detroit won Game 4 behind Morris' complete-game five-hitter, and Gibson drove in five runs the next day, helping the Tigers win Game 5 and the Series.

Benintende works as an information specialist for the San Diego County Credit Union, but his previous career as a music and film critic for newspapers and magazines took him away from San Diego for several years, including a brief stint in Los Angeles.

"After a fire, a riot, an earthquake, a flood and too many Dodgers fans, I moved back," he said. His two sons had a take-it-or-leave-it attitude toward baseball and developed other interests, but his daughter, the youngest, got hooked on the game.

"Every night when I tucked my daughter in, I would tell her three things: I will always love you no matter what, and you will always be my

Barry Benintende and his daughter, Shelby Joyce Joann, share a love of the San Diego Padres. "What keeps me coming back is the hope and possibility," he says (courtesy Barry Benintende).

one and only sweet babboo, and the Dodgers are pure, unfiltered evil. I'd say that every night, much to my wife's chagrin."

The daughter, Shelby Joyce Joann, now has plans to study massage therapy and sports medicine, with the dream of someday working for the Padres.

"I could not be more proud if she was elected president," Benintende said.

Shortly after Shelby Joyce Joann's birth, the Padres had their next glorious season, which led them to the 1998 World Series. It was a major achievement for a team that just five seasons earlier had lost 101 games.

The 1998 Padres still had Gwynn getting on base, for sluggers Greg Vaughn (50 home runs, 119 RBI) and Ken Caminiti (29 homers, 82 RBI). The pitching staff was anchored by starters Kevin Brown (18–7, 2.38 ERA) and Andy Ashby (17–9, 3.34) and closer Trevor Hoffman, who led the major leagues with 53 saves.

That Series against the powerhouse Yankees started strong with Gwynn blasting a two-run homer in the fifth inning of Game 1 to give the Padres a 4–2 lead.

"In my way of thinking, this was it," Vigeveno said, recalling her optimism at that moment. Vaughn batted after Gwynn and added to the giddy feeling, hitting his second home run of the game. All that good feeling soon disappeared. The Yankees piled up seven runs in the seventh inning, en route to a 9–6 victory.

"The wind just got knocked out of their sails," Benintende said. The Yankees swept the Padres with third baseman Scott Brosius, the World Series most valuable player, leading the New York offense with a .471 batting average and six RBI.

"It's like it was yesterday," Benintende said. "It still hurts."

As if that wasn't enough, more hurt awaited in 2007. The Padres held the wild-card lead with two games left in the season. That day they lost, 4–3, in 11 innings to the Milwaukee Brewers. The Brewers got a game-tying hit in the ninth inning from Tony Gwynn, Jr., son of the longtime Padres star.

"It seemed kind of eerie," Beattie said. Sure enough, the eerie feeling continued the next day, with an 11–6 loss to the Brewers. Meanwhile, the Colorado Rockies won for the 13th time in 14 games to tie the Padres for the National League wild-card spot. The teams met the next day in Denver to decide who would go to the playoffs and who would go home.

In a back-and-forth game, the teams were tied after nine innings. Neither team scored again until the top of the 13th when San Diego leftfielder Scott Hairston cracked a two-run homer, giving the Padres an 8–6 lead.

Hoffman, who ranks second in baseball history in career saves, took the mound for San Diego. He needed just three outs to send the Padres to the postseason. Instead, he yielded two doubles and a triple. Game tied, 8–8. After an intentional walk, Jamey Carroll lofted a fly ball to right field. Matt Holliday tagged at third base and raced home, trying to beat a strong throw by Padres rightfielder Brian Giles. Holliday slid headfirst into home, but his hand smacked into the foot of catcher Michael Barrett and it appeared to never touch the plate. Still, the call was safe, and the Rockies—not the Padres—were playoff bound.

"I like Matt Holliday, but every time I see him, I think of that play," Beattie said.

Benintende remembers his thoughts after the Padres took the lead in the 13th inning. "This is going to be great. This is going to be great. And then it wasn't. Safe, out, it didn't matter," he said of the Holliday play. "We should have done the job."

The 2010 season was just as challenging for Padres fans. San Diego led the National League West for much of the season, but a 10-game losing streak that started in late August and a mediocre September ruined it all. The Padres finished 90–72, missing the playoffs by one game.

"Every day was finding a new way to lose," Benintende said. "Every day was a new way to disappoint me. Every day was me trying not to swear in people's faces."

All of this may sometimes disappoint Vigeveno, but she lets her Padres faith shine through. She is president of the San Diego Madres, a group started by players' wives that has morphed into a fan club working to raise money for youth baseball and softball programs. It averages donations of $40,000 a year to make sure leagues have equipment and facilities for young players.

She grew up in Tucson, Arizona, where she would watch the Cleveland Indians during spring training. In 1951, she was hit by a foul ball off the bat of Joe DiMaggio. It was DiMaggio's final season and the only year that the Yankees held their spring training in Arizona. DiMaggio came over to make sure she wasn't injured. "I didn't know the difference, but my mother never forgot it," she said.

Vigeveno has spent two stints in San Diego, one that started in 1974 and included the first regular-season major-league game she ever saw. The baseball may not have been great, but she didn't mind. "I really was hooked. I liked the Padres. They were scrappers."

After a stint in Santa Barbara, California, and a second marriage in 1997, she returned to San Diego. "It wasn't a premarital condition, but it almost was, that we get season tickets," she said.

A recent 70th birthday party for her was worked around a date when the Yankees visited San Diego. Her three children, her grandchildren and other family and friends—18 in all—attended.

"We celebrated by beating the Yankees. We had a blast," she said.

Through the years, she has loved watching the players, from Gwynn, Jones and Winfield to the current stars. Jones is an ex-player who regularly attends Madres events. "It's more of a lovefest than anything else," she said of Jones' appearances.

And she loved listening to the talents of the late Jerry Coleman, the adored Padres announcer who was known for sometimes mauling the play-by-play just a bit. He once referred to Jones and his "Karl Marx" hairdo. Perhaps Coleman's most famous play-by-play call is this one of a deep fly ball hit by a Padres opponent: "Winfield goes back to the wall, he hits his head on the wall, and it rolls off! It's rolling all the way back to second base. This is a terrible thing for the Padres."

Benintende explained Coleman's broadcasts: "Listening to Jerry do a game, he could stick his foot in his mouth. It was as if he had too much knowledge and it was all spilling out."

It didn't bother Vigeveno. Coleman's work always made her smile. "It was so entertaining—that's the best word. He was so down to earth and unpretentious."

It has been just one of the joys of life in San Diego. Vigeveno wakes up every morning to a view of Point Loma and the Coronado Bridge.

"I get to look at this. That's how I deal with it. I don't really dwell on the past a lot. Hope springs eternal, and spring is the operative word. There may be doubts in the fall, but spring comes and spring training starts."

Benintende offered a similar philosophy. "It's kind of difficult to be miserable when the weather is always nice and the beach is 15 minutes away, and there are Mary's Donuts, which are the best doughnuts in the world."

Opposite top: Stevie Vigeveno is active with the San Diego Madres. The group, started by the wives of Padres players, now is a fan group that raises money for youth baseball and softball leagues (photograph by Henk Vigeveno). *Bottom:* Stevie Vigeveno met Jerry Coleman in 2007. Coleman, who died in 2104, was a San Diego Padres broadcaster for more than four decades and was known for his unique style. "It was so entertaining—that's the best word," Vigeveno says (photograph by Rick Zambori).

The losses hurt, he said, but he then referenced former major-league pitcher Joaquin Andujar, a Yogi Berra–like quote machine who has been attributed with saying, "There is one word in America that says it all, and that word is 'you never know.'"

"In baseball there is one word, 'you never know,'" said Benintende. "What keeps me coming back is the hope and possibility. In baseball, for many, it's wait till next year. I'm a Padres fan. It's wait till next decade.

"I will keep coming back because there will come a day when they win the World Series. I will be alive for it, and I will be the happiest man on the freakin' planet."

Family Ties

The Kansas City Chiefs

In January 1970, 9-year-old Lance Verderame was determined not to go along with everyone else in his New Jersey classroom. They were all picking the Minnesota Vikings to win Super Bowl IV. He decided to be the class contrarian.

"I was somebody who liked rooting for the underdog. Not really knowing anything, I said, 'The Chiefs are going to win,'" Verderame recalled.

That Sunday, he sat and enjoyed the first football game he ever watched as quarterback Len Dawson and the Kansas City Chiefs pounded the favored Vikings, 23–7. So began a family's three-generation love affair that has lasted 45-plus years.

After the Super Bowl, Verderame became such a passionate fan of the Chiefs that his mother and father, Liz and Charlie, became interested. He even taught his mother the finer points of the sport using an electric football game.

"She'd sit down and say, 'Show me again. I'm not getting this first-down thing,'" he said. Verderame set up the players on the game's playing field and explained how a 3-yard gain would turn first and 10 into second and 7; how a 15-yard pass on first down would create a new first down.

Unlike that first Super Bowl he watched by himself, he now had fellow fans—his mom and dad—to sit with whenever the Chiefs games were televised in New Jersey.

When it came time for Verderame to have a family of his own, a new generation of Chiefs passion was created.

"When I was born in 1988, I was indoctrinated right away," said Lance's son, Matt.

The Chiefs of Lance's youth were a strong team. Two seasons after the Super Bowl victory, the Chiefs went 10–3–1 and hosted the Miami Dolphins at home in a playoff game.

It was Christmas Day, a time for family, gifts and holiday spirit. On this day, with a 4 p.m. kickoff on the East Coast, it also was time for one of the National Football League's most memorable games.

Kansas City's Ed Podolak, a solid but not spectacular running back, had the game of his life, rushing for 85 yards, catching eight passes for 110 yards and returning kicks for another 155 yards. After Kansas City kicker Jan Stenerud, a future Hall of Famer, missed a field goal with 35 seconds left, the teams finished four quarters tied, 24–24. They were still tied after a first overtime.

Lance was watching all of this at his grandmother's house.

"The next thing I knew, relatives who weren't even football fans were in the room watching," he said. Along with all the action on the field, he had another memory of that game. During every key moment—and there were many—his mother was whacking his uncle in the leg.

"After the game, it was hard for him to walk," Lance said.

Midway through the second overtime, Miami's kicker, Garo Yepremian, ended the epic battle with a 37-yard field goal–82 minutes and 40 seconds after the opening kickoff. It remains the longest game in National Football League history.

"As a young kid, it turned out to be a devastating game. I remember a lot of crying in the back seat on the way home," Lance said.

While Lance and his relatives were watching on television in the Northeast, Dick Roseberry was at Kansas City's Municipal Stadium, cheering on the Chiefs with his son.

An Iowa graduate, Roseberry enjoyed the performance of Podolak, a fellow Hawkeye. Roseberry also was struck by the optimism in the stadium throughout the game. That disappeared with Yepremian's kick.

"Everybody kind of drooped. It was a big letdown," he said. There also was the postgame reaction, one that likely played out in homes across the Kansas City metro area.

"When we got home for dinner that night, my wife was a little unhappy. She had planned Christmas dinner for a couple of hours earlier."

Kansas City fans didn't know it at the time, but that loss marked the end of an era. With Dawson nearing the end of his career, the Chiefs would get a new stadium, Arrowhead, in 1972, but they wouldn't return to the playoffs for more than a decade.

"That stretch was a long, lonely one," Lance said.

The next visit to the playoffs in 1986 was over quickly. The Chiefs lost to the New York Jets, 35–15, but a few years later the team was on the upswing.

Marty Schottenheimer was hired as head coach, and he led the Chiefs to the playoffs seven times from 1990 to 1997. And in 1993, Joe Montana, one of the league's all-time great quarterbacks, arrived from the San Francisco 49ers.

The signing of Montana was such a big deal that Lance can still remember the exact spot where he was driving when he heard the news on the car radio.

Montana's first season in Kansas City saw the Chiefs beat the Pittsburgh Steelers and Houston Oilers in the playoffs. The playoff run made an impression on Matt Verderame, even though he was only 5 and living in Livingstone Manor, New York, more than 1,200 miles east of Kansas City.

He had been taken to the hospital before one of those playoff games. The problem turned out not to be serious, but Matt started crying in his hospital room, and his father asked him if he wasn't feeling well.

"I said, 'I feel fine, but we've got to get out of here. The game starts at 4,'" Matt said.

Father and son did get home in time. They watched the Chiefs win that playoff game, but they were separated for the AFC Championship Game against the Buffalo Bills on January 23, 1994. Lance did heavy timber repair work and on game day he was at an emergency renovation at an old theater in Fort Monmouth, New Jersey.

"I had to be there," Lance said of the job. "It killed me. We were in the AFC Championship Game, and I couldn't watch with my son. I promised him I'd call him as much as I could."

Lance kept his promise, even on a bone-chilling day in an era before cellphones were everywhere. During breaks, he drove to a nearby pay phone, called Matt and rolled up the car window as far as he could to hold out the bitter January air.

They didn't have many good moments to talk about. The Buffalo defense bottled up Montana before knocking him out of the game, and the Chiefs fell, 30–13. When Dad got home, he had to comfort his son.

"I remember crying my eyes out, saying they'll never get back [to the AFC title game]," Matt said. "My father said, 'Of course they will.' They've never been back."

Matt taped the game, figuring he and his father could watch together afterward. Since the Chiefs lost, they never did, but Matt still has the old VCR tape.

"I watch it in full every year to remind myself where I hope the Chiefs will get back to," he said.

Two years after that loss to the Bills, the playoffs ended in even more painful fashion for the Chiefs. In 1995, they were 13–3 and didn't lose a game at home all season. They were, in the words of Matt, "a juggernaut."

Because of their stellar regular season, the Chiefs got to host a playoff game against the Indianapolis Colts, who had finished the season 9–7. The Colts would have to play without injured second-year star running back Marshall Faulk.

Game day was one of those days that can sweep through the Plains states in early January. The temperature at kickoff was zero. The windchill was 15 below.

The Chiefs' offense was as frigid as the weather. Starting quarterback Steve Bono was 11 for 25 for 122 yards. He threw for a touchdown but also had three passes intercepted. Kicker Lin Elliott missed all three of his field-goal attempts.

"When he lined up for that third field goal, it was predestined," Matt said. "You knew there was no chance of that ball going through the uprights." It all ended in an ugly 10–7 loss for Kansas City. "They did what they always do—find a way to disappoint," Matt said.

There were other tough losses to come. In 1997, the Chiefs again finished with a 13–3 record, only to lose a home playoff game to the Denver Broncos, 14–10, thanks to a fourth-quarter touchdown drive led by Denver quarterback John Elway. In a defensive battle, the Chiefs couldn't stop running back Terrell Davis, who rushed for 101 yards.

"That was as devas-

Lance Verderame taught his son Matt about bowling at a young age. He also passed on a love of the Kansas City Chiefs (courtesy Matt Verderame).

tating a loss as that franchise has had since the Christmas Day game," Matt said. "That game destroyed people. That game is the most painful for me. You hate Denver. You hate Elway."

On Jan. 4, 2014, the Chiefs and Colts met in the playoffs again. This time, playing on the road, the Chiefs built a 38–10 lead. Even at 38–10, Matt wasn't comfortable, a feeling no doubt shared by thousands of other Chiefs fans. Kansas City was still up late in the third quarter, 41–31.

At that point, Matt, working in the newsroom of the Binghamton *Press & Sun-Bulletin* in New York, took a break and picked up his phone. "I called my father. I said, 'They're going to lose.' He said, 'I know they are.'" The Verderames were right. Quarterback Andrew Luck and the Colts completed the comeback, winning, 45–44.

If all of this sounds discouraging, it isn't for Lance and Matt Verderame. The father-son duo took off after Thanksgiving dinner in 2007 to make the 20-hour drive to see a game at Kansas City's Arrowhead Stadium.

Lance was struck by the enthusiasm of the fan base. It was displayed in full color when they stopped at a grocery store.

"It seemed like everybody was dressed in Chiefs red or Chiefs jerseys," he said. "It had the feel of a small-town high school game. It was just amazing."

The stadium was no different, with the Chiefs facing their most hated rival, the Oakland Raiders. It was a down season for both teams, who would each finish 4–12.

Kansas City running back Kolby Smith (150 yards and two touchdowns on 31 carries) dueled with Oakland's Justin Fargas (139 yards and one touchdown on 22 carries), but the Raiders won, 20–17.

"In Kansas City, they never sat down," Matt said. "Here's a team that's going nowhere playing a team that was going nowhere. It was three hours of people screaming."

Family ties and fans rooting together, no matter how dire the circumstances. Those factors help make up the essence of life for many devoted sports fans.

Roseberry and his family know that feeling. A Korean War veteran, he was a longtime season-ticket holder in Kansas City before moving to Florida in the mid–1990s. He was even selected by the team as its fan of the week for an Oct. 23, 1988 game. The game wasn't much, a 7–6 loss to the Detroit Lions, but he's still got the football he was given that day, even if it is a bit deflated.

Roseberry followed his daughter, Dana, to Florida, where they both live in Cape Coral, near Fort Myers. She runs her own marketing and advertising firm, and used some of those skills to get a Chiefs fan club started in southwest Florida.

The birth of the fan club came when her brother was visiting, and they decided to watch a Chiefs game at a bar in Fort Myers. They ran into a half-dozen other Chiefs backers, and one had a list of names of other fans.

Dana took charge, made some phone calls, and the fan club "just grew and grew and grew and grew," she said. It now has 300 families as members. These days, there are trips to Tampa Bay or Miami when the Chiefs are playing. Get-togethers at a local bar when the Chiefs are on television can draw 100 fans. There even have been specially named drinks: the Schottenheimer shot, after the onetime coach, and the Dave Szott shot, after the offensive lineman who played with the Chiefs from 1990 to 2000.

"It's so much fun to sit and watch a game and cheer and swear with other people," she said. "It's almost like you're there."

Her fan club attracted the attention of R.J. Huebert, who wrote about Chiefs fans in his thesis for a master's degree at the University of South Florida. The 2010 work focused on how fans used media to follow their team.

The spirit of the group captured the attention of Huebert, who is a Pennsylvania native and Pittsburgh Steelers fan.

"These guys were diehards, supporting week in and week out. It was crazy," Huebert said. "You're a Steelers fan in a Chiefs bar. They were completely welcoming."

Florida isn't the only state outside of Missouri where Chiefs fans gather on Sundays in the fall. George Perry of Rowlett, Texas, was an integral part of getting a weekly Chiefs tailgate started at Wizards Sports Café in Richardson, a Dallas suburb.

A huge tent, Chiefs flags, pennants and plenty of barbecue are set up outside Wizards, creating some Kansas City scenery for anyone passing by on the nearby highway.

"I pretend I'm at Arrowhead," Perry said of the get-togethers. It's a tribute to the Chiefs stadium and Kansas City's reputation as a great tailgating town. Perry recalled going to tailgates at Arrowhead soon after he was out of college, too poor to afford much of anything. People would give him free food, drinks and, if he was lucky, a ticket to the game.

The pregame tailgate at Wizards can draw 150 people. Even more may show up to watch the Chiefs game at the bar. It's all in good fun, even when Dallas Cowboys fans mingle with the Chiefs supporters.

"They're respectful to each other," said Wizards employee Mikaela Barnes. "They yell at the refs. They don't yell at each other."

Perry is a Kansas City native who grew up in the late 1960s and early 1970s, an era when every game wasn't shown on television. You watched your hometown team on Sunday. You waited until halftime of *Monday Night Football* to see highlights from the league's other games.

"That's why guys my age will watch the same replay 47 times," Perry said. "It's because we were denied for decades."

Perry moved to Texas in 1995. He met many gleeful Cowboys supporters, reveling in the fact their team was about to win its third Super Bowl in four years. Cowboys fans have cooled their act in recent years, Perry said, but when he first arrived in Texas, "they were the most obnoxious fans I met in my entire life, outside of Philadelphia. They were worse than the Raiders or the Broncos, and that's coming from an AFC West guy," he said.

When Dallas fans gave him a hard time about rooting for Kansas City, he would explain to them that the Chiefs actually started as the Dallas Texans. (The franchise played for three seasons in Dallas in the old American Football League before moving to Kansas City. In 1962, their last season in Dallas, the Texans won the American Football League championship, thanks to a stingy defense and a potent offense led by Dawson, running back Abner Haynes and wide receiver Chris Burford.)

If Dallas fans still weren't impressed, he would ask, "If you move to Canada, are you still a Texan? They would say, 'Damn right I am.' I'd say, 'It's the same thing.'"

Perry once said he wouldn't cut his hair until the Chiefs won again. He went almost a year between haircuts.

He suffered through the 15-year playoff drought of the 1970s and '80s. "It was difficult. You always hope—you brainwash yourself to hope."

And he watched with many other Chiefs fans in January 2014 when the team blew its 28-point lead to lose to the Colts in the playoffs. "With Chiefs fans, there's this thing," he said. "We're never safe until 10 minutes after the game is over. We've lived with this forever. It never seems to end."

Perry said he was well-trained for defeat watching a less-than-successful University of Missouri football team when he was a student there in the 1980s. (Sample season—1985: The Tigers went 1–10, beating only Iowa State and losing, 51–6, to Oklahoma.) "We cheered if they covered the spread. That's how miserable it was."

As he explained, "It's the essence of being a true fan—when you're there when they suck."

It's an attitude he takes to those tailgates every Sunday at Wizards. "I love sports. It's the camaraderie. There's so much crap in life. I tell people, 'Win or lose, we'll have fun.'"

That kind of enthusiasm also lives on in the Verderame and Roseberry families.

"I just love watching my team play," said Dana Roseberry. "I feel like I'm a Kansas Citian even though I've lived in Florida longer than I lived in Kansas City. I just hope to God that this is the year."

Her father has a pragmatic approach to his support for the team. Like other fans, he kept the faith during a 22-year stretch that saw the Chiefs lose eight straight times in the playoffs before finally beating the Houston Texans in January 2016. After beating Houston, the Chiefs got knocked out of the playoffs the next week when they had to travel to New England and face Tom Brady and the Patriots.

"I can't afford to throw away my Chiefs hats and shirts and buy new ones for another team," he said.

For Lance Verderame, there's a special connection with the Chiefs—memories of watching with Matt.

"The moments I've shared with my son, through the good times and the bad, will always link me to him," he said.

Matt recently moved to Chicago for his job as an NFL writer for the sports website FanSided, where his duties include writing and editing for a Chiefs blog, Arrowhead Addict. Being in the Windy City means he won't be watching the Chiefs on Sunday with his dad. "That will be the hardest part of the whole moving deal," he said.

Still, he will maintain his strong sense of how his dad and all other Chiefs fans feel.

"I think the losses have just bonded the fan base," he said. "With every loss, it just adds to the feeling that, hey, I've suffered through this. We're just hoping all the suffering will pay off in a glorious moment that everyone will remember forever.

"If you don't love sports, it's impossible to understand. If you look from the outside, you see the pain and the suffering and the high blood pressure. But it has become a religion. I can't imagine not watching every Sunday. They can't do anything to shake us."

More Cowbell

The Mississippi State Bulldogs

Christopher Walken has to be a Mississippi State fan. After all, his record producer in a famous 2000 sketch from *Saturday Night Live* demanded just one thing from Will Ferrell, Jimmy Fallon and the rest of the band: "I got a fever, and the only prescription is more cowbell."

He would fit right in at Davis Wade Stadium, where the cowbell is the noisemaker of choice. The clanging has driven opposing teams and Southeastern Conference officials crazy, but it's a proud tradition. "It's a constant reminder of Mississippi State and how awesome we are," said Anberitha Matthews (Mississippi State Class of 2010).

That awesomeness includes a passionate fan base for a team that has won only one Southeastern Conference title, and that was back in 1941. The conference is often the best in the country when it comes to football, but seven-plus decades are a long time to wait for a championship.

"I always tell everyone that if you're a Mississippi State fan, you're not there for the win. It's tradition. It's support. It's family. You just go," said Brandy Rea (Class of 2000).

The Bulldogs have been playing football since the late 1800s. Those early seasons included games against such schools as Samford and Cumberland and, of course, losing frequently to the Alabama Crimson Tide. Over the years, intense rivalries have developed, especially with that school 95 miles to the northwest, the University of Mississippi.

"I probably scream 'Roll Tide' louder than anybody when Alabama is playing Mississippi," said Matthews, who is a graduate student at Mississippi State in medical science research. "You know the saying, 'the enemy of my enemy is my friend'? That's our relationship with Alabama."

There were some great seasons in the early days of Mississippi State football. The 1913 team went 6–1–1 and finished the season in glorious fashion, beating Alabama, 7–0, on Thanksgiving Day.

In 1936, Mississippi State made its first bowl game appearance, finishing the regular season 7–2–1 to qualify for the Orange Bowl. It lost, 13–12, to Duquesne, then a national power. Four seasons later, Mississippi State went 10–0–1, including a 14–7 Orange Bowl victory over Georgetown, a school now known much more for basketball than football.

Mississippi State's glory year of 1941 featured shutout victories over Mississippi and Alabama, a season that would make any Bulldogs supporter happy. Mississippi State finished 8–1–1 overall, and its 4–0–1 conference record was good enough for first in the SEC. Japan bombed Pearl Harbor on December 7, 1941, and subsequent travel restrictions prevented the Bulldogs from going to a bowl game after such a terrific season.

Selecting a national champion in those days was murkier than it is today. The undefeated Minnesota Golden Gophers, who also did not play in a bowl game, were selected as national champions in the Associated Press poll as well as by nine other outlets that picked a champion.

Alabama went to the Cotton Bowl, a strange game that saw the Crimson Tide triumph despite getting just one first down and punting 16 times. Texas A&M helped out the Tide by turning the ball over 12 times.

But Alabama lost twice in the SEC—to Mississippi State and Vanderbilt—and finished 20th in the final AP poll. Still, one selector, the Houlgate Poll, found it in its heart to name the Crimson Tide the best team in the land.

Despite a single poll being the only site that selected the Crimson Tide No. 1, Alabama lists the 1941 season as one of its 16 national championships. This doesn't sit well with Mississippi State fans.

"We beat Alabama that year. We had a better record than Alabama. Why do they claim they're national champions?" Marc Anthony (Class of 1988) said. "I guess we didn't get the Slick Lizard Daily Gazette to pick us as national champions."

It's not as if State fans need any more ammunition to dislike Alabama. Entering the 2016 season, the Crimson Tide had a 79–18–3 record against Mississippi State.

"Alabama is the team we've got to figure out," said Justin Strawn (Class of 2001). "Every time we've had a chance to do something in the SEC, it's Alabama that's ruined it for us."

When it comes to Mississippi State vs. Alabama, there are few fans who have the in-depth perspective of Barbie Terry. She grew up in northern Alabama, wearing Alabama cheerleader outfits as early as age 2 on football Saturdays.

But, when it came time to pick a college, she opted for Mississippi

State. A few friends were going there, and when she visited the Starkville, Mississippi, campus, she fell in love with it.

"It was always just understood that I'd go to Alabama. I guess I've never done what I was expected to do," said Terry (Class of 2006, master's degree in public policy in 2010). When she told her grandfather that she was going to attend Mississippi State, "he just got up and left the table," she said. But he visited her during her first semester at the school and saw how much she loved the place. That Christmas she gave him a Mississippi State sweatshirt. "He still wears it," she said.

After graduating, mutual friends introduced her to Adam Terry, a University of Alabama graduate. How long did it take the topic of Mississippi State vs. Alabama to come up on their first date? "Probably about 20 minutes," she said.

Barbie and Adam overlooked their collegiate differences and got married. Their oldest child, son Eli, is a huge Alabama fan. Their daughter Avery, born in 2014, is still being molded as a football fan. On a Saturday in the fall, she may start the day in an Alabama dress, but "I'll put her in a Mississippi State outfit," Barbie said.

Barbie and Adam usually get to at least a couple of games each season at each of their alma maters. They may tease each other before the game, and, she said, "Sometimes it's debatable whether we should sit together during the game. I ring my cowbell, and it drives him crazy. But we're gracious toward each other after the game.... We believe God put us together when he did because we wouldn't have made it through a college relationship. We met when we were mature enough to realize it's only a game."

They lived in Mississippi until 2013 while Barbie continued to work for her alma mater as director of annual giving. They have relocated in northern Alabama, where they are both from, and she now works as director of development for the University of North Alabama.

She admits there are times she will root for Alabama for the sake of household harmony. When the Crimson Tide played Clemson in January 2016 for the national championship, Adam put out an Alabama sweatshirt for her to wear. "For that one game, I wore it," she said, "but I wore my State shirt under it."

And when Alabama plays Mississippi, there are no torn allegiances. "That's the one game of the year when I truly with all my heart root for Alabama," she said.

In the lopsided series with Alabama, Barbie is always pulling for her Bulldogs in that matchup. Despite Alabama's dominance, there have been

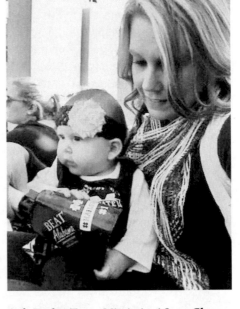

Left: **Barbie Terry, Mississippi State Class of 2006, is married to an Alabama graduate. She's trying her best to ensure daughter Avery is raised a Bulldogs fan (photograph by Lauren Roberts).** *Right:* **Avery Terry shows off the Mississippi State cowbell of her mom, Barbie. Ringing of cowbells during games is a proud tradition at the school (photograph by Lauren Roberts).**

some moments of glory in the series for Mississippi State, perhaps none better than 1980. The Crimson Tide, coached by legendary Bear Bryant, had won two straight national championships. Alabama was 7–0, carrying a No. 1 national ranking and a 28-game winning streak into the game. Mississippi State was 6–2, unranked and riding a two-game winning streak.

But on this day the Bulldogs limited Alabama's powerful rushing game to 116 yards, and Dana Moore kicked two second-half field goals to give Mississippi State a 6–3 lead. Alabama mounted a late drive, reaching Mississippi State's 4-yard-line with 25 seconds to go. On the next play, Alabama quarterback Don Jacobs rolled right and was hit hard by Mississippi State defensive end Tyrone Keys. Jacobs fumbled, Mississippi State's Billy Jackson recovered, and the Bulldogs had their first win over Alabama in 23 years.

"It's a game we all remember," Anthony said. There's plenty of proof of that. Newspaper clippings about the game hang on walls of restaurants and offices in Starkville. Some vehicles still display bumper stickers that show the game's final score.

"Nothing beats beating out Bear Bryant," Strawn said.

In 1999, the Bulldogs traveled to Tuscaloosa, Alabama, with an 8–0 record, ranked eighth in the country. The Crimson Tide was 7–2 and ranked 11th. This time, Alabama got the best of Mississippi State, winning 19–7.

But it was one of the few dark moments in a glorious season for the Bulldogs. Coached by Jackie Sherrill, they pulled off one improbable win after another. They won five games by three points or fewer, including an 18–16 victory at Auburn when backup quarterback Matt Wyatt threw two touchdown passes in the final 2:28.

Then there was the annual Egg Bowl against Mississippi, which ended the regular season. Both teams were ranked in the top 25 heading into the Thanksgiving game.

Playing at home, State trailed Ole Miss, 20–6, in the fourth quarter before quarterback Wayne Madkin led the offense to two touchdowns, the last a 38-yard pass with 27 seconds left to C.J. Sirmones. The extra point tied the game.

Rather than play for overtime, Mississippi tried a long pass in the final seconds, but the play was defended well by State defensive back Robert Bean. He deflected the ball, and as it fell to the ground, it hit Bean's foot and popped in the air. Defensive back Eugene Clinton snagged the errant ball and raced to Mississippi's 27-yard line. Scott Westerfield then kicked the game-winning field goal.

On the ESPN broadcast, Mike Tirico told the country, "The last-second Bulldogs do it again."

"It was one of the most unlikely plays you'll ever see," Strawn said of the interception. "It was the most unlikely comeback in a season filled with unlikely comebacks."

It was Rea's senior season, and she was at the game with friends and her parents on a frigid night in Starkville.

"Icicles were literally forming on our clothes, but we wouldn't leave," she said of herself and her friends. Her parents, however, did leave early. After all, Thanksgiving dinner awaited, and so did a warm apartment. They missed the Bulldogs' comeback.

"My roommates and I came back to the apartment after the game and gave them all kinds of grief. From that point forward, my parents swore they would never leave early again," Rea said.

The 1999 season was the best of Sherrill's 13 years at Mississippi State. The Bulldogs finished 9–2 and beat Clemson, 17–7, in the Peach Bowl.

Sherrill was a colorful character who once sought to inspire his players before a game with the Texas Longhorns by having a bull castrated at practice. In his time at Mississippi State, he turned around a struggling program, but his final three seasons were not good, ending with a 2–10 record in 2003. It was part of a six-year run from 2001 to 2006 in which the Bulldogs never won more than three games in a season.

Sherrill was followed by Sylvester Croom, the first black football coach in the Southeastern Conference. His first three seasons were lackluster, although Mississippi State had a knack for pulling upsets that got the opposing coach fired. Those dismissals created a new verb in Starkville— "You got Croomed." Croom found success in 2007, leading the Bulldogs to an 8–5 record and a 10–3 win over Central Florida in the Liberty Bowl.

The next year the team fell to 4–8, and it was an ugly season; Strawn described it as some of the most unwatchable play in college football history. There was a 3–2 loss at home to Auburn. There was the Egg Bowl disaster, a 45–0 crushing by Mississippi.

Croom was replaced by Dan Mullen, who soon had the Bulldogs winning again. After a 5–7 season in 2009, the Bulldogs made it to six straight bowl games from 2010 to 2015, a first in school history. The best season in that stretch was 2014, in which Mississippi State was ranked No. 1 in the country for five weeks, which was more unprecedented territory for the Bulldogs.

After a 9–0 start, the 2014 season ended with a thud. There were late-season losses to Alabama and Mississippi and a 49–34 loss to Georgia Tech in the Orange Bowl. The Bulldogs still finished ranked 11th in the country, and quarterback Dak Prescott placed eighth in voting for the Heisman Trophy, given to college football's best player.

"We weren't disappointed at the end," Rea said. "We were just glad to get some positive attention."

Rea and her family live in Philadelphia, Mississippi, about an hour south of Starkville, and are constant supporters of the Bulldogs.

"If it's a home game, we're there. If it's a road game that's not too far, we're there," she said. For other road games, they tailgate at home. Friends come over, the grill comes out and, if the weather behaves, the television is brought outside.

"There's lots of yelling and screaming at the TV," she said. "We're usually not happy with the commentators."

At Christmas, one of the trees in their home is devoted to Mississippi State. The decorative theme ranges from mini football helmets to school ornaments. "Everything is maroon and white," she said.

Top: Brandy and Richard Rea, with son Spencer and daughter Meagan, cheer for Mississippi State during the Bulldogs' 31–6 loss to Alabama in November 2015 (courtesy Brandy Rea). *Bottom:* Meagan and Spencer Rea show their Bulldog pride—and their cowbells—during Mississippi State's loss to Mississippi in the 2015 Egg Bowl (courtesy Brandy Rea).

Rea knows as well as anyone the depth of the rivalry between the Mississippi State Bulldogs and the Ole Miss Rebels. A therapist and forensic interviewer for abused children, she graduated from Mississippi State and got her master's from the University of Mississippi.

"My bachelor's degree is proudly mounted on the wall," she said. "My master's degree is hidden in my desk drawer. It's like a dirty, shameful secret."

She also knows the devotion of being a Bulldogs fan.

"Mississippi State is part of who I am. It's just like family. You don't give up on family," she said.

Matthews shares that devotion: "It's not always about the points on the board as much as it is about the heart of the team. They try hard. Win or lose, we're there to support them."

Strawn, a seventh-grade history teacher in northern Mississippi, agrees. "If you truly are a fan, you're going to always be there to support them," he said. "You don't do it as enthusiastically when they are bad, but

Richard and Brandy Rea enjoy Mississippi State's victory over Kentucky in October 2015. They are devoted fans and even have a Christmas tree dedicated to the Bulldogs (courtesy Brandy Rea).

you still do it. When they're having a bad time, you hope and pray they'll get better."

Being an alumnus brings you closer to the school. Strawn roots for professional teams, including the Los Angeles Dodgers, a team he was drawn to because he was fascinated with the story of Jackie Robinson, the player who broke the color barrier in major-league baseball.

"When I talk about the Dodgers, I don't ever say 'we,' but when I talk about Mississippi State, I say 'we' because I am a Bulldog. It's a part of who you are."

Terry said her love of the Bulldogs is based upon her philosophy of supporting Mississippi State in every way possible: "It's my love for the university as a whole. My experience there from day one was fantastic."

This Bulldogs passion is something that Danny P. Smith has been watching for many years. He's a Starkville native and sports editor of the *Starkville Daily News*.

"The fan support has always been there," he said, but it has gotten more boisterous in recent years. "A lot of that has to do with Dan Mullen. He keeps the energy alive."

Now about those cowbells.

They have been used by fans at games since the 1930s, according to Mississippi State's athletic website. The site says the exact start of the tradition is unclear, but the most popular legend is that a cow wandered onto the field during a game against archrival Mississippi. Mississippi State won, and students started bringing a cow to the games. Eventually, the cow was replaced by just the cowbells, thousands of them.

Opponents complained about the racket, and the bells were banned, although that didn't keep fans from sneaking them in and clanging away. In 2010, the Southeastern Conference approved the use of the cowbells, but prohibited their use when the visiting team is running its offensive plays.

Just how loud is it? "It's like nothing you've ever really heard before," Matthews said.

"When the center gets over the ball, it goes from cowbells ringing to just voices," Anthony said. "It's amazing to hear the whole tone of the stadium change."

Anthony knows a thing or two about cowbells. He makes them and sells them at his Starkville store, University Screenprint.

A good football season provides a big boost. He estimated that cowbell sales about doubled—to 17,000—thanks to the 2014 team.

"My business depends on whether the team wins or loses. I tell my friends I have a little different perspective [about football] than they do. It depends on whether I eat next week or not."

For State fans, the cowbells are a treasured tradition. Many use ones that have been handed down from generation to generation.

Anthony, who attends just about every home game, has used the same cowbell for more than four decades. "I make a lot of them, but when I go to a game, I grab that same one."

Each member of Rea's family has his or her own cowbell displayed on the mantel at home. "It makes me think of Mississippi State," Rea said. "It's home."

Strawn is also an energetic cowbell ringer. "It's part of our football tradition. We're perfectly OK with you hating it."

Terry got her cowbell, a maroon one with the phrase "Beat Alabama" on it as well as the Mississippi State logo, during her initiation to the Zeta Tau Alpha sorority. Her sorority sisters presented her with a cowbell because she is the first member of her family to attend Mississippi State.

When friends threw her a baby shower before Avery's birth, a sorority member gave Terry a cowbell for her daughter. It is pink, with Avery's initials on one side and a paw print on the other. "That was the only gift I cried about," Terry said.

Land of Snow and Dreams

The Minnesota Vikings

There aren't many National Football League fans who have had it tougher than those of the Minnesota Vikings. The list of pain is long: Super Bowls IV, VIII, IX and XI; Drew Pearson pushing off; Gary Anderson's miss; 41–0; Brett Favre's interception; Blair Walsh's miss; even the Metrodome roof collapsing.

Who could survive all this?

"I don't think I have a definitive answer other than this is my team," said Vikings stalwart Mike Sidders. "I mean that in the most personal sense. They feel like they're my friends. They're my family. You don't walk away from your friends and family when times are tough."

Sidders has been with this for more than four decades. He's not quite old enough to remember Joe Kapp's wobbly passes in Super Bowl IV, a loss to the underdog Kansas City Chiefs. He's plenty old enough to remember watching the other Super Bowl losses with his mom, dad, brother and sister.

Vikings games meant the family, who lived on the outskirts of the Twin Cities, was gathered around the television in the basement, with the fireplace blazing and enough popcorn to last the afternoon.

His dad, Pat, was a vocal fan. "My profanity vocabulary goes back to Sunday afternoon and football. It was a colorful part of my childhood," Sidders said.

That tradition even included selecting the right Mass on Sundays. The 11 a.m. one was a perfect fit. "The priest was also a massive Vikings fan," Sidders said. "On Sunday game days, he was making sure he was hammering through Mass so we could get home for the game."

Christopher Gates was born in Glencoe, a small town in south central Minnesota. "I heard more than once how I was born at halftime of a Vikings game," he said.

The family moved to Forman, a town of 600 in southeastern North Dakota, but he and his parents, both Vikings fans, continued their devotion to Minnesota's team.

Eric Meyer, who grew up in Minnesota and now lives in Colorado, also had an early introduction to the Vikings. He went to his first game when he was 2. He doesn't remember it, but he does have memories of a year or so later sitting on the lap of his dad, watching Kapp in action.

As he grew a little older, Meyer was enamored with the Vikings. It was the team that provided his first exposure to sports and the benefits of athletics. Meyer said he learned the virtues of discipline and hard work by watching the leadership of head coach Bud Grant, the scrambling of quarterback Fran Tarkenton and the determination of running back Chuck Foreman.

Grant, who led the Vikings to 158 wins and four Super Bowls in 18 seasons, also made an impression on young Sidders.

"He epitomized what it was to be a Minnesotan. He was stoic. He was no-nonsense. He was tough," Sidders said.

The players also made an impression. Sidders said that just about everyone he knew growing up had a number 10 jersey to honor Tarkenton. The wearers of number 10 even included Mary Tyler Moore, who donned that Vikings jersey while washing her car during the opening credits of her 1970s hit CBS show, which centered on life in the newsroom of Minneapolis' WJM-TV.

While many worshiped Tarkenton, Sidders gravitated toward defense. After all, it was the era of the Purple People Eaters, the Vikings' fearsome defensive line of Alan Page, Carl Eller, Jim Marshall and Gary Larsen. The four combined to make 19 Pro Bowl appearances and led a stout defense that was at the heart of the Vikings' success. Sidders was a Page fan. "He was my guy. He was *the* dude."

All of the successes of Grant, Tarkenton, Page and the rest ended in the four frustrating Super Bowl losses, including three in four years from 1974 to 1977. Here are the ugly details that many Vikings fans probably have tried to forget:

Super Bowl IV, January 11, 1970: With Kapp leading a steady offense, and the defense allowing a league low 9.5 points per game, the Vikings finished the regular season 12–2. The only losses were by one point to the New York Giants in the season opener and a 10–3 loss to the Atlanta Falcons in a meaningless final game of the regular season.

The Vikings edged the Los Angeles Rams and beat the Cleveland Browns to advance to the Super Bowl as a heavy favorite against the Kansas

City Chiefs, champions of what was considered by most the inferior American Football League. (The Vikings-Chiefs Super Bowl was the last game played before the American Football League merged with the National Football League.)

Kapp was a tough leader straight from the mold of his head coach, Grant. The quarterback spent eight seasons playing in the Canadian Football League before coming to Minnesota in 1967. During the 1969 season, he sparked the Vikings on their Super Bowl run, but the Chiefs contained him and the rest of the Vikings' offense all afternoon, limiting Minnesota to 239 total yards and forcing five turnovers.

Kansas City's Len Dawson threw for just 142 yards, but it was enough to earn him the game's Most Valuable Player Award. His third-quarter touchdown pass to Otis Taylor accounted for the final points in the Chiefs' 23–7 victory.

Super Bowl VIII, January 13, 1974: With a 33-year-old Tarkenton providing plenty of excitement with his scrambling and passing, the Vikings went 12–2 in the regular season. Again, the defense, built around the Purple People Eaters, was one of the best in the league, allowing only 12 points a game.

In the Super Bowl, though, the Vikings were no match for the defending champion Miami Dolphins. Led by Larry Csonka's 145 yards on 33 carries, Miami rushed for 196 yards. Dolphins quarterback Bob Griese threw just seven times, completing six passes for a mere 73 yards.

The Dolphins built a 24–0 lead before Tarkenton scored on a fourth-quarter run for the final points of the game.

Super Bowl IX, January 12, 1975: The Vikings used a familiar formula to finish 10–4 and return to the Super Bowl. Tarkenton led the offense, Foreman rushed for 777 yards and nine touchdowns, and the defense continued its stingy ways.

Once again, the Vikings' offense was shut down in the Super Bowl, this time by the Pittsburgh Steelers. The Vikings were held to 17 yards rushing and 119 total yards in a 16–6 loss. Minnesota's only points came on a blocked punt recovered in the end zone by defensive back Terry Brown. It was the Steelers' first of four Super Bowl victories in six seasons.

Super Bowl XI, January 9, 1977: After finishing the season 11–2–1, the Vikings had solid playoff wins over the Washington Redskins and Los Angeles Rams to set up a Super Bowl meeting with the Oakland Raiders.

It was a Super Bowl where little went right for the Vikings. Tarkenton threw a touchdown pass but was intercepted twice as the Vikings committed three turnovers. Oakland cornerback Willie Brown returned one of the interceptions 75 yards for a score. The Vikings' defense, so solid for so long, was blitzed by the Raiders, giving up 429 total yards. Ken Stabler threw for 180 yards and a touchdown and Clarence Davis rushed for 137 more yards as the Raiders waltzed to a 32–14 victory.

"I was young enough that it didn't sting," Sidders said of the Super Bowl defeats. "But as I grew up, there's that stigma that gets stuck to your back. As I get older, it stings more."

It's been a long time since the last Super Bowl appearance for Minnesota. Even so, Vikings fans have suffered through other heartbreaks.

Gates is too young to remember those Super Bowls. He was four months old when the Vikings lost their fourth one in 1977. "For some of the younger or newer Vikings fans, we've become more accustomed to receiving our disappointment in different ways, notably in NFC championship games," he said.

Whether it was a National Football Conference title game or an earlier exit from the playoffs, the Vikings have had plenty of excruciating postseason moments.

Take December 28, 1975. In a first-round playoff game at Minnesota's Metropolitan Stadium, the Vikings led the Dallas Cowboys, 14–10, with less than 2 minutes to go. The Cowboys started a final drive on their 15-yard line, and soon faced fourth down and 17. A pass from Roger Staubach to Drew Pearson picked up the first down and kept the drive alive. A few plays later, Staubach hoisted a pass from midfield to Pearson.

Pearson and Vikings cornerback Nate Wright battled for the underthrown ball. Wright ended up on the ground, and Pearson snagged the pass, pinning it on his right hip, for the winning touchdown. Pearson has insisted he didn't push Wright on the play. Minnesota fans still see the play differently.

"To this day, every Vikings fan is apoplectic that the penalty should have been called," Sidders said.

Talk about apoplectic. Just mention the miss by kicker Gary Anderson in the NFC Championship Game on January 17, 1999. That season, Anderson was to a football what Katniss Everdeen is to a bow and arrow. He made all of his 35 field-goal attempts and 59 extra-point tries, becoming the first National Football League kicker to have a perfect season.

He contributed to an offense that scored a league-best 34.8 points per game. It featured quarterback Randall Cunningham, who threw for 34 touchdowns and only 10 interceptions. Running back Robert Smith ran for 1,187 yards, and wide receivers Cris Carter and rookie Randy Moss combined for 29 touchdown receptions.

It was all part of a sparkling 15–1 regular season, and the glory continued in the Vikings' first playoff game, a 41–21 dismantling of the Arizona Cardinals that put Minnesota in the NFC Championship Game against the Atlanta Falcons.

Against the Falcons, Anderson made two field goals, Cunningham threw for two touchdowns and ran for another, and the Vikings held a 27–20 lead with 2:07 left. Out trotted Anderson to deliver the final blow, a 38-yard field goal that would give the Vikings a 10-point lead and send them to the Super Bowl.

It was a sure thing—a kicker who hadn't missed all year booting a relative chip shot in the indoor comfort of his home field, the Metrodome. There was just a slight problem. Anderson missed, barely to the left. It was his first and only miss of the season.

Chris Chandler then drove the Falcons 71 yards in eight plays, throwing a touchdown pass to Terance Mathis with less than a minute left. Morten Andersen kicked the tying extra point, and he soon finished off the Vikings in overtime with a 38-yard field goal—the same distance at which the Vikings' Anderson had missed.

When Anderson failed on the field goal that would have clinched the game for the Vikings, Meyer, watching at home, did his best impersonation of the kicker. He booted the dog's bowl, sending it and all its contents across the kitchen. "It took 20 minutes for me to clean it up," he said.

"That was crushing," Sidders said of Anderson's miss. "It still to this day gets a lump in my throat. The guy had been money all season. I can still see it. It's just terrible, just terrible."

Gates was watching in the United Kingdom, where he had just arrived for his first active-duty assignment as a meteorologist with the United States Air Force. For him, the defeat was tough to take because the Vikings had such a terrific season.

"Honestly, had they gone on to the Super Bowl that year and emerged victorious, we'd probably be talking about the 1998 Minnesota Vikings as one of the great teams in NFL history," he said.

Instead, these days the Anderson miss appears on such Internet lists as "The Greatest Choke Jobs in NFL Playoff History" and "The Worst 10 Metrodome Moments in Vikings History."

Two seasons later, the Vikings decided they weren't going to let an NFC Championship Game be decided by a last-minute field goal. They went on the road with a Super Bowl bid on the line and got trounced, 41–0,

Eric Meyer grew up in Minnesota but has lived in Colorado for years. The weather and his Vikings sweatshirt are reminders of home (photograph by Megan A. Greene).

by the New York Giants. While Vikings quarterback Daunte Culpepper was throwing three interceptions, New York's Kerry Collins was tossing five touchdown passes.

There was more disappointment in an NFC Championship Game on January 24, 2010, a 31–28 overtime loss to the New Orleans Saints. Playing on the road, the Vikings were tied with the Saints and had a chance to win late in regulation. But Favre threw an interception that sent the game to overtime, and the Saints won on a 40-yard Garrett Hartley field goal.

Shortly before the interception, the Vikings had drawn a penalty for 12 men on the field. It pushed them out of field-goal range, and Favre then threw the interception. Gates called it "one of the more ridiculous sequences in Vikings history, which is really covering some ground."

Sidders doesn't blame Favre for the loss. The quarterback, once a star with the rival Green Bay Packers, threw for 310 yards and survived a pummeling by a Saints defense that would help New Orleans beat Peyton Manning and the Indianapolis Colts two weeks later in the Super Bowl.

"I think he was an absolute warrior. New Orleans had a game plan to knock him out of the game," Sidders said. "Anyone else would have been on the sidelines."

Later in 2010, the pain for Vikings fans involved their stadium. In the midst of a classic Minnesota snowstorm, the Metrodome's Teflon-coated fiberglass roof collapsed under the weight of the snow on December 12. Video shows the snow filtering onto the field at first, looking like softly falling, sifted sugar. But the stress soon tore a hole in the roof, sending an avalanche onto the field.

The Vikings had been scheduled to play at home later that day against the New York Giants. The game was shifted to the next night and played in Detroit. The last home game of the season was moved to the University of Minnesota's TCF Bank Stadium.

"I had 83 people running into my office saying, 'You've got to look at this,'" Sidders said of the roof-collapse video. "To see that, it was like, really? That's our home."

There was more playoff heartbreak in 2016 when the Vikings met the Seattle Seahawks on a bitter cold January afternoon at TCF Bank Stadium. The day started with former coach Grant, 88 years old, walking out for the coin toss in short sleeves despite the minus-6 degree temperature at kickoff. The crowd loved it, as did Sidders. "Anything after that was gravy," he said.

Late in the game, the Vikings trailed the Seahawks, 10–9, but the offense moved 52 yards in six plays, helped in part by a pass interference penalty on Seattle.

The drive set up Walsh for a 27-yard field goal with 26 seconds left. Walsh had been perfect on the day, accounting for all of the Vikings' points with field goals from 22, 43 and 47 yards. But this time, in the wind and frigid air of a Minnesota January afternoon, he hooked the kick to the left.

"That sort of sums up my Vikings life," Meyer said. "Game over with a guy who missed three field goals [it was actually five] all year and chunk! Wide friggin' left! I was all alone in my house and I'm thinking we are actually going to win a playoff game and then … crushed once again."

"It was just heartbreaking," Sidders said. "They had worked so hard to get into position to win. I really couldn't believe it. Not only was it a miss, it was missed badly." It also brought up more than a few references to the Anderson miss from 17 years earlier.

But Sidders praised Walsh for standing up and answering all the questions from the media after the game, blaming himself for the loss. And Sidders remained optimistic: "We got a taste [of the playoffs]. Now we have to take the next step."

Aside from losses like that playoff game to the Seahawks, there have been some glorious moments along the way for Sidders, even if they come with tough lessons.

While in high school, he landed a ticket to a matchup with the Cleveland Browns late in the 1980 season. It was a game the Vikings needed to clinch a playoff spot. The wind-chill was 11, and Sidders watched as Cleveland quarterback Brian Sipe led the Browns to a 23–9 lead early in the fourth quarter.

Freezing and by himself, Sidders decided he had seen enough. Driving home, he listened as Tommy Kramer led the comeback, throwing three fourth-quarter touchdown passes, the last two to Ahmad Rashad. The winning score, a 46-yard pass, came on a last-play Hail Mary that deflected to Rashad as he backpedaled into the end zone.

"I still remember where I was on the road driving home," Sidders said. "Ray Scott, who was broadcasting the game, said, 'All you Vikings fans who left the game early, shame on you.' Ever since then, I've never left a game early, whether it's the Vikings, the Twins or anyone else."

Today, Sidders finds himself in Green Bay, Wisconsin, home of the Vikings' fierce divisional rival, the Packers. As he said, he's in the "belly of the beast," but he has started a Vikings fan club there. "It's a really small but passionate group."

He has little ill will toward Packers fans, who have treated him well on his visits to Lambeau Field.

"They're really kind of genuinely happy you made the effort to come," he said. "They've come up to me and said, 'Welcome to Lambeau.' While he has reservations about the crass, alcohol-fueled behavior at some NFL games, it's not a problem in Green Bay. "I absolutely would take a little kid to Lambeau Field. It's a really fun environment."

And it's not just the fans at the game who have impressed him. "I'm having conversations with grandmothers who know their stuff. It's really amazing to see the knowledge of football in the community."

As for the Vikings, he and other fans have a long-lasting devotion.

"When they do win it, it will be euphoric," he said. "Who wants to miss something like that because you were distracted?"

Gates eloquently expressed similar feelings.

Mike Sidders was at Lambeau Field in November 2013 to watch the Minnesota Vikings and Green Bay Packers play to a 26–26 tie. Being a Vikings fan in Green Bay might seem like a challenge, but he says he always gets treated well when he goes to Lambeau (courtesy Mike Sidders).

"I think the thing that keeps me coming back to the Vikings, if I may reference Andy Dufresne in *The Shawshank Redemption*, is hope. The hope that one day, somehow, this team is finally going to put everything together and get the job done, and that people who have been fans of this football team will finally get to experience that euphoria. I want to experience that euphoria with them.

"Sure, it would be a whole lot easier to jump on the bandwagon of a more successful team, but at this point a championship with one of those teams just wouldn't bring the same feeling of happiness that a Minnesota Vikings Super Bowl win might bring.

"I mean, if it came down to it, I'm sure I could live without cheering for the Minnesota Vikings. I'm just not terribly sure that I'd want to."

Here We Stay

The Sacramento Kings

Ask most any fan why he or she roots for the home team, and community pride is likely to be somewhere on the list. The players represent the city where you're from, so their victories become your victories.

But there's community pride and then there's what residents of Sacramento, California, have shown. When it appeared all but certain that the city's National Basketball Association franchise was headed elsewhere, residents helped put a stop to it. It's not every city that's been able to fight off the departure of a team, but Sacramento's story is one of civic pride, resourcefulness, hustle and having the right mayor in the right spot at the right time.

When efforts to build a new arena for the Sacramento Kings fell through in the 2000s, the team's owners, the Maloof family, started looking for new locations. Anaheim, California, was discussed, which would have given the league three teams in the Los Angeles area. Seattle, which had lost its SuperSonics to Oklahoma City, also was a possibility.

Fans were not accepting the loss of their NBA franchise quietly. When proposals for a new arena collapsed and talk increased that the team might move, it hit fans hard, according to Blake Ellington, a blogger who writes about the Kings. "That sort of set off a panic. There really was an uprising," he said.

Ellington got in touch with other bloggers, brainstorming about ways to give fans a forum to talk about their support for the team. One of the bloggers came up with a slogan for the movement, "Here We Stay," a play off the Kings' promotional slogan, "Here We Rise."

The phrase stuck. Soon, fans were taking part in letter-writing campaigns to city officials. They were flooding sports talk shows with calls. They were organizing chants during Kings game. The message was simple and clear: Don't take our Kings.

Mike Tavares was working another angle of the effort. The community college professor and counselor organized "Crown Downtown," a group that sought to educate residents about the benefits of a new arena, not just for the Kings but for other cultural events. Tavares worked to make sure City Council meetings were well attended by arena supporters whenever the topic was on the agenda.

The Crown Downtown group was part of an effort to bring a new arena in Sacramento, a crucial step in keeping the Kings (courtesy Mike Tavares).

Still, when the Kings played their final home game of the 2010–11 season against the Los Angeles Lakers, the team's departure seemed all but certain. In the arena that night, fans held signs with such slogans as "Take My Life But Not My Kings." They wept and hugged and chanted; they wore Kings hats, and the team's color purple was displayed in everything from T-shirts to shades of lipstick.

The game followed a plot similar to the trials and tribulations of Kings fans. Sacramento seemed hopelessly out of it, trailing by 20 points early in the fourth quarter. But the Kings rallied, outscoring the Lakers 29–11 in the final period, to stay alive, forcing overtime. The game did not have a happy ending, though; despite 33 points from Marcus Thornton, the Kings fell, 116–108.

Tavares was there and remembers what it felt like: "It was a somber moment for everyone in the arena—not just fans, but the staff. We knew if we lost the Kings, we'd never get an expansion team."

The Kings television broadcast team of Grant Napear and Jerry Reynolds fought back tears as they did their postgame show. Napear said, "There's a lot of uncertainty as we all know, but the one thing we do know is the love affair between this team and this city."

Kings fan Sharene Scott Josephs remembers that night well. "Tears rolled all over the city when we all watched what we thought was to be the last Kings game here," she said.

Tim Mikulin said, "It was like they were ripping our heart out. There was always that chance they'd be gone. I thought if they ever left, what would we do? There was big-time anger. There was sorrow. If you weren't a sports fan, you talked about it with a sports fan."

No one could accuse the Kings supporters of being fair-weather fans. All of this love was for a team that had just finished a 24–58 season.

The day after the season-ending loss to the Lakers, Sacramento Mayor Kevin Johnson flew to New York to meet with NBA officials. His sales pitch helped persuade Commissioner David Stern and other league executives to reconsider allowing the team to leave Sacramento.

Johnson is a Sacramento native, a onetime basketball star at Sacramento High School who went on to play at the University of California, Berkeley, followed by 12 seasons in the NBA, making the all-star team three times.

"His relationship with David Stern and the league in general helped," Ellington said. "The timing of having an NBA mayor was just right."

"His role was huge," Tavares said. "If it was any other mayor, the team wouldn't have stuck around."

The Here We Stay and Crown Downtown movements were being heard. There were fund-raising efforts to help keep the team. Billboards appeared around town. Residents wore purple when representatives of the NBA's relocation committee came to Sacramento.

Even the Here We Stay phrase morphed into a life of its own, sometimes to comic effect, Ellington recalls. There were tweets that ended with #HereWeWashOurCar, or from fans at Kings games, #HereWeMakeOur FreeThrows.

After all the letter-writing campaigns, chants during games, purple wardrobe days and lobbying, the league backed the Kings staying in Sacramento.

The Maloofs sold to a group led by Vivek Ranadive, founder of TIBCO Software, for $534 million, which set a record at the time for the price of an NBA franchise. A new downtown arena was built. "When I drive by there now, I think, man, all those City Council meetings were worth it," Tavares said.

"The community learned a lot about itself," Ellington said. "I think everyone learned a lot about what they could do." Ellington helped capture the spirit of the fan's uprising; he was a writer and producer for *Small Market, Big Heart*, a documentary film about the community bonding together to save the Kings.

Much like their fans, the Kings are a team that always seems to be fighting for attention. After all, no one has ever confused Sacramento with L.A. The Kings are on the West Coast, so their box scores don't make the morning papers in much of the country. Their highlights often run at the end of ESPN's *SportsCenter*, if they even make the cut. Yet, it's a franchise with a rich history that boasts one of the NBA's all-time great players, not to mention rosters that have included a pro football star and a point guard who would go on to become a legendary coach.

The franchise was playing basketball long before the Lakers and Celtics. And there's an NBA championship season in there. OK, it was a year before Dwight D. Eisenhower was elected president, and it was won in Rochester, New York, but it's still an official NBA title.

Those underdog feelings, along with a dash of Kings history, add to the passion of Sacramento's fan base. The Kings are the only major sports team in town, so there's plenty of love that gets sent their way in this city of a half-million people.

"It's been our only team. It's been incredible to have," said Mikulin, who has rooted for the Kings since their early days in Sacramento.

The Kings' route to the West Coast is a circuitous one. The franchise started in Rochester in 1923 as a semipro team called the Seagrams, sponsored by a local distillery. In 1945–46, the team, which had changed its name to the Royals, won a title in its first season in the National Basketball League, a predecessor to the NBA. The Rochester roster included Otto Graham, who would win seven championships as a quarterback with the Cleveland Browns in the All-America Football Conference and the National Football League.

By the late 1940s, the Rochester Royals joined the newly formed NBA, a league that back then was far different from what we know today. Teams in the league seemed to change annually, and they included squads such as the Sheboygan Red Skins in Wisconsin and the Tri-Cities Blackhawks, who played in Moline, Illinois.

In 1951, the Royals beat the Fort Wayne Pistons and the Minneapolis Lakers in the first two rounds of the playoffs. The Lakers, led by center George Mikan, were the league's powerhouse at the time, but the Royals prevailed, three games to one, with Arnie Risen scoring 26 points in the deciding game.

After disposing of the Lakers, the Royals met the New York Knicks in the NBA championship series. Rochester won, 4–3, with Risen averaging 21.7 points per game and guard Bob Davies adding 17. That Royals team included a point guard named Red Holzman, who two decades later would coach the New York Knicks to two NBA titles.

Six years after the Royals' championship, the franchise moved to Cincinnati and would soon draft University of Cincinnati star guard Oscar

Robertson. He became one of the best players in NBA history, even averaging a triple double (30.8 points, 12.5 rebounds and 11.4 assists) in the 1961–62 season.

Robertson teamed with Jerry Lucas, who had been a star at Ohio State, to give the Royals a potent combination. The team, though, was never quite good enough to advance in the playoffs past either the dynastic Boston Celtics or the Wilt Chamberlain-led Philadelphia 76ers.

The franchise had a couple more shifts—becoming the Kansas City-Omaha Kings in 1972 and then just the Kansas City Kings a few years later—before moving to and settling in Sacramento in 1985.

Jason Boggs, a lifelong Sacramento resident, was a young teen when the Kings arrived. He would take a transistor radio to bed and, when he should have been sleeping, listened to play-by-play announcer Gary Gerould broadcast Kings games. Thanks to those youthful memories, Boggs still loves the Kings on the radio.

Mikulin recalls growing up in Sacramento before the Kings arrived. Some fans leaned toward the Bay Area sports franchises in San Francisco and Oakland, but there was a diversity of support for teams from all over the country. Kids at school wore all kinds of different jerseys.

He took a liking to Boston teams, first because he got attached to the Red Sox during the dramatic World Series of 1975, which the Red Sox lost in seven games to the Cincinnati Reds.

"It ended up being a Boston obsession," he said. He didn't know anyone in Boston, and he had never been to Boston, but he became a passionate fan of the Red Sox and the Boston Celtics.

When the Kings moved to Sacramento, Mikulin was attending the University of the Pacific, but he made sure he got tickets for the February game when the Celtics made their only visit that season to Sacramento.

Boston, led by star forward Larry Bird, came to town with a 38–8 record, en route to that season's NBA title. The Celtics were heavy favorites to beat the Kings, who were struggling at 20–30. Bird had 29 points and Dennis Johnson and Robert Parish each added 19, but it wasn't enough for the Celtics. The Kings, led by 27 points from Mike Woodson, pulled off the upset, beating Boston, 105–100.

"The place went crazy," Mikulin said. "At that moment I became a Kings fan, and the Celtics were my second-favorite team. Since then, it's been a definite love affair. I don't miss anything."

Despite finishing that first season in Sacramento 37–45, the Kings made the playoffs, although they were swept in the first round by the Houston Rockets. It would be a decade before the Kings returned to the

Good seats for a Kings game—it's a good night for (left to right) Justin McLarty, Trevor Mikulin, Nathan Mikulin and Tim Mikulin (courtesy Tim Mikulin).

postseason, with a team led by sharp-shooting Mitch Richmond and a lot of hard-working players such as Brian Grant and Michael Smith. They finished the season 39–43, but that was good enough for an eighth seed in the Western Conference playoffs.

"They were usually out-talented, but they had a lot of heart," said Ellington, who became a fan that season. They also fell quickly in the playoffs, losing in the first round to the top-seeded Seattle SuperSonics.

Josephs joined the Kings fan base soon after moving to Sacramento from Los Angeles in the early 1990s. She found herself drawn to the team in her new town. "It was just exciting," she said. "And I like watching a bunch of good-looking guys running around the court."

As the late 1990s approached, the team got good. There was a special draw for Mikulin. His grandfather, 17 years old at the time, had arrived in Sacramento in 1917 from Yugoslavia. "He came looking for an uncle and found my grandmother," Mikulin said. Those Kings teams from the late '90s and early 2000s featured Serbian Vlade Divac and Croatian Peja Stojakovic, providing a connection to Mikulin's family roots.

The Kings made a playoff run all the way to the Western Conference finals in 2002, and fans had to get used to a whole new world of success. "Those were fun times," said Tavares. "It was beautiful basketball. We were kind of like, 'Pinch yourself. Is this really happening?'"

"We've always played second fiddle to San Francisco and Oakland," Boggs said. "When we got that team, there was so much civic pride. There was a buzz throughout the city."

The 2001–02 Kings featured Divac and Stojakovic as well as high-scoring forward Chris Webber and smooth point guard Mike Bibby. After disposing of the Utah Jazz and Dallas Mavericks in the playoffs, the Kings played the Lakers in a memorable Western Conference finals series.

The Kings held a 2–1 lead and led, 99–97, in Game 4 with seconds remaining. The Lakers missed two shots near the basket, but the ball then was swatted out to Robert Horry, who drained a 25-foot jumper to sink the Kings, 100–99. It was one in a series of last-second shots by a guy who made a career of clutch playoff moments.

Ellington recalls watching those final moments of Game 4 while a student at Sacramento State. "I remember looking at my roommate, and I said, 'I don't think this is going to end well.' I think it was 8 o'clock. That shot went up in slow motion. When it went in, I just turned off the TV and went to bed."

"We thought we had won," Boggs said of Game 4 and Horry's shot. "The air went out of the whole city. Still to this day you can't talk to anybody about that shot. He's still one of the most hated men in Sacramento."

The Kings regained the series lead by winning Game 5, 92–91, thanks to a late shot by Bibby. That set up a Game 6 that is not easily forgotten by Kings followers. In a close contest that saw neither team lead by more than five points in the fourth quarter, the Lakers eked out a 106–102 victory. Los Angeles went to the foul line a remarkable 27 times in the fourth quarter, helping to erase a late Sacramento lead.

Shaquille O'Neal and Kobe Bryant combined for 72 points for the Lakers, including going 24 of 28 from the foul line. Webber was Sacramento's leading scorer with 26.

NBA conspiracy theorists sometimes speak of fixed games and referees favoring the big-market teams at playoff time. The theme of those theories is it's a favor to the television networks that pay millions to carry the games because the networks want big names and big cities in the finals. Game 6 of the 2002 Sacramento–Los Angeles series, with all of those Lakers foul shots, fueled those conspiracy fires.

A story on the Grantland website looked at the entire Kings-Lakers series, and it included a number of comments that were made after Game 6.

Former Washington Post columnist Michael Wilbon wrote, "I think officials are the most unfairly criticized people in sports … but that game was an abomination."

Bibby spoke of being called for a foul on a play where he took a Bryant elbow to the nose: "It pissed me off because when I got up, I thought they called a foul on him. I didn't know what happened. I remember saying, 'You called a foul on me?' And my nose was bleeding, and I blew some of my blood out onto the court just to show them."

Kings forward Chucky Brown put it simply: "We got robbed that game."

Fans share those feelings. "It was heartbreaking. It was horrible," Josephs said. "If we had won, it wouldn't have been enough star power [for television]. Who cares about Sacramento?"

"It felt like it was being pulled right out of our hands," Mikulin said.

Tavares remembers the game this way: "Terrible officiating; where Bibby's nose fouls Kobe's elbow."

Laura Good knows that game well, even though she moved to Sacramento and got interested in the Kings several years after that Western Conference finals series with the Lakers.

"If you mention the year 2002, not even in the context of basketball, everyone will think about the series with the Lakers. Everyone associates that year with a basketball event," she said.

With O'Neal and Bryant again dominating, combining for 65 points, the visiting Lakers beat the Kings in Game 7, 112–106. Los Angeles then romped over the New Jersey Nets to win the NBA title in a four-game sweep. Mikulin believes that season's Kings team also would have easily handled the Nets.

"That series still affects us," he said of losing to the Lakers. "Now that they [the Kings] have fallen apart, it feels like that was our moment."

After the loss to the Lakers in 2002, the Kings continued to be a solid team, returning to the playoffs in the following four years. But Webber suffered a serious knee injury in the 2003 Western Conference semifinals, a series the Kings would lose in seven games to the Dallas Mavericks.

"That pretty much closed our window," Tavares said of the Webber injury. By the 2006–07 season, most of the key players of the Kings' golden era were gone. Divac played his last game in the NBA in 2005. Webber went to the Philadelphia 76ers in a six-player deal in February 2005, a month after guard Doug Christie was sent to the Orlando Magic. Stojakovic was traded to the Indiana Pacers in January 2006. Even coach Rick Adelman was gone. His contract was not renewed after the 2005–06 season.

The 2006–07 Kings fell to 33–49. In the following season, Bibby, one of the holdovers from 2002, was dealt to the Atlanta Hawks for four players and a draft pick. It was the start of a long run of misfortune for the franchise, which did not win more than 29 games in a season from 2008 to 2015.

In the 10 seasons that followed Adelman's departure, the Kings employed eight head coaches, two of whom were interim. Three of those coaches—Paul Westphal, Reggie Theus and Mike Malone—were all fired less than one-third of the way into a season.

But with a new arena shining downtown, California's capital city continues to show its love of the Kings with a special touch—being known as having some of the loudest fans in the league.

Mukilin, a salesman for a title insurance company, has seen opposing coaches screaming out plays in the huddle, trying to outshout the Sacramento crowd. "If you asked coaches what's the toughest place to play, I guarantee it would be Sacramento," he said.

He is proud to say he's a key contributor to the din. "I can whistle louder than anybody." While at a playoff game against the Dallas Mavericks, Mukilin and a handful of others caught the eyes—and ears—of a security guard for Dallas owner Mark Cuban. The security guard came over and asked them to tone it down a bit, including easing up on the ringing of cowbells. "It made us ring them louder," Mukilin said.

Through the years, Mukilin has enjoyed the positives, such as the point guard magic of Jason Williams, the accurate shooting of Richmond and the "Rattle Seattle" T-shirts from the 1996 playoff series against the SuperSonics.

He has passed on his love of the Kings to his three children, Maddison, Trevor and Nathan. "They grew up with pennants in their rooms, posters and the games on TV."

Mukilin and his children will watch games together. As often happens with fans of teams that have limited success, there's always an eye on the future, in this case the NBA draft.

"You root and root and root and then they lose, and we look at each other and say, 'Well, we get more pingpong balls,'" he said. The NBA selects teams' positions in the draft by drawing pingpong balls.

Josephs also has passed on her love of the Kings to her daughter, Aubree, who was dribbling a basketball at age 2 and later became a big fan of Bibby after attending his basketball camp.

As a member of Congregation B'nai Israel, the oldest temple in Sacramento, Josephs has cheered on Omri Casspi, a Kings forward and the first Israeli player in the NBA. "He just has a great attitude," she said. Above all else, she keeps her Kings support alive with her own positive attitude.

"We always have a lot of hope that it will get better. You have to support the guys. It's not always their fault. We've had so many coaches come and go."

In a city that rose to the challenge of keeping its team in town, it's no surprise what theme comes up repeatedly when fans are asked why they keep rooting, even as the Kings battle to overcome a long playoff drought.

Sharene Scott Josephs has passed on her love of the Sacramento Kings to her daughter, Aubree. Here they are at a Kings game against the Houston Rockets in November 2015 (courtesy Sharene Scott Josephs).

"When I moved here from L.A. to escape the sprawling, impersonal, earthquake-rocked metropolis that it is, I was impressed most by the friendly, small-town, neighborly community feel of Sacramento," Josephs said. "That sense of community and city pride shines unequivocally at each and every Kings game."

Ellington said, "It really is just a matter of civic pride.... Everybody still has a taste of that Lakers series [from 2002]. Everybody wants to have that back."

"I like being part of the community," Good said. "I like being known as a Kings fan and a supporter of this community."

Good is a business consultant who previously lived in the Bay Area and attended games of the San Francisco Giants, Golden State Warriors and Oakland Athletics. She enjoyed those teams, but she didn't follow any of them the way she follows the Kings, a devotion she picked up from her sister Peggy, a huge Kings fan.

"Seeing the passion from the city for this team got me interested," Laura said. "It feels more to me like high school. You care about your team. It's like high school pride."

For Boggs, a restaurant owner in the city, there are two reasons he keeps pulling for the Kings. "It's a love for the game and a love for the city," he said. "The Kings' love runs deep in this town.

"We've been long-suffering since 2002. People in Sacramento are huge basketball fans, but a lot of it is civic pride. You have that name Sacramento on the jersey. It means a lot to us."

Hot Summer Nights

The Texas Rangers

When the Texas Rangers were playing at home in the early to mid–1990s, there was a good chance that Brian Silverstein and Jeremy Goldberg were there.

The friends, members of the debate team at Greenhill High School in nearby Addison, would soak up the action, being among those willing to take on the triple-digit heat of a Texas summer evening to watch the Rangers fall short of the playoffs again. Sometimes, their debate club pals Doug Moore and Andy Szygenda would join them. For $4 each, they would buy bleacher seats and then move to better locations in the often half-filled ballpark.

"We talked baseball, girls and what's this alcohol stuff that people are drinking," Silverstein said. "That was a whole night's worth of entertainment. That's where my personality grew from. Those nights are something I cherish."

Silverstein said the group would try not to miss Dollar Dog Nights at the ballpark, which he described as "the greatest invention ever for a teenager on a budget." They'd scarf down as many $1 hot dogs as they could.

Szygenda, now a lawyer in Dallas, said he was more a fan of individual players, especially Nolan Ryan, than of the team. But he remembers that when they were running late to a game, the debate team members would have lively discussions about the best route to take.

"Once a road had been passed, that usually ended the discussion," he said.

Those Rangers outings helped cement their strong friendships, the kind that form so solidly in high school. They also got to watch a team that had many years of struggle, both on the diamond and in the Dallas marketplace, trying to grab just a bit of attention away from the National Football League's Cowboys.

The Rangers were a bit of an oddity from the start. When the Washington Senators moved to Minnesota and became the Twins, baseball in 1961 awarded Washington an expansion team, also called the Senators. The team lasted just 11 seasons in the nation's capital before moving to Arlington, Texas, on the outskirts of Dallas.

Within their first two years in Texas, the Rangers were managed by three memorable baseball figures—Ted Williams, who hit 521 home runs with the Boston Red Sox; Whitey Herzog, who would manage the St. Louis Cardinals to a title in 1982; and Billy Martin, who would lead the New York Yankees to a championship in 1977. Williams had led the team for three seasons in Washington but left managing after the first season in Texas ended with a 54–100 record. In his first stint as a manager, Herzog was hired by the Rangers in 1973 and fired in September after a 47–91 start. He was replaced by Martin.

Under Martin, the Rangers had a respectable season in 1974, led by American League most valuable player Jeff Burroughs, who batted .301 and drove in 118 runs.

The next two decades were filled with many ordinary seasons. The Rangers did win 94 games in 1977, but they finished 8 games behind the Kansas City Royals in that pre–wild-card era. The 1986 team went 87–75, 25 wins better than the previous season, but the playoffs were still a long way away. It was in this stretch that Silverstein and his pals were starting to notice baseball.

Silverstein said that he started paying attention to baseball box scores at age 4, helping him learn to read.

"I was hooked on the daily minutiae of the sport," he said. He enjoyed the constant addition to a player's seasonal statistics as each game passed. He was the kind of young fan who would use a video game to play out an entire baseball season, keeping statistics of the players as he went.

For Silverstein's early years as a baseball fan, bedtime was much too early. He saw little of the Rangers night games on television, so the radio was his friend.

"I would fall asleep listening to the sounds of the Rangers games," he said. If the team was on the West Coast, he might have to wait until the afternoon newspaper arrived to find out the final score, hard to imagine in today's world of instant information.

Often, the news wasn't uplifting. "The Rangers were never good when I was young. I didn't know what good was," Silverstein said.

Goldberg got hooked through his father, Ken, who grew up in Cleveland as a long-suffering Indians fan before relocating to Texas.

"As an Indians fan, he was OK with me rooting for a franchise that hadn't won in a long time," Goldberg said.

Goldberg, his dad and his younger brother, Josh, were all into baseball. The Rangers games would be on the car radio. They would be on the radio by the pool. When Goldberg went to summer camp, his dad would mail him care packages that included newspaper sports sections.

In those year, the Rangers had rosters full of players who could hit–Julio Franco, Ivan Rodriguez, Rafael Palmeiro, Juan Gonzalez and Ruben Sierra.

"It made going to the games really fun," Goldberg said. "It felt like a five-run inning was always around the corner."

The flip side was the Rangers seldom had enough pitching. They did, however, have Ryan for the last five seasons of his career, from 1989 to 1993. As a Ranger, Ryan would win his 300th game, notch his 5,000th strikeout and toss his sixth and seventh no-hitters. While Ryan was a star, the team's overall pitching struggles often meant the Rangers were hopelessly out of the pennant race.

"The reality was when you were back in school, the summer was over, and the Rangers had faded because they were so far back," Goldberg said. Talk turned to the National Football League. "Remember, this is Dallas. The Cowboys rule," he said.

During Goldberg and Silverstein's high school years, though, baseball in Dallas/Arlington took some interesting twists. In 1994, the Rangers opened a new stadium, then known as The Ballpark in Arlington. The park paid tribute to other historic baseball sites, including a white frieze along the upper deck similar to Yankee Stadium, and a dark, angled right-field rooftop that resembled the one in Detroit's old Tiger Stadium.

A labor dispute ended the 1994 season on August 12 with the Rangers in first place. Yes, they had a less-than-sparkling 52–62 record, but that was good enough for first in the anemic American League West.

"Of course, the one year they're in first place, the season ends," Silverstein said. "It's not Murphy's Law. It's the Rangers' Law."

The new stadium and the '94 season signaled a turnaround. The Rangers were in contention annually. Silverstein remembers attending a game in June 1995 when the Rangers trailed the Kansas City Royals, 8–1, heading into the bottom of the eighth inning. The Rangers strung together seven hits for six runs in the eighth and tied it in the ninth on a Benji Gil home run. They won in the 10th when Rusty Greer belted a Billy Brewer pitch out of the park. Silverstein and company stayed until the end even though it was a school night, earning a big payoff to reward their devotion.

Silverstein recently pulled out his high school yearbook and took note of all the signatures from classmates that referenced the Rangers—messages such as "Next year is our time."

Those yearbook forecasts weren't all that far off. In 1996, the Rangers made the postseason for the first time after winning the American League West with a 90–72 record.

The playoffs started well. Texas went into Yankee Stadium and beat the New York Yankees, 6–2, behind John Burkett's complete game and home runs from Gonzalez and Dean Palmer. But the Yankees won Game 2 in 12 innings and then rallied to win the next two games in Arlington, taking the best-of-five series, 3–1.

Goldberg was a student at Georgetown and flew home for Games 3 and 4. "The energy was indescribable," he said. "The flip side was losing two games we should have won."

He returned to school, where his roommate was a New Jersey resident and Yankees fan. The roommate had that attitude of many Yankees fans, an approach that comes with steady success—he expected to win.

"He looked at me like, 'Oh, man, I'm sorry.' We didn't talk about it too much. When it was over, we returned to our Cowboys-Giants rivalry," Goldberg said.

The Rangers returned to the playoffs in 1998 and '99. Both times they met up with the Yankees. Both times they were swept. Looking back, it wasn't a disastrous performance by Texas. Those Yankees teams won four World Series from 1996 to 2000.

It took the Rangers 11 more years to get back to the playoffs. This time, there was some progress. The Rangers knocked out the Tampa Bay Rays in the first round, winning the deciding Game 5 thanks to a complete game by Cliff Lee and three RBI from Ian Kinsler. That victory set up a rematch with the Yankees in the American League Championship Series.

"For the Yankees, we were a gnat on their shoe. That was the top of the hill that we couldn't get over," Silverstein said.

The playoff reunion with the Yankees looked like a trip back to the 1990s for the Rangers in Game 1. They blew a 5–0 lead to lose at home, 6–5. The storyline quickly changed, though. Texas won the next three games, including Games 3 and 4 in Yankee Stadium, and ended up winning the series in six games. Colby Lewis won his two starts, and Josh Hamilton was the series' most valuable player, hitting four homers and driving in seven runs.

Goldberg, now living in New York, went to the games there. "Nothing was better than beating the Yankees, and doing it at Yankee Stadium."

For the World Series, he flew home, attending one game with his father, brother and his mother, Sharon, who had expressed some disinterest in the past about baseball. "She was as into it as anyone," Goldberg said.

Silverstein had searched for World Series tickets for Game 3, the first one to be played in Texas, but had come up empty. He got home from work, prepared to watch that game at home with his wife, Lauren. As he walked through the door, she told him that she had bought him a single ticket for that night's game.

"I think I was literally in shock," Silverstein said. "I didn't say anything. I froze. She said, 'I know how much this means to you.' I said, 'Oh, my God.' She said, 'Now stop, get dressed and go.'"

Silverstein soon got to take in the mixed message of a World Series crowd. The energy level was off the charts. "It's just different," he said. "The anticipation is just remarkable." But he also was struck by the corporate feel of many in attendance. "None of them had been coming in the heat of July and August when we were losing, 8–2."

The San Francisco Giants won the series, 4–1, but Rangers fans took some joy in the moment. "We had been building, building, building for 30 years. Finally we got a five-year plan that got us to the World Series," Silverstein said.

Not that the loss didn't hurt. Goldberg, who is a technology entrepreneur, had to make a business trip to San Francisco shortly after the World Series. He was walking to a meeting in downtown San Francisco when he was stopped by the Giants victory parade.

"It was like God was taunting me," he said.

The Rangers returned to the World Series the next season, this time against the St. Louis Cardinals. After the Cardinals took a 2–1 lead by pounding the Rangers, 16–7, in Game 3, Texas responded with a 4–0 victory behind a brilliant start by left-hander Derek Holland.

Silverstein had seats behind home plate, just below the press box, to watch Holland's performance. "For me, that night was the pinnacle. That was the happiest, most satisfied I've been as a baseball fan. Everything was perfect."

He and most Rangers fans continued to feel just about perfect after Texas won Game 5. Then it all fell apart in painful, inexplicable fashion. The Rangers led, 7–5, with two outs and two on in the bottom of the ninth of Game 6. They were one strike away from a championship when Cardinals third baseman David Freese lifted a fly ball to right that probably should have been caught. The ball eluded rightfielder Nelson Cruz and fell for a two-run triple.

The Rangers grabbed a 9–7 lead in the top of the 10th, but once again the Cardinals tied the game with two outs. Freese finally ended the Rangers' misery, belting a leadoff homer in the bottom of the 11th for a 10–9 Cardinals win.

At one point, Goldberg's wife, Jenna, was filming him, ready to capture his ecstasy as his Rangers finally won the title.

"You see me collapse and scream. I'm holding my head," he said. "The next day at work, I was just a zombie. No one wanted to talk to me."

With the Rangers leading in both the ninth and 10th innings of Game 6, so close to winning the title, Silverstein tried to keep a promise to his son, Ethan, that he would wake him so he could see the Rangers win the World Series. Both times Ethan couldn't be awakened. Perhaps he just knew it was better not to watch.

"It was as gutted and deflated as a person could be," Silverstein said of the Game 6 loss. "All I could think was, it's a good thing he didn't have to watch this."

The Rangers provided a brief burst of hope in Game 7, taking a 2–0 lead in the first inning, but they were soon bulldozed by the Cardinals, losing 6–2.

The next season saw the Rangers give up a 13-game lead in the American League West. Instead of winning the division, they ended up in a newfangled, one-game wild-card playoff, which they lost to the Baltimore Orioles, 5–1. And in 2015, after rallying to make the playoffs, the Rangers won the first two games of their American League Division Series in Toronto. They lost Games 3 and 4 to the Blue Jays at home, then committed three errors in an inning to lose the decisive Game 5.

Two lost World Series, including one they probably should have won, followed by a horrific September collapse, followed by a heartbreaking loss in the American League Division Series—that's a lot of pain over a six-year period for any fan base to take. Silverstein looks at it this way: "It was fun as heck to watch it all. It would have been nice to win the World Series, but I wouldn't give it back. There's still that piece that we haven't got yet. That keeps me watching."

After the 2015 playoff loss to Toronto, Silverstein talked to a number of Rangers fans. "There are two camps," he said. "One camp is, 'I can't watch this team anymore. They're a bunch of chokers.' The other camp, which is the one I am in, is that this team was picked for last place and it made the playoffs. As frustrating as it was to lose, it was fun having your team in the playoffs when they weren't supposed to be there. All that spirit is back like it was in 2009 through 2011."

Like all Rangers fans, Goldberg is waiting for his baseball team to win a title just as the other Dallas teams have—the Cowboys in the NFL, the Mavericks in the National Basketball Association and the Stars in the National Hockey League. He still roots because of his roots.

"When you're a young kid and these are your memories with your dad and your brother, you don't abandon that. It's foundational. The Rangers have become like family. They're never going to go away."

In recent years, Silverstein, who works as a pharmaceutical representative, has had to adjust to the concept of the Rangers being in the pennant race, battling until the end for postseason positioning.

"To actually care about the Rangers at the end of the season is a new phenomenon. When my friends and I went to a game, it seemed we were the only ones there. Sometimes we really were the only ones there."

For him, the losing years are offset by the benefits of being a fan. "I never thought about not being a Rangers fan. It's that tied to my inner core."

Silverstein's passion for baseball is something he has dreamed of passing on to son Ethan and eventually Ethan's younger sister, Brinley. He and Ethan have taken in a number of Rangers games, providing some one-on-one time for father and son.

"I'm hoping as he grows up, we'll have that commonality," Silverstein said. So far, so good. When asked about the Rangers, Ethan said, "I love going to games with my dad."

Ethan may eventually join his dad as a fan of Jamey Newberg, who writes a popular blog about the Rangers, "The Newberg Report."

"He's the Rangers fan for all of us," Silverstein said.

Newberg's roots with the Rangers date to the mid–1970s, when he was 6. It was just a few years after the team had moved from Washington. "They may have been a bad team, but they were my team," he said.

Since those early years, Newberg has shared in the pain of 1985—a 99-loss season—and the joy of being a contender in the 2010s.

When the Cowboys faltered in the mid- to late 1990s, after winning three Super Bowls in four years, the Rangers were there to pick up the slack, making the playoffs three times from 1996 to 1999.

"For folks like me, who suffered through two and a half decades of losing, the fact that we were in the playoffs was huge," Newberg said.

Like Silverstein, Newberg shares the passion of baseball with his children. As a boy, Newberg started a baseball card collection that now numbers in the thousands. His son has started his own collection.

Newberg, who is a lawyer in Dallas, has traveled to many of the

Rangers playoff road games. But, in 2011, when the Rangers took a 3–2 lead in the World Series, he had no desire to travel to St. Louis.

"If we're going to win this thing, I wanted to be with my kids," he recalls thinking at the time. He and his wife, Ginger, watched with son Max and daughter Erica. They cheered when the Rangers built a 7–4 lead in the seventh inning. They watched in horror as Cruz failed to catch Freese's fly ball in the ninth.

"When Freese hit it, my initial thought was, 'It's staying in the park. We just won the World Series,'" Newberg said. Then he watched Cruz drift and drift and eventually not make the catch.

"I remember looking at my son. He was shell-shocked," Newberg said. "At that moment, I had no words. I'm a pretty vocal sports fan. At that moment, I had nothing."

The family watched in even more horror when Freese homered in the 11th to win Game 6 for the Cardinals.

The next day, Newberg wrote in his blog: "I woke up this morning to the dismal realization that, in fact, that happened. Baseball is still the greatest game, but on some nights it's the hardest to take."

Those memories still are haunting ones, he said. "All you have to say in this market is 'Game 6' or 'Nellie should have caught it,' and it brings up a flood of painful memories."

Still, in a football-crazed state, Newberg knows the Rangers have a fan base that he calls "very loyal." They watch a team that hasn't won it all yet, but they also see a Rangers front office that never stops trying. Newberg pointed to the Rangers' trade of a bundle of prospects for Philadelphia ace pitcher Cole Hamels in July 2015. At the time of the deal, the Rangers were in third place and two

Jamey Newberg writes a blog about the Texas Rangers, whose fans have had some rugged moments in recent seasons (courtesy Jamey Newberg).

games below .500, normally not a position in which a team makes such a huge move.

"This is a go-for-it front office. That has rubbed off on the fan base," Newberg said. Texas may still be a Cowboys state first and foremost, he said, but "there are a whole lot of people like me who have plenty of room for this baseball team."

The Ones
That Got Away

The Atlanta Hawks

Kris Willis admits it. There was a time when he lost interest in the Atlanta Hawks.

When you're a teenager and your favorite team has just traded your favorite player, it's hard. It's even more difficult when that player is Dominique Wilkins, a player so flashy he earned the nickname "The Human Highlight Film."

Wilkins averaged 24.8 points and 6.7 rebounds per game in his 15-year National Basketball Association career, but he was much more than that. His leaping ability and creativity led to an assortment of dunks that truly were suited for any NBA highlight film.

"I was captivated by watching him," said Willis. "A shot would go up, and two or three of his teammates would go up for the rebound. He'd come out of nowhere, one hand above everybody else, and throw it down."

Willis became devoted to basketball as a young teen in the mid–1980s. His family had moved to an apartment building in Summerville, Georgia, in the northwestern corner of the state. Willis hadn't yet made any friends in the new neighborhood, but the apartment complex was in a converted day care, with a play area that had a basketball hoop.

"It was something I could do by myself," Willis said. "A lot of evenings, I'd be out there shooting hoops until dark." Some of that time was spent emulating Wilkins, the young, crowd-pleasing star of the Hawks. He loved the rest of the team as well. "I lived and died with every loss," he said.

A growth spurt from seventh to eighth grade turned Willis from small—5-foot-2—to basketball size—6-foot-2—big enough that he eventually played center and power forward on his high school basketball team.

"It was like I found my niche," said Willis, who now works as a youth recreation program director. "I cherish those times. I look back on how much joy I took from playing the game."

Meanwhile, he was cheering for his Hawks and Wilkins, who was a nine-time all-star in Atlanta. That changed on February 24, 1994, when Wilkins, who was 34 and nearing the end of a contract, was traded to the Los Angeles Clippers for Danny Manning.

It was a stunning move by the Hawks, who were in first place. "I don't want to compare it to a funeral, but that's how it felt," Willis said. "That really knocked me back. That was the only time I questioned my fandom." He stopped watching Hawks basketball. Heck, he stopped watching all NBA games.

"You kind of understand it now, but back then you're talking about my idol. At the time, it was crushing. Traded to the L.A. Clippers of all places—about as far away as you could get."

Willis wasn't the only fan who felt the sting of that Wilkins trade. Jason Walker remembers hearing the news while watching television in his home at the time, a Gainesville, Florida, apartment.

The atmosphere for the day was fitting, Walker recalls. The late afternoon sky in Florida was darker than normal, creating a pall over the Sunshine State's landscape. "Every time I think of it, I think of that dark living room at twilight, and me staring straight ahead. The only thing that could have made it more Shakespearean was if a thunderstorm dumped six tons of rain," he said.

Vicki Kremer had just moved to Atlanta a few years before the Wilkins deal, but that didn't ease her pain.

"It was awful. He's your best player. How do you trade away your best player? And then to the Clippers? And then to get Danny Manning?"

It was one of those trades that didn't work out for either team. Wilkins played 25 games in Los Angeles before signing after the season with the Boston Celtics. He wouldn't make another All-Star Game. Manning, who had been a great college player at the University of Kansas, was solid in the NBA, though limited by knee injuries. He finished the season in Atlanta before signing with the Phoenix Suns.

After the trade, the Hawks got knocked out in the second round of the 1994 playoffs by the Indiana Pacers. The Clippers finished that season with 27 wins.

Worst of all for Hawks fans, it was the end of a thrill-a-minute era in Atlanta. Wilkins had bedazzled fans, memorably going head-to-head with Boston's Larry Bird in Game 7 of a 1988 Eastern Conference semifinal series. Wilkins finished that day in Boston Garden with 47 points, making 19 of his 23 shots. Bird scored 34, 20 of those coming in the fourth quarter, to lead the Celtics to a 118–116 victory. The two stars dominated the game in the final 12 minutes.

"The one thing I was filled with was pride," Walker said of Wilkins' performance against Bird. "He was our guy. That showdown still resonates to this day."

Willis said of that Game 7 loss to Boston, "It was excruciating fun. I was having a ball, but it was like a punch to the gut." That Game 7 loss to Boston is a showcase of Atlanta Hawks basketball. Through the years, the team has been solid, but seldom sensational.

Still, the Hawks have been good enough to win back a fan like Willis. After the dark days and his self-imposed NBA blackout following the Wilkins trade, he soon came around. His return to the league was helped when the Hawks signed free-agent center Dikembe Mutombo in 1996. The native of the Democratic Republic of the Congo had been a star at Georgetown University and showed off his defensive skills for five seasons with the Denver Nuggets before coming to Atlanta.

Meanwhile, Walker's fandom never wavered. He had grown up in Florida in the 1970s before the NBA had found its way to that state. His first basketball love was Julius Erving, the high-flying forward with the signature Afro who was then playing in the American Basketball Association with the New York Nets.

Erving, known as "Dr. J," was the early version of Michael Jordan, creating moves in mid-air as he flew to the basket for rim-rattling dunks. Walker loved everything about him.

"I tried to talk my mom into letting me grow an Afro," Walker said. "She had to break it to me that my hair was not going to grow that way."

While always keeping an eye on Erving, Walker eventually gravitated to the team in Atlanta and a shot-blocker from that era, Tree Rollins.

"When I played an imaginary game, I was Tree Rollins, blocking 15 shots," Walker said. "I had no idea how limited his offensive game was. I loved him."

Kremer moved to Atlanta in the late 1980s from Independence, Iowa. She loved her Iowa Hawkeyes, and she had grown up as a fan of Magic Johnson and the Los Angeles Lakers, but she was excited to move to a city with its own professional sports teams. Her first move was to buy season tickets for the Atlanta Braves baseball team. Fans she met at Braves games talked to her about trying out the Hawks as well.

The Braves beat the Cleveland Indians to win the World Series in

Jason Walker roots for the Atlanta Hawks, but he was first a fan of Julius Erving. He even asked his mother if he could let his hair grow into a Dr. J–like Afro (courtesy Jason Walker).

1995, and Kremer went to every home game that year. She even flew to Cleveland for the Series games played there. "If they're going to win it, I want to be there," she said.

After the Braves won, she thought, "I need something to do now." She called the Hawks and bought season tickets. "I've never looked back. I've been a fan ever since."

What Walker has seen since the 1970s, Willis since the '80s and Kremer since the '90s is a team that has had much regular-season success, but not a lot of postseason glory. That's been the pattern for the Hawks, who started as a franchise in 1946 as the Tri-Cities Blackhawks, playing in Moline, Illinois, as a member of the National Basketball League.

The franchise soon joined the new National Basketball Association, and Red Auerbach coached the team during that first NBA season. After the Blackhawks went 29–35, Auerbach moved to Boston, where he soon would lead the greatest dynasty in NBA history.

The Blackhawks moved to Milwaukee in 1951, shortened their nickname to the Hawks and experienced four unsuccessful seasons. There was one shining moment in Milwaukee, though. In 1954, the Hawks used the second pick in the draft to select Bob Pettit, a 6-foot-9 center from Louisiana State University.

Pettit averaged 20.4 points and 13.8 rebounds per game as a rookie. It was the start of a remarkable career. Pettit would be named an all-star in each of his 11 seasons in the NBA and received the league's first Most Valuable Player Award in 1956.

In 1955, the franchise moved to St. Louis and in its third season there won the NBA title, beating Bill Russell, Bob Cousy and the Boston Celtics in six games. Pettit averaged 29 points and 17 rebounds a game against Boston, and he got plenty of help from teammates Cliff Hagan (25.2 points per game) and Slater Martin (12.2 points per game).

It would be the first and, so far, only championship for the franchise. What made it even more remarkable was beating the Celtics, a team in the early stages of winning 11 championships in 13 seasons. Two of those titles, in 1960 and '61, came by beating the Hawks in the finals.

After making the finals three of four years, the Hawks plummeted to a 29–51 record in 1961–62, a season that saw three different coaches run the team, including Pettit as player-coach for six games. The Hawks bounced back to make the playoffs every season from 1963 to 1973, losing six times in the Western Division finals, four times to the Los Angeles Lakers and twice to the San Francisco Warriors.

During that stretch, the franchise made another move, settling in Atlanta in 1968. Walker was born the following year, and it didn't take him long to discover Erving. From there, he found out about the Hawks and Rollins, the big, shot-blocking center he loved so much. There was plenty more he liked about the team.

"Steve Hawes, Charlie Criss, they may as well have been all-stars to me," he said. Then there was the curly-haired head coach. "Hubie Brown cursed a blue streak. I could listen to him talk about basketball all the time."

Brown would lead the Hawks from 31 wins in his first season, 1976–77, to 50 in his final full season in Atlanta, 1979–80. He was succeeded by Kevin Loughery, who had played 11 seasons in the NBA and later coached the New York Nets and Erving to two ABA championships.

"It was the classic stepdad syndrome for me," Walker said. "He was a good coach, but for me, he wasn't Hubie Brown."

Willis came aboard as a fan in the 1980s, a decade that saw the Hawks make the playoffs seven times under Loughery and his successor, Mike Fratello. Once again, there were no playoff runs beyond the second round as the Hawks couldn't get past Eastern Conference powerhouses like the Detroit Pistons, Boston Celtics and Milwaukee Bucks.

The most painful loss was the 1988 Eastern Conference semifinals matchup with Boston. In Game 5 of that series, the Hawks got 27 points and 14 rebounds from Kevin Willis, 25 points from Wilkins and 21 from Doc Rivers to win in Boston, 112–104. It gave the Hawks a 3–2 lead, one game from advancing as they came home to Atlanta.

The Celtics held off a late rally by the Hawks and won Game 6, 102–100, thanks to 26 points from Kevin McHale, 23 from Bird and 22 from Danny Ainge. It was just enough to overcome more stellar performances by Wilkins (35 points) and Rivers (32).

Game 7 was the classic Wilkins-Bird showdown, with the Hawks falling just short. "To lose that game and have Dominique play so well was just heartbreaking," Walker said. "When we lost that series and didn't advance, I felt the Hawks wouldn't get there. It's still crushing. There's still a black armband on every Hawks fan for that series. It defines being a Hawks fan—good, but not good enough."

Kris Willis still has that Boston-Atlanta series on DVD.

"I watch it now, and my heart still gets pumping," he said. Of the Game 7 showdown, he added, "It's still one of the best games I've ever watched."

There was one other showdown in that season that is talked about by basketball junkies. Wilkins and Michael Jordan faced off in the Slam Dunk contest during the 1988 all-star weekend. The contest was in Chicago, on Jordan's home court, but many thought Wilkins should have won the event. A teenager at the time, Willis felt Wilkins was the clear winner. Now, he's not so sure, but one thing he's certain of: "It was the golden age of the NBA."

As the 1990s arrived, so did Kremer as a Hawks fan. With Wilkins traded to the Clippers, Mookie Blaylock and Steve Smith took over much of the scoring. The decade featured seven straight playoff appearances, but as usual they all ended by the second round.

"I was happy to be in the playoffs, but it was frustrating. You don't want to be known as the Buffalo Bills of basketball," Kremer said, referring to the pro football team that lost four straight Super Bowls. "They got to a championship. We haven't even done that."

Still, the '90s were better than what awaited. In June 1999, Blaylock was dealt to the Golden State Warriors for Bimbo Coles and Duane Ferrell. The teams also exchanged first-round draft picks. In August, the Hawks traded Smith and Ed Gray to the Portland Trail Blazers for Jim Jackson and Isaiah "J.R." Rider.

Atlanta still had Mutombo as a defensive presence, but this newly constructed team just didn't work. The Hawks fell to 28 wins in the 1999–2000 season. They would miss the playoffs for eight straight seasons, including 2004–05, when the Hawks won just 13 games.

That Hawks team was 28th in the league in scoring and 29th in the league in points allowed, not a formula for success. A nine-game losing streak that started in early November got the season off to a rugged begin-

Vicki Kremer moved from Iowa to Atlanta in the late 1980s. Since then, she's become a big fan of both the Hawks and the Braves (photograph by Dennis E. Kelly, Jr.).

ning. That was no match for what happened from February 10 to April 8 when the Hawks lost 27 of 28 games.

The team had some talent, including Antoine Walker and Al Harrington to handle the scoring. The Hawks often were in games right until the end, losing five in overtime and another 14 by five points or fewer.

Still, as Kremer said, "Oh my goodness, I've got to tell you. It was awful. It was ugly. It was really ugly."

For Willis, "That 13-win season was painful, but it wasn't as painful as it would have been for the 15- or 16-year-old me."

And Kremer managed to pull out her silver linings playbook through all of this. "I looked at it as there's always tomorrow. There was never anything to make me say I'm giving up my tickets. I just thought we've sunk as low as we can go."

It turns out she was right. The Hawks traded Walker in the second half of the 2004–05 season, and in the off-season acquired Joe Johnson from the Phoenix Suns. Johnson took over Walker's role as the team's leading scorer while displaying a bit more sensibility in his shot selection.

The Hawks' win total doubled in 2005–06 and steadily grew as the team made a handful of other key moves, trading for Mike Bibby in 2008 and Jamal Crawford in 2009 and drafting Al Horford out of the University of Florida in 2007. Josh Smith, a Georgia native whom the Hawks drafted out of high school in 2004, developed into a solid NBA player, adding to the Hawks' depth.

The franchise that had won 13 games in 2004–05 won 47 in 2008–09 and 53 the following year. Johnson averaged 21.3 points per game to lead the offense in the 53-win season, and Josh Smith, Horford, Bibby, Crawford and former first-round pick Marvin Williams were all key contributors.

"That was a fun team because we no longer sucked," Walker said.

Amid its sparkling downtown towers and modern vibe, Atlanta can be a tough sports town. Many residents aren't native to the city, so their interests can turn elsewhere when the local teams take a downturn. Kremer remembers those who questioned her when she went to every game in a 13-win season. She recalls the joking comments during those dark years from folks asking whether Atlanta still had an NBA team.

When those people showed up to support the new and improved Hawks, Kremer was accepting. "I didn't care. I said, 'You guys can jump on this bandwagon.'"

Once again in 2010, after winning 53 games in the regular season, the Hawks struggled in the playoffs. They rallied in the first round, winning

Games 6 and 7 to edge past the Milwaukee Bucks. But in the next round, they were blitzed by Dwight Howard and the Orlando Magic, who swept the Hawks in four games.

"We couldn't knock that manhole cover off and breathe the fresh air of a conference finals," Walker said. "To never get past the second round was so bizarre, especially with all those great players. You'd think it would just happen by accident."

The pattern continued for several more years. Then came the 2014–15 season. A team that generally had been pretty good suddenly got great.

The season started slowly with three losses in the first four games. It warmed up from Thanksgiving to Christmas, a stretch that saw the Hawks win 14 of 15. Then it got sizzling. The Hawks lost to Milwaukee the day after Christmas and didn't lose again until February 2, a streak of 19 wins.

"At first, I felt this was a hot streak. Then I had to say this team is pretty dang good," Willis said. It was a team built on stingy defense and sharing the ball on offense. There were no superstars. It was five guys playing together for 48 minutes.

"What sealed the deal was when they didn't lose a game in January," Kremer said. "Then it started to hit home—this team is special."

The Hawks finished with 60 wins, the best in the Eastern Conference and second in the NBA to the Golden State Warriors. Four players—Horford, Kyle Korver, Paul Millsap and Jeff Teague—made the all-star team.

"You could just feel something going on, something changing," Kremer said. "But did I expect them to win 60 games? Never in a million years."

Walker also noticed a change. "There was a vibe across Hawks Nation and across social media that hadn't been there since the '80s. I'm getting goose bumps just thinking about it. They had been waiting for something real to believe in again. You don't realize how much you miss something like that until you get it again." But, he added, "sixty wins didn't matter if we couldn't get past the second round of the playoffs."

The New Jersey Nets put up a fight in the first round, but the Hawks advanced, winning in six games. The Washington Wizards won two of the first three games in the next round, one on a last-second shot by Paul Pierce. With Teague scoring 26 points, the Hawks bounced back to win Game 4 in Washington.

Back in Atlanta, Game 5 was a defensive tussle that came down to the final possession. Horford grabbed the rebound of a missed Dennis Schröder shot and scored with 1 second left to give Atlanta an 82–81 win.

In Game 6, Millsap, DeMarre Carroll and Teague combined for 65 points, and the Hawks won again in Washington, 94–91. It had happened.

For the first time in decades, the Hawks had won two rounds of playoff basketball.

Walker, who is a software engineer, remembers attending a training session in California and running back to his hotel room so he wouldn't miss Game 6 between the Hawks and Wizards. He said that after the Hawks' victory, "I know I spent an hour on Twitter. I'm not sure I said anything intelligible. It was a great feeling."

The Eastern Conference finals against the Cleveland Cavaliers proved to be a struggle. The Hawks already were without one of their key substitutes, Thabo Sefolosha, who had been injured in an altercation with New York City police in April. (Sefolosha later was cleared of charges of obstruction, disorderly conduct and resisting arrest.) Carroll was hobbled by a knee injury suffered in Game 1 against Cleveland, and Korver's season ended when he hurt his ankle in Game 2.

The Cavaliers played part of the series without their star point guard, Kyrie Irving, but they had LeBron James, one of the league's most dominating players. Cleveland swept the Hawks in four games. It was a tough way to end a 60-win season, but for Willis, Walker and Kremer there was plenty of joy in a year that had been more successful than any they had seen.

Kremer, who is a manager in store operations for Home Depot, recalls how on many nights in the past she couldn't even tell she was in Atlanta because there were so many fans rooting for the visiting team. There was no such feeling in 2015 as all those people who had joked with her about the Hawks now were sitting around her in an energized Philips Arena.

There is one other oddity that can be a challenge for Hawks fans. All professional sports teams can regret trading or releasing players who later become stars with other teams. The Hawks have a list that can match most anyone's.

Along with once having Auerbach as a coach, the Hawks drafted Bob Cousy, a star point guard at the College of the Holy Cross, with the third pick in the 1950 NBA draft. Being unable to sign him, they sold him to the Chicago Stags.

In 1956, they drafted Bill Russell, who had won two national championships at the University of San Francisco, with the second pick in the draft. The Hawks immediately traded him to the Celtics for Cliff Hagan and Ed Macauley, two good players who would be part of the Hawks' 1958 championship team. But Cousy and Russell became two of the league's all-time greats, teaming up in Boston to start the Celtics dynasty.

In 1972, the Hawks signed Erving, Walker's boyhood hero. However, the Milwaukee Bucks drafted Erving, and the ABA's Virginia Squires claimed they still had the rights to Dr. J. A legal battle followed, and Erving eventually returned to the Squires.

If the Hawks had somehow landed Erving, he would have ended up on a team with two other showy offensive stars, Lou Hudson and Pete Maravich. "What kind of team would that have been?" Walker wondered. "They wouldn't have defended much, but they would have been fun to watch."

As much as he would have loved to see Erving in a Hawks jersey, the move Walker laments the most just might be the 2001 NBA draft. With the third pick, the Hawks selected Pau Gasol, a talented big man from Spain. He was immediately dealt in a five-player trade with the Vancouver Grizzlies. The key piece coming to Atlanta was Shareef Abdur-Rahim, again a good player, but Gasol became a five-time all-star who won two championships with the Los Angeles Lakers.

The 28th pick in that draft was a point guard from France named Tony Parker, who was taken by the San Antonio Spurs. Many teams, the Hawks included, regret passing on Parker, a six-time all-star and four-time champion with the Spurs. The following year, the Hawks were seeking point guard help and pulled off a draft-day trade to get Dan Dickau, who had been a fine player at Gonzaga University before the Sacramento Kings selected him. Dickau played 73 games in Atlanta before the Hawks traded him in 2004. In his six-year NBA career, Dickau averaged 5.8 points per game.

"That's the kind of era it was for the Hawks," Walker said. "They passed on Tony Parker, but the next year they got Dan Dickau."

There may have been painful trades in the past, and too many early exits from the playoffs, but these fans stick with it.

For Willis, it's a matter of city pride. "I've never been the kind of guy who can go to Philips Arena and wear a Lakers jersey. It's a sense of duty. It's my sense of responsibility. If you ask who my favorite baseball team is, it's the Atlanta Braves. If you ask who my favorite football team is, it's the Atlanta Falcons."

For Kremer, it's a dedication to her teams. She has had to answer to friends who wonder why she keeps going when her teams are bad, but she seldom misses a Braves or Hawks game. In 2015, she skipped a Braves game to go to a Hawks playoff contest. The next night, people who sit near her at Braves games and even folks in the dugout asked where she had been. "I held up my Hawks playoff shirt and said, 'I have to support my Hawks.' I'm one of those people that if they are playing, I'm going."

For Walker, it goes back to memories of his youth. "It was those days growing up in Lakeland, Florida, with a black-and-white TV showing Hubie Brown and the Hawks. These are your guys. You can try rooting for someone else, but it's not the same.

"That's the team you pretended to be when you were growing up, shooting a Nerf ball into a laundry basket. That's what keeps you going through a 13-win season. That's the team that's in your heart."

Showing Their Stripes

The Cincinnati Bengals

The pain of being a Cincinnati Bengals fan might best be summarized in one play, and it is a 66-yard pass completion. The date: January 8, 2006. The place: Cincinnati's Paul Brown Stadium. The event: A first-round play-off matchup with the division rival Pittsburgh Steelers.

It had been a glorious season for the Bengals; for the first time in 15 years, they were playing in the postseason. They had finished 11–5, tied with the Steelers for first place in the American Football Conference's North Division. It was a vast improvement over the previous two seasons, in which the Bengals finished 8–8 each year. The season before that, they had gone 2–14.

The turnaround had been led by Carson Palmer, a former first-round draft pick out of the University of Southern California. In 2005, his second season as a starting quarterback, Palmer threw for a league-high 32 touchdowns while completing more than two-thirds of his passes.

In the playoff game against the Steelers, Palmer dropped back for his first pass attempt of the game. He unleashed a long toss that hit Chris Henry in stride for that 66-yard completion. But, on the play, Steelers defensive lineman Kimo von Oelhoffen came in low and crashed into Palmer's left knee, sending the quarterback to the ground, writhing in pain.

Max Gollobin was at that game, happy to be watching the Bengals in the playoffs for the first time in his young life. "It was horrible," he said. In these pre–Twitter days, no one in the crowd was sure at first how serious the injury was. A newspaper website soon posted an item about Palmer. "You just heard whispers in the crowd, 'Palmer tore his ACL,'" Gollobin said.

The injury was even more extensive—tears to both the anterior cruciate ligament and the medial collateral ligament as well as other damage to the knee. In a later interview, von Oelhoffen said that when he collided with Palmer's knee, it "sounded like a gunshot." There was speculation the injury would end Palmer's career, although he did recover in time to return the following season.

The play was felt by Bengals fans everywhere. Dan Marks was watching in his Amelia, Ohio, home and shook his head as he saw Palmer and Henry, who left the game a few plays later, knocked out with injuries. "I remember thinking that we had just been cheated out of a Super Bowl victory."

Matthew Willson had just returned from Christmas break to his dorm room at Clarion University in western Pennsylvania. "It was one of those times we said, 'What do we do now?'"

John Phythyon, Jr., was at home in Lawrence, Kansas. "I came flying off my couch," he said of his reaction to the long completed pass. "Then they cut back to Palmer on the ground. It screwed us as usual."

After the injuries to Palmer and Henry, the Bengals fell to the Steelers, 31–17. In the next two weeks, Pittsburgh beat the Indianapolis Colts and the Denver Broncos to advance to Super Bowl XL, where they defeated the Seattle Seahawks. Bengals fans were left wondering what might have been.

That Bengals team was loaded on offense, with Palmer throwing to Henry, Chad Johnson and T.J. Houshmandzadeh. Those three combined for 22 touchdown receptions, and running back Rudi Johnson rushed for 1,458 yards and another 12 scores.

"A lot of Bengals fans saw this team as being capable of what the Steelers did—going on to win it all," Willson said.

That injury-riddled loss to Pittsburgh is just one in a string of postseason frustrations for the Bengals and their fans. The team has lost two Super Bowls, both to the San Francisco 49ers, the league's most powerful team in the 1980s. The Bengals had a stretch of eight straight playoff losses from 1991 to 2016. Seven of those were under coach Marvin Lewis, an NFL record for most consecutive playoff losses by a head coach.

This is how bad that playoff losing streak became. Shortly before Lewis lost his seventh straight playoff game in 2016, Associated Press reporter Joe Reedy asked actress Susan Lucci how Lewis must feel. Lucci, the longtime star of the soap opera "All My Children," earned some additional fame for being nominated 19 times before winning her first Emmy Award. After a 2012 playoff loss, Lewis said he was starting to feel like Lucci.

"I certainly hope the best for him," Lucci told Reedy. "I'm sure he has a familiar feeling to what I had—how do you do your work better and grow?"

All these frustrations are from a franchise that started well. As an expansion team in 1968, the Bengals built themselves from the ground up. Paul Brown, who won seven championships as coach of the Cleveland Browns in the 1940s and '50s, was the Bengals' first coach and general manager. The team's first-ever draft pick in 1968 wasn't a flashy wide receiver or record-setting college quarterback. It was a center, Bob Johnson from the University of Tennessee. He spent his entire 12-year career in Cincinnati, and his number 54 is the only one the franchise has retired.

The first two seasons were the rugged ones you would expect for a new team (3–11 and 4–9–1), but the Bengals went 8–6 and made the play-offs in their third season. They soon won at least 10 games in three out of four seasons from 1973 to 1976.

It's not every fan that gets his own bobblehead, but Dan Marks has one, dressed of course in Cincinnati Bengals gear (photograph by Carolyn Marks).

"Paul Brown was an excellent coach," said Marks, a Cincinnati native who has followed the team from its early days. One of the first stars for the Bengals was quarterback Ken Anderson, whom the team drafted in 1971 out of tiny Augustana College in Illinois. The only other Augustana alum to play in the National Football League is George Lenc, an end who spent one season with the Brooklyn Dodgers in 1939.

Anderson led the league in passing yards twice and took the Bengals to the Super Bowl after a 12–4 season in 1981. Their matchup was

Dan Marks gets to hang out with the Cincinnati Bengals' mascot. Marks went to his first Bengals game in 1970, the team's third season (photograph by Carolyn Marks).

Even Dan Marks' dog has a Bengals wardrobe and a Bengals-themed name, T.J. Poochmanadeh, a play off the name of the retired wide receiver (photograph by Carolyn Marks).

a tough one—the San Francisco 49ers, who were at the beginning of a decade they would dominate.

"When they ran out of the tunnel, they looked star-struck," Marks said of the Bengals. Apparently, they were, committing three first-half turnovers. San Francisco quarterback Joe Montana ran for one touchdown and passed for another, and the 49ers held a 20–0 lead at the break.

Anderson led a comeback, but his touchdown pass to tight end Dan Ross late in the fourth quarter ended the day's scoring. It wasn't enough as the Bengals fell short, 26–21.

Phythyon remembers the frustration: "My dad was grumping around. My mom asked, 'What's wrong? You don't normally get this upset. He said, 'Because it's the first time in 16 years I give a damn about who wins the game.' I turned and said, 'Yes, exactly that.'"

Seven years later, the teams met again in Super Bowl XXIII. It was expected to be the culmination of a special season in Cincinnati. One year after winning just four games, the Bengals had gone 12–4 to win the AFC

Central. Quarterback Boomer Esiason threw for 28 touchdowns, and the offense also got a spark from a three-pronged running attack. Ickey Woods rushed for 1,066 yards and 15 touchdowns, doing his scoring dance, "the Ickey Shuffle," after each one. He got help from James Brooks (931 yards, eight touchdowns rushing and six touchdowns receiving) and Stanley Wilson (398 yards and two touchdowns).

They beat the Seattle Seahawks and Buffalo Bills in the playoffs, setting up a Super Bowl rematch with the 49ers. From there, not much went right for the Bengals.

The team's downfall started the night before the Super Bowl when Wilson had a relapse with cocaine, a habit that already had led to his suspension in 1987. He would not play in the Super Bowl, or ever again in the NFL.

Early in the game, Tim Krumrie, the Bengals' standout defensive tackle, broke his leg. Even without Krumrie, Cincinnati's defense played well, giving up yardage but few points. What everyone figured would be an offensive showdown was a 3–3 game at the half.

Esiason and the Bengals' offense never got untracked. They were limited to 229 yards in the game, but two field goals by Jim Breech and a 93-yard kickoff return by Stanford Jennings gave Cincinnati a 13–6 lead late in the third quarter.

Early in the fourth quarter, Bengals cornerback Lewis Billups dropped an interception in the end zone. "Montana hits Billups right in the numbers. If he catches that, the Bengals win the game," Phythyon said.

On the next play, Montana connected with Jerry Rice for a game-tying touchdown. As well as the Bengals had played, Rice had been a problem all afternoon; he finished the day with 11 catches for 215 yards.

The Bengals' offense had one more burst of life, moving into scoring position. When the drive stalled, Breech kicked his third field goal of the day, a 40-yarder, to give the Bengals the lead with 3:44 left. But the most painful moments of the entire day awaited Cincinnati diehards.

Starting at his own 8-yard line, Montana completed three straight passes followed by two short runs by Roger Craig. Still, with two minutes to go the 49ers were 69 yards from the end zone.

But Montana kept his team rolling, completing two passes each to Rice and Craig before hitting John Taylor with the game-winning 10-yard scoring pass. The play came with 34 seconds left.

"Every time I watch the replay of that game, it kills me," Phythyon said. "Montana is Montana. For 58 minutes, the Bengals had him hemmed in, but he does what he does. The fact that seven years later we lost to that same team, quarterbacked by that same guy, it was gut-wrenching."

Marks recalls, "At the two-minute warning, I said, 'We're going to win this thing.' When the game ended, I was sitting there with my family. I was dumbfounded."

As painful as that Super Bowl loss was, Bengals fans soon would be longing for the good old days of playoff appearances and winning records. Starting in 1991, the Bengals went 14 years without a winning season, bottoming out with that 2–14 record in 2002.

Phythyon blames the long, cold stretch on the Bo Jackson curse. Jackson, a Heisman Trophy winner when he played at Auburn University, was a tough running back in the four seasons he played for the Oakland Raiders. His football career ended in January 1991, when he suffered a hip injury in a playoff victory over the Bengals. Later that year, the Bengals' losing ways began.

Phythyon was living in Kansas during that losing era, out of range of Sunday broadcasts of Bengals games. He recalls tuning in to ESPN to see its roundup of NFL action.

"I'd cringe when I watched the Bengals' highlights. This is not supposed to be who these guys are. I'd say, 'C'mon man, what happened to the days of Ken Anderson and Boomer Esiason?'

"There are years and years and years of clownish football. It was just painful to watch—week after week after week of this."

That 2–14 season led to Palmer, which led to a return to the playoffs in 2005. "Carson Palmer was somebody a lot of people were excited about," Willson said. "He really did give a spark to the offense."

The Bengals made the playoffs again in 2009 and then five straight seasons from 2011 to 2015. But that stretch was part of the run of eight straight playoff losses.

Palmer was traded to the Oakland Raiders in 2011, after the Bengals had drafted a new quarterback, Andy Dalton, who put up spectacular passing numbers leading a fast-paced offense at Texas Christian University.

It's been a frustrating time for Bengals fans. Their team is a long way from that 2–14 squad of 2002, but being pretty good only gets you so far.

"It's great they're making the playoffs, but they don't give out championship rings for making the playoffs," Marks said.

"It's tough because you become a laughingstock in the NFL," Gollobin said. It has also been tough on Dalton, who has taken much of the heat for the Bengals' playoff failures.

Gollobin mentioned how Dalton took part in a celebrity softball game during baseball's 2015 all-star event, which was held in Cincinnati. Dalton was booed by his home crowd at that softball contest. "How ruthless is that?" Gollobin asked.

These fans have taken different routes to their love of the Bengals.

Willson, now a car salesman in the Pittsburgh area, was born in Cincinnati and attended his first Bengals game at Riverfront Stadium when he was 4. When he was 10, his family moved from the Cincinnati area to Moline, Illinois, and then Lancaster, Pennsylvania. So there's been pressure to root for the Chicago Bears, the St. Louis Rams and the Pittsburgh Steelers, not to mention there is a branch of his family that cheers for the Minnesota Vikings.

"I really never swayed from the Bengals," he said. He credits that to his upbringing. "I had exposure to the Bengals pretty much every day. As a kid, you felt the disappointment when they lost, but you didn't fully understand 3–11."

Willson displays his support of the team as a co-editor of the Fan-Sided website www.stripehype.com. "It's stress relief to write about something I love," he said.

Like Willson, Phythyon had a nomadic existence in his youth. He was born in Columbus, Ohio, but the family moved to West Virginia and then settled in De Pere, Wisconsin, where his father taught biology at St. Norbert College.

"Our father did not let the passion for Ohio sports teams die in our household," said Phythyon, an author who writes fantasy fiction, including the Wolf Dasher series. It was easy to carry on that passion in the 1970s. Ohio State football was a national title contender with Woody Hayes as coach. The Cincinnati Reds were in their "Big Red Machine" mode, winning back-to-back championships in the middle of the decade. Even the floundering Indians

Matthew Willson attended his first Cincinnati Bengals game at Riverfront Stadium when he was four years old (courtesy Matthew Willson).

had a couple of winning seasons. And the Bengals, of course, were just getting started but already proving they could make the playoffs.

Being a kid, though, Phythyon searched for a pro football winner. He had no interest in the nearby NFL team, the Green Bay Packers, who had fallen off sharply from their glory years of the 1960s.

"I remember doubting that the Packers had ever been any good." When he took a trip to the team's Hall of Fame, he read the history of Green Bay's domination under coach Vince Lombardi. "My mouth was agape. I said, 'You've got to be kidding me? This team?'"

Phythyon found a winner in the Dallas Cowboys, who were regularly getting to Super Bowls in the '70s. He always kept an eye on the Bengals, though. He collected football cards as a boy, and the first card he ever got was of Ken Riley, a solid defensive back with the Bengals. It came in a loaf of Wonder Bread.

"To this day, he's my favorite player. All my jerseys have been number 13," Phythyon said.

His affair with the Cowboys lasted until Jerry Jones bought the team and fired longtime head coach Tom Landry. "I was furious," he said. "How do you do that to traditions?" From then on, he was all in with his Bengals.

Marks was just out of the Air Force when his brother took him to his

Max Gollobin knows one thing about Cincinnati fans—they are loyal to their teams (photograph by Tess Davis).

first game in 1970 in Cincinnati. He recalls that pro football games back then were formal events. "It was a dress-up occasion. It was a whole different atmosphere than today," said Marks, a retired construction supervisor with Duke Energy.

From the play on the field to the energy in the stands, it made an impression. "From going to that one game, I got hooked." Within three years, he owned Bengals season tickets. The price for each game back then? Eight dollars and 25 cents.

Gollobin is a Cincinnati native who got interested in

sports at an early age. He is young enough that he wasn't paying attention just yet through the dark years of the 1990s and the early 2000s.

He's a big enough fan that he traveled from New York City, where he now works in banking, to attend a Bengals game in Baltimore against the Ravens in 2015. He met up with fraternity brothers from his alma mater, Vanderbilt University. Their tailgate group included a few fans of the two-time champion Ravens who gave Gollobin a hard time about his Bengals' past failings.

He has learned to take such taunting in stride. "Cincinnati has been the little brother in professional sports," he said. "The Reds, despite their success, have been the [St. Louis] Cardinals' little brother. The Bengals have been the Steelers' little brother."

For this game day, Gollobin wore the number 18 jersey of Bengals wide receiver A.J. Green. The white, orange and black color scheme stood out in a sea of Ravens purple heading toward Baltimore's M&T Bank Stadium.

But Gollobin was not alone in the crowd on this day. Jackie Bonds traveled from her home in Stafford, Virginia, to cheer on a Bengals team she has rooted for since she was a girl growing up in Cincinnati.

Like Gollobin, she wore a Green jersey. She talked about the days when Bengals fans wore paper bags over their heads at games, a now-standard show of disappointment during a team's lousy season.

"I was a Bengals fan when they were called the Bungles. I'm a diehard. Everything is about home," she said, recalling growing up with parents who were always watching the Bengals. "No matter what the record is, I'm for the Bengals."

Denny Smith and several relatives drove from Independence, Kentucky, just outside of Cincinnati. It was about a nine-hour drive, part of a family tradition of taking a trip each season to see the Bengals away from home. They'll continue that tradition, no matter what the team's record is.

"You want to feel joy and pride and get a chance to celebrate," he said.

The Bengals fans celebrated on this day. Dalton threw three touchdown passes, including a go-ahead scoring toss to Green with 2:14 left, as the Bengals edged the Ravens, 28–24. The victory was the third in an 8–0 start by the Bengals, en route to a 12–4 record. It was a good season for the Bengals, one that provided hope to a fan base that needs a blast of it from time to time.

"We are all sitting around, waiting for the other shoe to drop," said Phythyon, during the middle of that hot 2015 start.

"Being a Bengals fan, I distrust anything good happening," Gollobin said. "I expect to be punched in the balls with two minutes to go."

Phythyon and Gollobin's words proved to be prophetic. Dalton, in the midst of a fine season, broke his right thumb in a December 13 game, an injury that kept him out the rest of the season.

Backup quarterback AJ McCarron was the starter the rest of the way, including a wild-card–round playoff game at home against the Pittsburgh Steelers on Saturday night, January 9, 2016. Of all the Bengals' consecutive playoff losses, this one would prove to be the most inexplicable.

The Bengals took a 16–15 lead when McCarron hit Green with a 25-yard touchdown pass with 1:50 left in the game. Cincinnati seemed to wrap the game up when it got the ball back deep in Steelers territory after an interception by linebacker Vontaze Burfict. But Bengals running back Jeremy Hill fumbled, and the Steelers moved the ball to Cincinnati's 47-yard line with 22 seconds left.

Then came a play that will leave Bengals fans shaking their heads into the next millennium. A pass from Ben Roethlisberger to Antonio Brown was incomplete, but Burfict was flagged for unnecessary roughness because of a vicious hit on Brown. In the scuffle after the play, Bengals defensive back Adam Jones was penalized for unsportsmanlike conduct. The two 15-yard penalties moved the Steelers to the 17-yard line, giving Steelers kicker Chris Boswell an easy field goal to win the game. Final score: Pittsburgh 18, Cincinnati 16.

"Saturday night was rough," Gollobin said of the loss. "By Sunday, I was OK. When I got to work on Monday, all anybody wanted to talk about was the Bengals' meltdown." Co-workers razzed him about the rowdy behavior of Cincinnati fans during the game. "I told them, 'I wasn't there. I was in New York on my couch.'"

Despite moments like this, Gollobin won't be changing his rooting stripes. "I'm a diehard. I can't get enough of it. One trait of Cincinnati, whether it pertains to the city itself or its sports teams, is loyalty. It's what separates true fans from the front-runners. When they finally break through, it will be well worth the wait."

Phythyon has a similar approach to why he supports the Bengals, even during their darkest days. "Number one is loyalty. I bleed stripes because my father taught me to root for Ohio teams. My job is to root for this team."

But he admits the 2016 playoff loss to the Steelers took its toll. A couple of months after that defeat, he said, "I have been unable to recover from the latest loss in the playoffs. Aside from my stocking cap, which I have worn because it's been cold and it's the only one I own, I have not been able to bring myself to wear any of my Bengals gear."

Phythyon remembers other painful moments. "I can recall watching the draft, and when the Bengals made their pick, you'd stand up and say, 'What?'"

He attended graduate school in the early 1990s at the University of Kansas and stayed in the area until moving back to Ohio in 2014. In the leanest years, he would walk around Lawrence, Kansas, sporting a Bengals sweatshirt. "People would say, 'Dude, you're a Bengals fan? Who would root for that team? I'm so sorry.'"

Shooting Stars

The Houston Astros

To grasp the passion of Houston Astros fans, one simply has to know the reactions of brothers Brandon and Brian del Castillo to a certain post-season home run.

Let's set the stage. It was Game 5 of the 2005 National League Championship Series at Houston's Minute Maid Park. The Astros, three outs away from their first World Series, held a 4–2 lead over the St. Louis Cardinals as the ninth inning began.

The packed stadium was rocking as closer Brad Lidge struck out the first two Cardinals he faced in the ninth. Then, David Eckstein singled and Jim Edmonds walked, bringing up baseball's most feared hitter of the time, Albert Pujols.

The crowd was nervous, and with good reason. Pujols blasted Lidge's 0–1 pitch onto the train track above the left-field stands. ESPN's Home Run Tracker estimated the ball hit 95 feet above the playing field and would have traveled 470 feet if it hadn't smashed into the upper reaches of Minute Maid Park. What had looked like a pennant-clinching party for the Astros became a crushing loss.

"When he hit it, I didn't even turn to see where it went," Brian del Castillo said. He and Brandon were there with their family—father Hector, mother Barbara, younger sister Brianna—all devoted Astros fans. "We had to be there. It was our chance to see something we'd never seen before—going to the World Series," Brian said.

Brandon's reaction to the Pujols homer was more intense. "I was so sick to my stomach, I had to lie down," he said. The family, which held season tickets, was watching from a club box that included a couch. That's where Brandon went, curled up, as the Astros were retired quietly in the bottom of the ninth inning.

Brandon and Brian's younger sister remembers that moment well.

"It was just heartbreaking for everyone—the fans, the players," Brianna del Castillo said. "I knew the players would get over it. I wasn't sure my brothers would."

The pain did not disappear quickly. Two nights later the teams met for Game 6 in St. Louis. An Astros victory would win the pennant. A Cardinals victory would force a gut-wrenching, winner-take-all Game 7. Brandon, a lawyer, had made a business trip that day to Corpus Christi, Texas, and his return flight to Houston landed just about the time the game started. As he walked through the terminal, he found a spot with no television coverage of the game.

"I walked past the airport chapel and I said, 'You know what I'm going to do? I'll hang out here for a while.'" After two hours—and many prayers—he emerged.

On the drive home, he worked up the courage to turn on the car radio. As he recalls, it was just like a scene from a movie—as soon as the radio came on, he got an instant update from the play-by-play broadcaster.

When the Houston Astros played in the 2005 World Series, the del Castillo family was there, including (from left) Brianna, Brian and Brandon. "The family that has baseball in its heart is a healthy family," says their father, Hector del Castillo, Jr. (photograph by Hector del Castillo, Jr.).

"He said, 'Well, if you missed it, it's 4–1 Astros, and [Roy] Oswalt has been pitching a gem.'"

Oswalt and the Astros would win, 5–1, and Houston was headed to its first World Series. It's a victory Astros fans refer to as "the bulldozer game." Team owner Drayton McLane promised Oswalt a bulldozer if he won. In December, the piece of heavy equipment was delivered to the star pitcher, complete with a giant red bow on its cab.

The 2005 World Series appearance was 43 years in the making for a team that started as the expansion Houston Colt .45s. From the start, it's a franchise that has found a way to be overlooked.

In their first three seasons, the Colt .45s were bad, losing 96 games each year. Their fellow expansion buddies, the New York Mets, were worse, though, drawing all the attention with a 120-loss season in 1962.

Houston did generate some buzz when it moved into the Astrodome in 1965, replacing its first home, mosquito-laden Colt Stadium. With the move came a name change from the Colt .45s to the Astros.

The Astrodome, called by some "The Eighth Wonder of the World," was the first domed, air-conditioned sports arena. It covered 1 million square feet, and the roof protected fans and players from the heat and humidity of a Houston summer.

The stadium, which would remain the Astros' home for 35 years, opened April 9, 1965, with an exhibition game between the Astros and New York Yankees. President Lyndon B. Johnson and Lady Bird Johnson, the first lady, watched as the Astros won, 2–1.

Three days later, the Astros and Philadelphia Phillies played the first regular-season, major-league game held indoors. Dick Allen hit the first indoor home run, a two-run shot that was all the offense in the Phillies' 2–0 win.

The early Astros teams had some exciting players, including pitcher Don Wilson, second baseman Joe Morgan and outfielder Jim Wynn, but they wouldn't have a winning season until 1972 and wouldn't make the playoffs until 1980. Some of that early suffering was the pain expected for an expansion team. Some of it was bad decision-making, such as trading Morgan, a future Hall of Famer.

The 1980 playoff team featured a pitching staff that included Joe Niekro, Nolan Ryan and J.R. Richard, who saw his career end in late July at age 30 when he suffered a stroke. The lineup had little power—Terry Puhl led the team with 13 home runs—but it had steady hitters in Puhl, Cesar Cedeno, Art Howe and Jose Cruz.

The Astros lost a memorable series to the eventual World Series champion Philadelphia Phillies. Four of the five games went extra innings, including the deciding Game 5, which the Phillies won, 8–7, on Garry Maddox's 10th-inning double. The Astros didn't hit a home run in the series but hung in there thanks to Puhl, who hit .526, and Cruz, who had a .609 on-base percentage.

That 1980 series also saw the birth of a baseball axiom: If you want an exciting postseason series, make sure you invite the Astros.

In 1986, the Astros met the Mets in the National League Championship Series. The Mets won in six games, but it was no easy task. Game 5, a 2–1 New York victory, went 12 innings. It was topped by Game 6, which went 16 innings before New York won, 7–6, scoring three in the top of the 16th and then limiting the Astros to two in the bottom of the inning.

The win was a crucial one for the Mets because Houston had Mike Scott lined up to pitch Game 7. All Scott had done that year was finish with 18 wins, a 2.22 ERA and 306 strikeouts, and he pitched a no-hitter in late September to clinch the National League West title for the Astros. Scott was all of that against the Mets in the playoffs, limiting New York to one run in two complete games. A few weeks later, he would be named the National League Cy Young Award winner.

It was around this time that Jose Nogales began noticing the Astros. He was a reluctant fan at first. His stepfather, Miguel, would always watch the Astros on television, but Nogales and his stepbrothers weren't all that interested.

"It was long and boring," he said. "When you're a kid, all you want to watch is cartoons."

But, as Nogales started playing the sport, he took more notice of the Astros, especially as they found success in 1986.

Brandon del Castillo was also starting to pay attention. His dad had been a physician in the Navy, so the family had been in Virginia and Florida before settling in Houston in the mid–1980s.

Brandon enjoyed watching an Astros pitching staff that was led in 1986 by Scott, Ryan and Bob Knepper. He appreciated how they would work the count and baffle batters with an assortment of pitches. "That's when I fell in love with the thinking part of baseball," he said.

Brian del Castillo, five years younger than his brother, soon came on board. He remembers growing up with the Astros and having his picture taken while being carried on Knepper's shoulders. There's another photo of Brian shaking hands with former New York Yankees great Yogi Berra, then an Astros coach.

Brian is a little too young to remember 1986, so his earliest Astros memories are of a team that struggled through the late 1980s. There soon was hope with the arrival of Craig Biggio and Jeff Bagwell, two young players whom the Astros would build around for the next decade and a half.

Bagwell was named National League rookie of the year in 1991 and most valuable player in 1994, a year that saw him drive in 116 runs in 110 games before labor troubles brought the season to an end on August 12.

The Astros found success again in 1997, which started a run of four postseason appearances in five years. The 1998 team was one that raised hope with a 102-win season. "Everybody was on the bandwagon back then," Nogales said.

The Astros made the bold move of trading with Seattle for star pitcher Randy Johnson in late July of 1998. It was one of those go-for-broke baseball trades that provides fodder for sports talk shows and barroom debates—trading potential to win now. The Astros gave up a chunk of their future by dealing prospects John Halama, Freddy Garcia and Carlos Guillen, all of whom would go on to have productive major-league careers. What Houston got in return was one of the best pitchers in baseball, a 6-foot, 10-inch flamethrower who in two months with the '98 Astros went 10–1 with a 1.28 ERA.

Ryan Dunsmore was with his father and sister for Johnson's first home start as an Astro. They were in the top row of the Astrodome and could touch the back wall of the stadium. One of the seats was behind a pillar.

"But we were in the stadium," Dunsmore said. "It was as electric as that place has ever been." And that includes plenty of Astros highlights as well as exciting moments with running back Earl Campbell and the National Football League's Houston Oilers.

Along with a boost from Johnson, the 1998 Astros were bolstered by a terrific season from Moises Alou, who batted .312 with 38 home runs and 124 RBI. He had a sparkling OPS (combined on-base and slugging percentage) of .981. In true Astros fashion, Alou was overshadowed that year by the Mark McGwire vs. Sammy Sosa home run chase. Sosa would hit 66 homers and win the National League Most Valuable Player Award. McGwire would hit 70 and finish second in the voting. Alou was third.

With hopes high, the Astros met the San Diego Padres in the first round of the playoffs. Houston was swiftly knocked out.

"There was no way we were going to lose," Brandon said. "We ran into [San Diego pitchers] Sterling Hitchcock and Kevin Brown. We couldn't hit them at all. That was pretty heartbreaking."

The gamble on trading for Johnson reaped what turned out to be a short-lived benefit. He was a free agent after the '98 season and signed with the Arizona Diamondbacks, a team with whom he would win a World Series in 2001.

"The ultimate kick in the teeth was he didn't want to come back," Brian said.

Dunsmore said, "It was the only time in my life I called in to sports radio. My 10-year-old brain couldn't wrap itself around why Randy Johnson didn't want to come back."

The other three Astros playoff appearances from 1997 to 2001 ended with losses to the Atlanta Braves. "It was kind of a bummer to lose to [Greg] Maddux, [Tom] Glavine and [John] Smoltz," Brian said, referring to the starting pitchers who made the Braves a force in the National League for more than a decade.

Once again, in 2004, the Astros met the Braves in the playoffs. Houston hit four home runs to win Game 1 and also took Game 3. Atlanta won Game 2 in 11 innings and erased an early 5–2 Houston lead to win Game 4. This time, with a deciding Game 5 in Atlanta, the Astros finally got past the Braves, winning, 12–3, thanks to a five-RBI game from Carlos Beltran.

Next up were the St. Louis Cardinals, who had won 105 games and were considered by most to be the best team in baseball that season. The Astros lost the first two games in St. Louis, then won the next three at home, including rallying to wipe out a 4–1 St. Louis lead in Game 4 and getting a combined one-hitter from Brandon Backe and Lidge in Game 5. The game was scoreless in the bottom of the ninth when Jeff Kent won it for the Astros with a three-run homer.

"That walkoff homer, my brother and I were there," Brian said. "I don't think we've ever been that excited."

The Astros tied Game 6 in the bottom of the ninth on a Bagwell single but lost in the 12th inning when Jim Edmonds crushed a two-run homer. In Game 7, the Cardinals rallied in the sixth inning and eventually won, 5–2.

Houston fell despite Beltran batting .417 and scoring 12 runs in the seven games. Lance Berkman drove in nine runs.

It was a series that had everything you could ask for—great pitching, dramatic home runs, solid defense. It was overshadowed by what was going on in the American League Championship Series, where the Boston Red Sox rallied from a three-games-to-none deficit to beat the New York Yankees in seven games.

"I remember thinking how great this series is, and no one is going to see it," Brandon said of the Houston–St. Louis matchup.

Dunsmore, who is now a sportswriter, said the loss to the Cardinals was a good example of just how hard it is to win in postseason baseball.

"You do everything right. You get all the pieces on the roster. Carlos Beltran is playing out of his mind, and it just doesn't happen," he said.

The next year the Astros started so badly—19–32—that the Houston Chronicle ran a large picture of a tombstone on the front page of its June 1 sports section. Its inscription was "RIP Astros' season."

The Astros dug out of that early June hole, going 70–41 the rest of the way to make the playoffs. And they added to their revenge on the Braves, winning the divisional series against Atlanta, 3–1. It wasn't as easy as it sounds. In Game 4, the Astros fell behind early, 4–0, and they couldn't get much offense going against Atlanta starter Tim Hudson.

The del Castillo brothers, of course, were there watching as the Braves grabbed the early lead. "I turned to my brother and said, 'Let's have some drinks at the bar, watch the [Houston] Texans' game, then we'll come back and watch the big comeback,'" Brandon said.

Somehow, that's just how it played out. The del Castillo brothers were back in their seats in the bottom of the eighth inning when the Astros, trailing 6–1, got a grand slam from Lance Berkman off reliever Kyle Farnsworth. An inning later, Brad Ausmus, who had hit three homers all year, hit a game-tying shot off Farnsworth. Suddenly, there was a little less interest in the Texans, who would lose their National Football League matchup that day with the Tennessee Titans, 34–20.

The Astros and Braves battled for nine more innings. As the game wore on, Houston even brought in starter Roger Clemens to throw three innings of relief. "That was superhero kind of stuff," Brian said.

In the bottom of the 18th inning, outfielder Chris Burke, who had hit five homers all year, belted one to win the series for the Astros. "That was probably my favorite Astros moment," Brandon said.

"I went to work the next day, and my legs didn't work," said Brian, an IT manager. "I had been standing for hours."

The axiom about the Astros and exciting postseason baseball was holding true. The next series brought that painful Pujols homer followed by Oswalt's masterful "bulldozer" game that gave Houston its first National League pennant.

Nogales, who is a carpenter, remembers watching the Game 6 victory in the National League Championship Series at a bar. When the Astros won, many patrons gathered in a circle and jumped around together. Then

Nogales headed to a nearby store to buy an Astros National League champions T-shirt. By the time he got there, the line was three wide and around the block.

The World Series was a letdown in an odd way. The Astros played four tough, tight games against the Chicago White Sox—and lost all four. Two were decided by one run; the other two, one of which went 14 innings, were decided by two runs.

"We were disappointed, of course," Nogales said. "For three or four days, you walked around going, 'Dammit, couldn't we win one?'"

Shoulder troubles limited Bagwell's role in the World Series, and he soon retired. Biggio followed in 2007, and the Astros began a wicked slide that culminated in 111 losses in 2013. "It was brutal," Brian said.

Dunsmore started covering the team for an SB Nation website in 2011. "I picked a great time to start writing," he said. From 2011 to 2013, the Astros lost 324 games, but he was struck by the cluster of fans who didn't give up.

They would send emails and exchange photos, including posters with the face of an Astros player Photoshopped into the action. One of Dunsmore's favorites was Arnold Schwarzenegger's *Terminator* becoming pitcher Lucas Harrell as the Walk-i-nator. Harrell allowed 88 walks in 2013 to lead the major leagues.

"We were on the same wavelength that no matter what the result is, we're going to watch our Astros. They were a joke, but they were our joke," he said.

A batch of young, talented players, including George Springer, Jose Altuve, Dallas Keuchel, Lance McCullers and Carlos Correa, helped push the team back into contention in 2015 in the American League. (The Astros switched leagues in 2012 so that each league would have an equal number of teams.)

The Astros qualified for the one-game, wild-card playoff matchup, which saw them travel to New York to face the Yankees. Behind six masterful innings from Keuchel, the Astros won, 3–0. In the next round, the Astros led two games to one over the Kansas City Royals and were ahead, 6–2, at home heading to the eighth inning. They were six outs from advancing to the next round when the Royals exploded for five runs in the eighth and two more in the ninth. The series shifted to Kansas City, where the Royals wrapped up the series, winning 7–2.

"While it was kind of a downer, it wasn't devastating," Brandon said of the loss to the Royals, who went on to win the World Series. "Baseball happens. We've got to grow from that and learn."

Making the playoffs was a huge step for a team that had lost 111 games two seasons earlier. "I'm loving it," said Brandon of the rebounding Astros. "This is what we live for as fans."

It's a fitting reward for a fan base that has survived a track filled with hurdles: the Astros' gaudy rainbow uniforms worn from the mid–1970s to mid–1980s; the 2005 start that generated a tombstone on the newspaper's sports section cover; the angst of a classic intrastate rivalry—Houston vs. Dallas. "I was proud that we were the first Texas team to make the World Series," Brandon said. The fans have savored dramatic postseason, extra-inning victories, and suffered through agonizing postseason, extra-inning losses.

Through it all the del Castillo family was there. Brianna has fond memories of all five of them piling into the car for their regular trips to see the Astros.

"The game started even before we got there," she said. "My brothers were spouting statistics the whole way. They are the biggest Astros nerds I've ever met in my life. I love that about them."

The brothers show their love for the 'Stros and all things baseball with a series of YouTube videos under the name HouBaseBald, a tribute to their shaved heads. The two talk about baseball issues of the day— those that involve the Astros as well as other topics that don't. The room where they film is a shrine to their team. The camera angle shows a framed Biggio jersey, a Bagwell portrait, bobbleheads and an Astros coffee mug with the team's shooting star logo.

Brianna has left the Houston area to study traditional Chinese medicine in California, but she hasn't lost her love of the baseball team of her youth.

"The Astros have been the background of our whole lives," she said. "For me, the Astros are a touchstone with how I relate to my family and to Houston."

She and other fans were rewarded in 2015 when they got to see Biggio become the first Astro inducted into the National Baseball Hall of Fame. "The Biggio induction was a huge victory for us," Brian said. It is that kind of victory that keeps Brian and others pulling for the Astros.

"This is part of me," he said. "I always felt that people who switched teams are cowards. I took offense with people who said, 'I'm a Yankees' fan now,' or 'LeBron [James] went to Miami, so I'm a Heat fan.' It's part of your personality to be a diehard for your hometown team.

"I'm a proud Houstonian. I love this city. I love everything that comes with it."

Those aren't empty words for Brian. He still has an Astros T-shirt that was once his father's. It includes the rainbow colors of those famous Astros uniforms and reads "Western Division 1986 champs."

"I wore that to every big game we had," he said. "I stopped wearing it when it stopped working."

But, like the true Astros fan he is, he hasn't given up. He has saved the shirt.

"It's tucked away for my kids to have someday."

Cleveland Rocks

The Cleveland Browns, etc.

Go ahead and make snarky jokes about the past failings of the Cleveland Browns if you'd like. But remember this if you ever make light of the team's supporters. Despite zero championships since 1964, there's an awful lot of worldwide love for this franchise.

The official fan club of the team, Browns Backers Worldwide, has 355 chapters in 14 countries. Around the world, Browns fans cheer for a franchise that had two of the most painful playoff losses in back-to-back seasons. They root for a squad that went two and a half decades with only a few winning seasons, and, perhaps most amazingly of all, they holler and scream after a team abandoned the city and left it football-less for three long, lonely seasons.

There are the Browns Backers of Scandinavia in Oslo, Norway, and the Taipei Browns Backers in Taiwan, not to mention the Royal Perth Browns Backers of Western Australia. On this Sunday, the location is a bit less exotic—the Glory Days Grill in Towson, Maryland, meeting place for the Baltimore Browns Backers, Chapter 51.

An enclosed patio at Glory Days is set aside for Browns fans. A poster outside reads: "From behind enemy lines—the Baltimore Browns Backers." It is illustrated with the image of Cleveland team mascot Brownie the Elf with his hand around the neck of a Raven, the mascot of Baltimore's football team.

Inside, the color scheme for the party is, of course, brown and orange, with Browns posters decking the walls. Two televisions are tuned into the pregame show as Cleveland prepares for a home game against Peyton Manning and the Denver Broncos.

Bill Eaton is president of this local chapter of Browns diehards. He's a Baltimore-area native who grew up a fan of the Baltimore Colts, a team that was revered for its years of success and its list of great players, including quarterback Johnny Unitas, running back Lenny Moore and offensive lineman Jim Parker.

But, in the middle of the night in March 1984, the Colts bolted town and moved to Indianapolis. It was a move that broke the hearts of Colts fans throughout the region.

Eaton, a utility company worker, left town a few years later, moving to Akron, Ohio, in 1989. "I became a Browns fan in 30 days," he said. He was struck by the devotion of the team's followers. "Their fans have always supported them for all these years. Browns fans show up every week. It's sellout after sellout." When Eaton returned to the Baltimore area in 2001, he stuck with the Browns, snubbing the Ravens, the team that moved from Cleveland and replaced the Colts in 1996.

The Browns crowd at the restaurant is a little slow in arriving for the weekly event painstakingly put together by Eaton and his fellow club officers, but soon after kickoff the patio area is packed. The audience ranges from children to gray-haired, longtime Browns backers. The brown-and-orange color scheme is enhanced by Browns hats, T-shirts and sweatshirts. There are jerseys that range from the old—Bernie Kosar (19) and Jim Brown (32)—to the more recent—Isaiah Crowell (34) and Paul Kruger (99). Some women sport orange ribbons in their hair. One wears eye black with a Browns accent. There are "We Are Cleveland" pins.

Kosar seems to be a particular favorite. He is an Ohio guy who was a college star with the Miami Hurricanes before the Browns selected him in the first round of the National Football League draft in 1984.

Steve Bochenek wears a Kosar jersey he's had since high school. Bruce Rurka recalls how Kosar was a favorite for him and his father when they would watch Browns games together. "Those are some of my fondest memories of my dad," he said.

Eaton tells anyone who makes a comment about the Browns' lack of success that the franchise has won eight championships. He's right on target, although seven of those championships were before 1956, long before most in the room were born.

The Browns were the scourge of the All-America Football Conference, a league that challenged the NFL but existed for just four seasons, from 1946 to 1949. The Browns, led by quarterback Otto Graham, won the championship all four years. The conference's final title game was against the San Francisco 49ers, and the Browns won, 21–7, getting a 68-yard touchdown run from Marion Motley.

When the All-America Football Conference folded, three teams from the league—the Browns, 49ers and Baltimore Colts—joined the NFL in

1950. The switch to the more established league did nothing to slow the Browns. In their first NFL season, they again won the championship, beating the Los Angeles Rams on Christmas Eve in Cleveland's Municipal Stadium. The Browns trailed, 28–20, heading into the fourth quarter but won, 30–28, thanks to a Graham touchdown pass to Rex Bumgardner and a 16-yard field goal by Lou Groza.

The Browns made it to the championship game in 1951, '52 and '53 but lost all of them. They then won the next two titles, including a 56–10 thrashing of the Detroit Lions in 1954, a game in which Graham threw for three touchdowns and ran for three more.

Graham retired after the 1955 season with a remarkable legacy. He played in the championship game in every one of his 10 professional seasons, winning seven titles.

The Browns got one more taste of a championship, beating the Colts, 27–0, on December 27, 1964. Cleveland's Jim Brown, one of the most rugged running backs in NFL history, was the star of the team, rushing for 1,446 yards that season. But in the title game, the offensive hero was wide receiver Gary Collins, who scored all three touchdowns on passes from Frank Ryan. The defense limited the great Unitas to 95 yards passing, and the Colts' offense gained a meager 181 yards.

That's been it for the Browns. In fact, that was it for all Cleveland teams until the Cavaliers beat the Golden State Warriors in 2016 for the NBA title. It ended a streak of 52 years without a championship for the city.

In a 2014 Associated Press story, Brown, the great former Cleveland running back, addressed the long non-winning spell. "It's hard to believe," he said. "Because when you look back at 50 years, something's wrong because somebody should've figured out something.... We've got money and we've got a new building and we've got green grass and we can draft players, and we can't do any better than that?"

The long drought is a fact that doesn't go unnoticed in this crowd.

"If you're a Cleveland team, I'm a fan," said Sarah Twiggs. "I just torture myself."

Doug Fisher said, "Maybe we appreciate it more because we've been waiting so long. You wonder how it will be when they actually win. All the Cleveland teams seem to be cursed."

Despite the frustrations, Browns fans are devoted. "The loyalty and passion the city and the fans have, it's hard to explain, but it's contagious," Twiggs said.

On this day, these fans are happy to be here. Eaton mans a bullhorn with a siren that gets blasted when the Browns make a big play. He makes announcements about raffles and charity donations. On days when Cleveland wins, the Browns Backers celebrate with a conga line through the main area of the restaurant, kicking and strutting through a room filled with Ravens fans.

The primary server for the room gets into the spirit, wearing a Browns jersey; it's a number 10 with "Quinn" on the back. That would be 2007 first-round pick Brady Quinn, who had a lackluster NFL career in Cleveland and points beyond. No one seems to mind the reminder of another failed draft pick as the server jokes along with the crowd and gets plenty of smiles in return.

These fans also are happy to share their stories. Twiggs grew up in a Browns-loving household in Zanesville, Ohio, about two and a half hours south of Cleveland. Her father, Howard, is from Cleveland and has always cheered for the Browns. So have her mom, Aimee, and sister Michele.

"You can count our dog, too. Our dog's a Browns fan," Twiggs said. She recently moved to the Baltimore area after landing a job as assistant commissioner of the Landmark Conference, a group of nine Division III schools, including nearby Goucher College. When she found she had gotten the job and would be moving, she had her priorities straight. "Forget the apartment. Is there a Browns Backers Club? That's one of the first things I looked up," she said.

Fisher was born and raised in Cleveland until he spent his teenage years in Columbus. He was born the year before the Browns won their last title in 1964. "I was alive for the championship," he boasted. He moved to Maryland in 1986, and his support for the Cleveland teams has not wavered.

Patrick Sloat grew up in Philadelphia as an Eagles follower. But, as a boy, he attended an Eagles-Browns game and went looking for autographs afterward. A Philadelphia player blew him off, but Cleveland's Kosar signed for him.

"The seeds were planted there," he said. While he still keeps an eye on the Eagles, he has grown to love the Browns. "The fan base always treated me right. Win, lose or draw—and especially through the heart-breaking losses—they are there," he said.

Bochenek is a Baltimore-area native who was 14 when the Colts left town. He never forgave that franchise and never got interested in the Ravens. Instead, he latched onto the Browns, a team that had first caught his attention in 1980, the season of the "Kardiac Kids." That 1980 Browns team, which had eight of its games decided by a field goal or less, was led by Brian Sipe, who threw 30 touchdown passes and was named the league's most valuable player.

The Kardiac Kids' season ended in early January with a playoff loss to the Oakland Raiders. Playing in Cleveland's Municipal Stadium, the frigid air was enhanced by winds topping 20 miles per hour. The NFL's website lists the game temperature at 5 below, which makes it the fifth coldest game in league history.

The frozen air and the wind limited both offenses. Trailing, 14–12, in the final minute, the Browns drove to Oakland's 13-yard line, close enough to kick a go-ahead field goal. Instead of kicking, the Browns ran one more play to try to score a touchdown, and Sipe's pass intended for Ozzie Newsome was intercepted by Mike Davis. For Browns fans, the play call, "Red Right 88," is one of those phrases you don't ever mention. It's like taunting Boston Red Sox fans with the name Bill Buckner or Chicago Cubs fans with references to billy goats.

It was a sad end to a marvelous season for Sipe. He was 13 of 40, and that last-second interception was his third of the day. It also was the start of a decade and a half of painful moments for Browns backers.

There was "The Drive." After the Browns beat the New York Jets in double overtime in a first-round game, all that good karma turned bad the next week in the American Football Conference championship, held January 11, 1987. Cleveland led the Denver Broncos, 20–13, with 5:43 left. Broncos quarterback John Elway then took over. He led a 98-yard drive that ended with a 5-yard touchdown pass to Mark Jackson with 37 seconds left. In overtime, the Broncos won on a 33-yard field goal by Rich Karlis.

"It was hard, but it was acceptable," Bochenek said of the Elway drive. "They beat us down the field."

The next year, there was "The Fumble." The Broncos and Browns met again in the AFC title game, and Elway and the Broncos' offense shot out to a 21–3 halftime lead. Kosar, who would end the day throwing for 356 yards, got the Browns back in the game in the second half. His fourth-quarter pass to Webster Slaughter tied the score at 31.

Elway came right back with a scoring drive that ended with a 20-yard touchdown pass to Sammy Winder. The Browns responded quickly, driving down the field. With the ball on the 8-yard line and a little over a minute left, Kosar handed off to Earnest Byner, who cut to the left. Byner had been superb all day, rushing for 67 yards, catching seven passes for another 120 yards and scoring two touchdowns. So, it was a cruel choice of the football gods to put Byner in the late spotlight in the worst possible way—he fumbled just short of the goal line. The Broncos recovered, and the Browns' game-tying drive was over, as was the game and their season.

"The fumble was brutal. We wouldn't have been back in the game except for him," Bochenek said of Byner.

Of "The Drive," Rurka said, "I remember my dad and I sitting on the couch. My dad grabbed a pillow and threw it down on the ground. He wasn't a real emotional guy, but you could see it took the wind out of us. When 'The Fumble' happened, he took that same pillow and threw it at the television."

Worst of all for Browns fans, there was the move. In November 1995, team ownership, lured by a sweet deal involving a new stadium, announced it was abandoning Cleveland for Baltimore. Left behind were the memories of Jim Brown bowling over linebackers, Gary Collins catching those touchdown passes from Frank Ryan, and the Dawg Pound, that rowdy bunch of Browns fans camped out in the end zone for home games, barking after every Cleveland touchdown.

"It was such a huge thing for me and my dad," Rurka said of their love of the Browns. "It was like they took a part of us away."

Twiggs had a similar reaction. She knew the Browns' move was the end of a family tradition—gathering around the television set on Sunday to watch the team play. "I was young. I was upset because my dad was upset and my mom was upset."

Eaton said of the move, "It's hard to put into words; disheartening is the best."

Football returned in 1999 when the city was awarded an expansion team, one that was allowed to keep the Browns nickname as well as the uniform colors, team records and history.

"It was great," Twiggs said. "We could have that tradition back. Cleveland is a football city. It was severely missed."

These Maryland-based Browns fans have little interest in the Ravens, the current team in their home state. After all, Baltimore did take their original Browns, something that is hard to forgive. Plus, the Ravens have managed to win two more Super Bowls than the Browns. After one of those Ravens' titles, Bochenek's daughter asked whether he would take her to the parade to honor the new champions. "I told her I'd rather burn the house down. I told her if she could name five Ravens, I'd take her. Thank goodness, she couldn't do it."

The Browns can be the target of cruel comments, thanks to few winning seasons since 1999. Their city also receives plenty of slings and arrows. There are images of snowy winters and the Cuyahoga River catching on fire. And there are the references to the "Mistake by the Lake," a phrase that's been directed both at the Browns' old home, Municipal Stadium, and the entire city.

But today's Cleveland has a downtown bursting with energy. There are spacious apartments overlooking Lake Erie, sparkling sports arenas and the Rock and Roll Hall of Fame.

And Cleveland fans have maintained a sense of humor through it all. More than once a photographer has captured the image of a Browns fan holding a sign with this message: "Hey Baltimore, can you take this team, too?"

There is the video of Cleveland comedian Mike Polk, Jr., standing in front of the Browns' stadium and ranting about the team's inability to be any good. He ends his outburst shouting at the stadium, "You are a factory of sadness," and then turns and walks away, spouting the words that Browns fans have uttered for ages: "I'll see you Sunday."

There was a social media posting late in the abysmal 2015 season that addressed the Browns' ongoing, futile efforts to find a winning combination. The posting included a picture of Ron Burgundy, Will Ferrell's pompous anchorman, delivering the breaking news: "Browns fire coaches, GM, players, fans, relatives related to Browns, anyone wearing Brown, the color Brown and Charlie Brown."

The folks gathered at the Glory Days Grill aren't dwelling on any negativity, although you can't entirely shake that feeling in a room filled with brown and orange.

"It's the passion we all share," Twiggs said. "And to wallow in the misery we sometimes have; it's nice to do that in a group."

Throughout the game, the crowd is lively. As you'd expect, there is some complaining about the officials' calls and the coach's play calling. Some fans gripe about past personnel moves made by the Browns. After all, this is the team that in 2012 used the third pick in the draft on Trent Richardson, a running back from the University of Alabama who had a decent rookie season but did little else in Cleveland. In that same draft, the Browns used the 22nd overall pick to grab Brandon Weeden, a then–28-year-old quarterback out of Oklahoma State who quickly played his way to backup status.

"Kevin Costner is not our general manager," Sloat said, a clever reference to the 2014 movie *Draft Day*, in which Costner plays a crafty Browns executive who pulls off the mother of all trades on NFL draft day.

The crowd gathered on the patio erupts when linebacker Karlos Dansby intercepts a Peyton Manning pass just 3 minutes into the game.

Bruce Rurka's passion for the Cleveland Browns has inspired his wife, Jessica, and their daughter, Kiersten (photograph by Bruce Rurka).

There are a few fearful shouts and then silence when Denver cornerback Aqib Talib picks off a Josh McCown pass and returns it 63 yards for a touchdown. There's a buzz of satisfaction when the Browns' defense stiffens and forces a long field-goal try at the end of the first half. The kick misses, and the Broncos' lead at the break is 10–0.

Early in the third quarter, the loudest cheers of the day so far fill the enclosed patio when McCown hits tight end Gary Barnidge with an 11-yard touchdown pass. Barnidge scores again in the fourth quarter, and soon after Dansby returns his second interception of the day for a touchdown.

Sadly, though, there will be no conga line on this day. The Browns tie the game late on a Travis Coons field goal, but in overtime the Broncos get a field goal from Brandon McManus to prevail, 26–23.

It's pain those on the patio have all felt before. "You have to have a strong heart to be a Browns fan," Fisher said.

Rurka has been watching the action with his wife, Jessica, and young daughter Kiersten. He once bought Jessica a Browns T-shirt that reads, "I married into this." For Kiersten, who has caught the Browns fever, Rurka thinks back to watching a difficult Browns loss with his dad. "I remember him turning to me and saying, 'It's tough to be a Browns fan.' I tell the

Just like her father and grandfather, Kiersten Rurka is a Cleveland Browns backer (courtesy Bruce Rurka).

same thing to her. If you're going to be a Browns fan, it's tough. She gets harassed about it at school, but she's a good sport about it." Kiersten is enjoying it, being part of the circle of life as she cheers on the Browns team that her father loves and for which her grandfather once cheered.

This is all poignant for Rurka, whose father died in 2009 from complications of Alzheimer's disease. "Being a Browns fan is a part of him I still have."

Emerald City Ennui

The Seattle Mariners

When the City Council of Clyde Hill, Washington, decided to honor City Administrator Mitch Wasserman in 2010 for his 20 years of service, it didn't want to give him just another plaque to hang on his wall. Instead, it got the perfect gift for the Seattle Mariners–loving official—a framed photograph of Ken Griffey, Jr., sliding home with the winning run to beat the New York Yankees in a 1995 American League Division Series.

It's a lasting image in baseball history—one of the game's great players scoring a series-winning run, moments before he is mobbed by his teammates as a Kingdome stuffed with fans erupts in celebration.

"Every day I look at that and I remember," Wasserman said. For him and all Mariners fans old enough to remember, the Griffey slide home is *the* moment. It gave the Mariners a win in the franchise's first postseason appearance—knocking off the always-powerful Yankees, no less. It's a moment Mariners fans dream of seeing again as they root for one of only two teams that has never played in the World Series.

Baseball's birth in Seattle was a laborious one. The city was awarded an expansion team that began play in 1969 and was named the Pilots. There was some talent—Tommy Harper stole 73 bases in that first season and Don Mincher slammed 25 home runs—but the roster was a mediocre mix of young and old that finished the season 64–98. It was a colorful crew, though, entertaining enough to be at the heart of pitcher Jim Bouton's classic baseball book, *Ball Four*.

But plagued by money problems and poor attendance—slightly more than 8,300 a game in tiny Sick's Stadium—the team bolted Seattle after one year for Milwaukee.

John Marchione, the mayor of Redmond, Washington, was just a young boy when the Pilots left town. "I was told they were sold to a used car salesman and moved to Milwaukee. It was said with a loathing in the voice."

It took eight years before another expansion team arrived in Seattle. Dan Weedin recalls the excitement of knowing the city was getting another team. He submitted his entry—the Aces—in a contest to name the new squad. "I remember when they announced it would be the Mariners. As a 12-year-old boy I thought, 'What a dumb name.' Now I think it's a cool name."

He listened to the first Mariners game on the radio. He can recall the Seattle starting pitcher—39-year-old Diego Segui, who would finish the season with a 0–7 record. Weedin also can remember the final score: a 7–0 win for the California Angels.

There were plenty more games like that in the first few seasons for the Mariners, who seemed to be trying to out-Pilot the Pilots. In its first two years, the team lost 98 and 104 games. "You get an expansion team and you realize it isn't easy to win," Weedin said.

Marchione was on board with the Mariners from the start. He and his three younger brothers attended the team's public workout held in the Kingdome the day before the Mariners' first game. He remembers his youthful view of the baseball world during those first few seasons of Mariners futility: "They'd win two in a row, and I'd look and see they were 18 games out [of first place]. I'd say, 'How come we're that far out?' Before that, we'd lost 14 of 16."

As the 1980s arrived, the Mariners got a little better, but not much. "My memory was they were always on the verge of turning the corner—that was probably me more than the team," Marchione said.

Terry Moreman, executive director of the Mercer Island Chamber of Commerce, arrived in Seattle about the same time as the Mariners. She remembers the struggles of those early years well.

"It's not like it's hard to stick with them, but you just get discouraged. Those guys don't go out there to play badly," she said. The losing seasons were a transition for her because she had lived in Los Angeles, witnessing the great Dodgers teams of the late 1950s and the '60s.

There were other differences. She watched as the Mariners blew through nine managers or interim managers in the 1980s. The Dodgers had one manager—Walter Alston—for 23 seasons (1954 to 1976). Those nine Mariners managers included Maury Wills, whom she had watched play shortstop for the Dodgers, and Rene Lachemann, with whom she went to high school in Los Angeles.

And, after having watched the Dodgers play in sunny Chavez Ravine, she was stunned when she and her family went to their first Mariners game at the Kingdome. "We went into this concrete tomb. There were about

6,000 people there. I said, 'I don't think I can do that again.' But we did go back. We went back a lot of times." Soon, her allegiance shifted from the Dodgers to the Mariners.

Despite all the losing seasons, there were some bright spots in the 1980s, including Alvin Davis, who was an all-star in his rookie season and drove in 100 or more runs two times. Phil Bradley and Jim Presley added some thump in the lineup, and pitcher Mark Langston was a rising star.

But the Mariners did like to strike out. They led the American League in that category in 1985 and '86 and famously were the victims when Boston Red Sox right-hander Roger Clemens tied the record for most strikeouts in a game (20) on April 29, 1986.

During the '80s, the good moments—Gaylord Perry winning his 300th game in 1982; the Mariners almost getting to .500 in 1987—were overshadowed by the bad, including a 102-loss season in 1983 and an entire decade without a winning record.

Fans also found frustration in other areas. Weedin recalls the trade of outfielder Dave Henderson, who was a former No. 1 draft pick of the Mariners and had shown some potential in his first several seasons. He was dealt along with shortstop Spike Owen in August 1986 to the Red Sox for shortstop Rey Quinones, a hot prospect, and several players to be named later.

"I can't remember to take the trash out, but I remember the Rey Quinones trade," Weedin said. Quinones had two average seasons in Seattle before he was dealt to the Pittsburgh Pirates, and the three players to be named later didn't add much to the Mariners' win total. Meanwhile, Owen and Henderson helped bring the Red Sox within a strike of the championship in 1986, and Henderson went on to win a championship and become an all-star with the Oakland A's.

The late '80s did have two golden moments for the Mariners. Thanks to their 67–95 record in 1986, the Mariners had the first pick in the 1987 baseball draft. Most analysts expected they would select Griffey, a high school star in Cincinnati. Some fans weren't quite so sure.

"We all disliked the [Mariners] owner, George Argyros, so we were all afraid he was going to blow it," Marchione said. The Mariners didn't blow it. "It seemed like there was a cheer in the city when they drafted Griffey," Marchione said.

Then, in May 1989, the Mariners took a gamble, trading their best pitcher, Langston, to the Montreal Expos in a deal that landed Randy Johnson. The 6-foot, 10-inch Johnson, then 25, could throw as hard as anyone in the game, but at that point he had won just three major-league games.

Members of the Wasserman family pose with fellow Seattle fan Mariner Moose. With the mascot (left to right) are Barb, Liz, who is holding daughter Jordyn, Mitch and Rob, who is holding son Logan (courtesy Mitch Wasserman).

At 19, Griffey made it to the big leagues in 1989. By his second season, he was selected to the all-star team, an honor he would receive 12 more times in his career.

A year after Griffey came to the Mariners, Wasserman moved to the Seattle area. He had grown up in Chicago as a fan of the White Sox, but he soon would be switching allegiance, along with his young sons, Rob and Scott, to the Mariners.

"We grew as fans simultaneous to Griffey growing as a player," Wasserman said. "It happened like wildfire. You could see the genuine spark he provided."

In the 1991 season, Griffey batted .327 with 22 home runs and 100 runs batted in. Johnson won 13 games and struck out 228 hitters in 201⅓ innings. For the Mariners, those contributions helped the team to an 83–79 record, the franchise's first winning season in its 15th year of existence. "It was a very big deal that we won Game number 82," Weedin said.

The Wassermans show their support for Seattle pitcher Felix Hernandez at a recent game. Left to right are Rob, Mitch, Barb and Scott (courtesy Mitch Wasserman).

It took another four seasons before the franchise reached another milestone, making the playoffs for the first time in 1995. It took some doing.

Griffey fractured his wrist while making a spectacular catch in a late May victory over the Baltimore Orioles. Robert Bean is too young to remember much of the 1995 season, but he does recall he was at that game with his parents. They left early and heard the news of the Griffey injury on the radio during their drive home. "I cannot leave a game early now. I think it's because of that," Bean said.

On August 20, the Mariners were 53–53, languishing in third place, 12½ games behind the first-place California Angels. The Angels fell apart, losing 14 of their next 16 and soon followed that with a nine-game losing streak in mid–September. The second-place Texas Rangers also faltered, losing nine of 10 from late August into early September.

The Mariners, led by manager Lou Piniella, took full advantage, going 19–8 in September, including a 14–2 stretch that started with a 4–1 win over the Kansas City Royals on September 8. During the late-season push, Mariners outfielder Jay Buhner made a comment that the team wasn't

Mitch Wasserman and his granddaughter, Jordyn, take to the field during a Fan-fest event at Seattle's Safeco Field (photograph by Barb Wasserman).

playing for the wild card, a playoff position given to the league's second-place team with the best record. The Mariners wanted to win the division, Buhner said. "It lit their fire," Wasserman said. "It lit the feelings of the fans as well."

It was a finish—and a season—filled with improbable comebacks and a Kingdome full of energy. "Refuse to lose" became the team's—and the city's—mantra.

Seattle first baseman Tino Martinez, who would go on to win four championships with the New York Yankees, told the *Seattle Times* in 2005, "That was just the greatest run I've ever been a part of, as far as winning every day when it counted."

The Mariners and Angels finished tied at 78–66 in a season shortened by a labor dispute, with the Rangers third, four games back. Those records were not good enough for the American League wild-card spot, so the Mariners and Angels met on Monday, October 2, at Seattle's Kingdome to decide the American League West. The winner would go to the playoffs; the loser would go home.

The one-game showdown matched the two starting pitchers once traded for each other—Johnson and Langston. Johnson was superb, giving up three hits and one run while striking out 12. Langston pitched well for six innings, but the Mariners got to him in the seventh inning and then pounded the Angels' bullpen. It all added up to a 9–1 Seattle victory and the team's first trip to the postseason.

"It's hard to put into words how exciting that time was," Weedin said. Marchione recalls driving home one night during one of those late-season 1995 games: "There wasn't a soul on the street. You could hear the game blaring from the bars. You could have shot a cannon off in downtown Seattle and not hit anyone."

After a season of improbable wins and wild comebacks, the Mariners somehow topped it in their playoff series against the Yankees.

The best-of-five series started with two games in New York. The Yankees won Game 1, 9–6, and Game 2, 7–5, on Jim Leyritz's two-run homer in the 15th inning. The winning pitcher in that game was a Yankees rookie reliever named Mariano Rivera.

In Game 3, Johnson struck out 10 in seven innings and Tino Martinez homered and drove in three runs as the Mariners cruised to a 7–4 victory.

If Game 3 was a cruise, Game 4 was an ocean journey in a rowboat with swirling seas pounding from all directions. The Yankees jumped to a 5–0 lead in the top of the third inning, looking as if they would be the team cruising into the American League Championship Series. But the Mariners answered with four runs in the third inning, powered by a three-run homer from their superlative designated hitter, Edgar Martinez.

Seattle got a run in the fifth and a Griffey home run in the sixth to take a 6–5 lead, but the Yankees tied the game in the top of the eighth when Randy Velarde scored on a Norm Charlton wild pitch.

The Mariners started the eighth with a walk, a single and a hit batter, loading the bases for Edgar Martinez. On a 2–2 count, Martinez launched John Wetteland's pitch over the center-field fence, giving the Mariners a 10–6 lead. Buhner came up two batters later and homered off Steve Howe. The Yankees scored two in the ninth and brought the tying run to the plate, but the Mariners held on for an 11–8 win, forcing a decisive Game 5 the next afternoon in Seattle.

In Game 5, a two-run homer by Paul O'Neill and a two-run double from Don Mattingly helped the Yankees build a 4–2 lead heading into the eighth inning. Once again, the Mariners found a way to rally, tying the score in the eighth inning on a Griffey solo home run and a bases-loaded walk to Doug Strange. Ball four to Strange was the 147th—and last—pitch of the day by Yankees starter David Cone.

The game moved to extra innings, and the Yankees grabbed a 5–4 lead in the top of the 11th on a Velarde single off Johnson, pitching his second inning in a rare relief appearance.

Three outs from their season being over, the Mariners started the bottom of the 11th against Jack McDowell, another starter pitching in relief, with back-to-back singles by Joey Cora and Griffey.

That brought up Edgar Martinez, who ripped the second pitch he saw from McDowell into left field. While leftfielder Gerald Williams sprinted to get the ball as it bounced up against the wall, Cora scored easily and Griffey raced around third base.

"I remember thinking, 'He's going to score,'" Weedin said. "Maybe it was the Junior mystique. He was not going to be thrown out. I've never seen him move like that."

Marchione had seats in left field for that game. On the Martinez hit, he couldn't see the ball in the left-field corner, but he could see Griffey flying around the bases. "He rounded third, and I thought, 'Oh my gosh, he's going to score.'"

Williams had played the ball well in left field and hit the cutoff man with his throw, but the relay throw home never had a chance. Griffey slid across the plate and soon disappeared in a pile of Mariners. The first player who jumped on him was the on-deck hitter, Seattle's 20-year-old shortstop, Alex Rodriguez.

Marchione had clapped so much and so hard during that game that his wedding ring had left a welt on his right hand. He had to visit a doctor to relieve the pressure.

"Every one of those games was an electric moment with Edgar hitting the grand slam and coming back in each game. It was surreal," Wasserman said. He recalls attending those games with his sons. "After the games, you were friends with 45,000 people," he said. People stuck in their cars in the parking lot honked their horns and shared the joy.

Of his sons, Wasserman said, "They couldn't wait to get to the ball-park the next day to see it happen again. Sure enough, it did happen again."

Seattle's offense pounded New York pitching in the series. Griffey batted .391 with five home runs. Tino Martinez hit .409; Buhner batted .458. None, however, could match the performance of Edgar Martinez, who hit .571 with 10 RBI.

The American League Championship Series wasn't quite as much fun. A strong Cleveland Indians team beat the Mariners in six games. "We were sad because we thought we were a team of destiny," Weedin said. "People thought this is the new 'it' team."

Still, the fond memories of 1995 remained. When the Mariners built Safeco Field, which opened in July 1999 to replace the Kingdome, the team offered fans a chance to buy bricks to be installed at the park.

Wasserman purchased a brick that is part of the concourse floor in left field at Safeco. It reads, "Never forget 1995 / The Wassermans."

When the Wasserman family goes to Safeco Field, it pays tribute to the family brick in the left-field concourse. "I'm glad I did that," Mitch Wasserman says of the brick. "It's worth a lot more than $25" (courtesy Mitch Wasserman).

"Every time we go, we pay homage to our brick. And we reminisce about that season," he said. They sprinkle a little water on the brick and clean it off, and "we all have to step on it."

His wife, Barb, and his two sons have been part of the ceremony. Now, the tribute also includes the Wassermans' two young grandchildren. "The deep-seated feeling you get from that—passing that love to the next generation—is priceless," he said. "I'm glad I did that," he said of the brick purchase. "It's worth a lot more than $25."

As often happens in sports, the joy of a 1995 can be followed with some pain. After making the playoffs again in 1997, Seattle struggled the next season. On July 31, 1998, the Mariners, tied for last place, traded Johnson to a contending team, the Houston Astros, for pitchers Freddy Garcia and John Halama and infielder Carlos Guillen.

Following the 1999 season, Griffey, the foundation of the Mariners for a decade, said he wanted to be traded, and the Mariners dealt him to the Cincinnati Reds in February 2000 for four players, including outfielder Mike Cameron and pitcher Brett Tomko. "I felt betrayed," Wasserman said.

And, as also often happens in sports, the down times are followed by a revival. In 2000, the Mariners were without Griffey and Johnson, but they were playing their first full season in sparkling new Safeco Field. Unlike the Kingdome, it offered a view of the downtown skyline and the blue sky above. On days when rain pelted the Emerald City, a retractable roof kept fans dry.

"I've been to a lot of baseball stadiums. It's one of the best, if not the best," Moreman said.

The Mariners finished the 2000 season 91–71 and got to the American League Championship Series again before falling to the Yankees in six games.

After the 2000 season, Rodriguez also left. The young shortstop who had been the first to hug Griffey after his series-winning slide in 1995 had blossomed into one of the game's best players. He had become a free agent, and he cashed in, signing the biggest deal baseball had ever seen at that point—10 years, $252 million—with the Texas Rangers.

Despite all the stars' departures, everything worked for the Mariners in 2001. Garcia, acquired in the Johnson trade, went 18–6. The ageless Jamie Moyer, 38 at the time but still nine seasons from the end of his career, won 20 games. Centerfielder Cameron, acquired in the Griffey trade, had the best season of his career, belting 25 homers and driving in 110 runs. So did second basemen Bret Boone, who hit 37 home runs and drove in 141.

There were radio contests to predict when the Mariners would win their 100th game. That 100th victory came on September 5, and the Mariners would tie a major-league record with 116 wins. They edged Cleveland in the American League Division Series, but the Yankees easily handled the Mariners in the championship series, winning in five games.

The Mariners dropped the first two games at home, but then went into New York and won Game 3, 14–3, with Boone driving in five runs. When Game 4 went to the ninth inning tied, 1–1, there seemed to be hope for the Mariners. That was crushed when New York second baseman Alfonso Soriano hit a game-winning, two-run homer in the ninth.

Bean wasn't yet a teenager, but he remembers that moment well: "Alfonso Freakin' Soriano. It was heartbreaking."

"That was a huge disappointment," said Weedin, who is a business consultant and author. "I think we could have lived with a World Series loss. But to lose, 4–1, to the Yankees in the American League Championship Series was a low point."

It also marked the start of a long dry spell as the Mariners failed to make the playoffs again throughout the first decade and a half of the 21st century. They had matching 101-loss seasons in 2008 and 2010. "It's not easy to get to the playoffs," Wasserman said. "But, for goodness' sake, it shouldn't be this hard."

The Mariners were favorites to win the American League West in 2015. They finished the season 76–86, solidly in fourth place.

"Growing up in Seattle, we don't win a lot," said Bean, a bartender in the city. "We don't expect to win. With all the hype [in 2015], I appreciated it, but it didn't feel right."

Seattle saw its SuperSonics win a National Basketball Association title in 1979, but the team left the city behind when it moved to Oklahoma City in 2008. The beloved Seahawks won the Super Bowl in 2014. "I went to the parade," Weedin said. "You can't put into words how many people were there. It was the biggest celebration this region has seen in my lifetime."

But Mariners fans have to keep waiting for their time of glory. While they wait, they have plenty of great moments and memories to keep them cheering. They've embraced the team slogans, from "Refuse to Lose" to "Two outs, so what?"

"It's those memories," Weedin said. "We may not have made the World Series, but I've watched Hall of Famers. I've seen epic games." Like other Mariners fans, Weedin was thrilled when Griffey was elected to baseball's Hall of Fame in 2016. He is the first player in the hall to have a

Mariners cap on his plaque. (Johnson, inducted in 2015, played for six teams in his career and has an Arizona Diamondbacks hat on his plaque.)

Moreman is the kind of fan who always buys a program so she can keep score at the game. She brings her radio outside to listen to the Mariners when she's doing yard work on a summer afternoon. She once attended a 19-inning game and stayed for every pitch.

"The one thing about baseball is every spring you have a clean slate," she said. "Hope springs eternal. I say that every year so one of these days, I'll be right. There are times—like when Lou Piniella was here—that it was really fun. Those kind of things keep you going, even when you're not winning. Then you have a winning season or two and you think, 'OK, this is it. We're on our way.'"

Marchione remembers his son Andrew once announcing in the 1990s that he wanted to change his name. "I want it to be Martinez," he said. "That's a baseball name." Marchione and his wife, Debbie, reacted quickly. "We introduced him to the concept of Joe DiMaggio" as well as the idea Andrew could make Marchione another good Italian baseball name.

Weedin recalls seeing Johnson's 1990 no-hitter, barely. He couldn't find anyone to go to the game with him until his wife suggested he bring her sister's fiancé. The future brothers-in-law went and saw Johnson work his magic, even if it wasn't the cleanest no-hitter in history. Johnson walked six.

"If I had not gone to that game, I'm not sure I could have lived with myself," Weedin said.

Those Mariners memories echo in the words of Dave Niehaus, the team's play-by-play announcer who died in 2010. His trademark calls included "My, oh my" and "Get out the rye bread and mustard, Grandma, it's grand salami time" after a Mariners grand slam.

"Dave Niehaus was—I get chills saying it—he was the best. He became an iconic figure in the Pacific Northwest," Weedin said. "He had a great way of calling a game so you could visualize it. He was a reason— probably the main reason—in the doldrums of a losing season people kept listening."

Rapper and Seattle native Macklemore pays tribute to Niehaus and the Mariners in his song "My Oh My." It's not the only pop culture reference to the team. A *Seinfeld* episode includes a scene in which Yankees owner George Steinbrenner (voice by Larry David) visits Frank and Estelle Costanza to deliver the erroneous news that their son George, a Yankees employee, has died. Jerry Stiller, playing George's father, is less concerned about the report of his son's death than he is at yelling at Steinbrenner for

trading Buhner to Seattle. ("What the hell did you trade Jay Buhner for?...
You don't know what the hell you're doing!")

It all adds up to devotion for a Mariners team that has done a lot
more losing than winning in recent years.

"You continue as a good fan to look toward the positives and hope
for the best," Wasserman said. "At some point you realize we're not the
'refuse to lose' team; we're just going to lose. Even that's OK because you
love the team and you love the game."

**John Marchione, mayor of Redmond, Washington, throws out the first pitch at
the city's new baseball/softball field at Grasslawn Park in 2008 (courtesy the City
of Redmond, Washington).**

Wasserman hopes all the hours he spent instilling a love of baseball in his children will pay off years from now: "I will expect them to wheel me into the games. That was my way of assuring I could still go."

Bean described Safeco Field as "my favorite place to be in the world. For me, I'm never not going to a game. If I have a free night and there's a game, I'm there."

"I guess it's like a bad habit," Marchione said on a January day. "Pitchers and catchers report in six weeks. The fact I know that shows what kind of habit it is."

New York State of Mind

The New York Knicks

When basketball devotees discuss their beloved sport's history, the conversation is bound to turn to New York. After all, it's the city that gave the world Kareem Abdul-Jabbar and Connie Hawkins, Chris Mullin and Nate "Tiny" Archibald. If you want to go back a generation, it has also produced Bob Cousy, Richie Guerin and Lenny Wilkens. Heck, even Carmelo Anthony, who grew up in Baltimore, and Michael Jordan, so closely associated with North Carolina, are New York City natives.

When it comes to basketball and New York, it's more than the great players the city has birthed. There are pickup games at Rucker Park and the hundreds of other asphalt courts in the city. It's the National Invitation Tournament back when it was *the* tournament. It's St. John's taking on the beasts of the Big East in Madison Square Garden.

Or as it's better known, The Garden, the place that has hosted politicians and Pope John Paul II; the spot where Joe Frazier handed Muhammad Ali his first professional boxing defeat in 1971; the building that has had its walls rocked by U2 and Springsteen and the Stones. It is best known, though, as one of basketball's historic arenas and the home for a professional team that has had spurts of greatness surrounded by years of mediocrity—and worse.

The New York Knicks. Clad in their white jerseys with the distinctive orange numbers and lettering and blue trim, they play before full houses that feature plenty of celebrity glitz. On any given night, the crowd probably will include Spike Lee and Woody Allen, but you also might spot Jon Stewart or Tracy Morgan or Kristin Chenoweth or Jerry Seinfeld.

"With the Knicks also comes Madison Square Garden," said Raul Aristud, a Queens resident and lifelong Knicks fan. "The energy is amazing when you're watching a game there. The energy is there no matter how bad the team is."

There have been times when the Knicks have been bad—the 17–65 disaster of 2014–15 comes to mind. But there have been plenty of highlights for the Knicks, one of the original teams in the old Basketball Association of America. After three seasons, the league merged in 1949 with the National Basketball League to form the National Basketball Association.

In their first season in the NBA, the Knicks lost in the Eastern Conference finals to the Syracuse Nationals. The next three years they got to the NBA Finals, losing once to the Rochester Royals and twice to the Minneapolis Lakers, a team in the midst of winning five titles in six years.

Those early Knicks teams had a balanced offense led by point guard Dick McGuire, a city native who was a star at St. John's, helping the school win the NIT in 1944. When McGuire died in 2010, the *New York Times* wrote: "His nickname was Tricky Dick, a nod to the blind feeds and needle-threading bounce passes that became his trademark. His philosophy was the epitome of old-school team basketball; he preferred passing to shooting."

McGuire and the rest of those early Knicks were coached by Joe Lapchick, who had been McGuire's coach at St. John's. Lapchick led the Knicks from 1947 to 1956, finishing with a record of 326–247.

From 1950 to 1957, the Knicks' roster included Nathaniel "Sweetwater" Clifton, a power forward and one of the first African-American players in the NBA. Clifton played decades before Karan Madhok was born. Still, the team's acquisition of Clifton struck a note with him. "It makes me very proud. It's awesome that even back then, the Knicks were doing the right thing. If I was around, I would have chosen them for my fandom in the 1950s, too," said Madhok, a writer who splits his time between Washington, D.C., and his native India.

The Knicks reached the playoffs several more times before they hit a serious skid in the 1960s, finishing with losing records for eight straight years. McGuire was the head coach in 1966–67 when the Knicks won 36 games, their most in the decade to that point, and made the playoffs, getting knocked out by the Boston Celtics in the first round. McGuire was replaced during the following season by Red Holzman, and it proved to be part of a turnaround for the franchise.

A key to the Knicks' uprising was the 1967 draft, in which they used the fifth pick to select Walt Frazier, a guard from Southern Illinois. The 1967–68 season also saw rookie forward Bill Bradley begin his NBA career in December, having delayed his entry into the league to study at the University of Oxford as a Rhodes scholar. Frazier and Bradley joined a solid core that included Willis Reed, a quality big man in his fourth season;

Cazzie Russell, a second-year player who provided scoring punch off the bench; and Dick Barnett, a veteran left-handed guard with an awkward-looking but effective jump shot.

Donald Scardino was a teenager at the time, living in Tuckahoe, New York, in Westchester County. He recalls going to Knicks games in the early 1960s, an era when the NBA was scrambling to attract fans. In those days, the Garden would sometimes host an NBA doubleheader with the Knicks' game as the featured event.

Scardino visited the Garden on November 16, 1962, when the Knicks hosted the San Francisco Warriors. One of his youthful thrills was getting to see the Warriors' star 7-foot-1 center, Wilt Chamberlain, in the lobby. What was even more impressive was Chamberlain's performance that night. He scored 73 points. "It seemed like every time you turned around, he was dunking," said Scardino, now an operations manager in wholesale distribution who lives in White Plains, New York.

After watching the Knicks struggle through most of the '60s, fans were happy to see the arrival of Frazier, Bradley and company. "Everybody was feeling like this team was starting to get better," Scardino said. "It was exciting to see them turn the corner."

The Knicks added another essential piece in December 1968, trading Walt Bellamy and Howie Komives to the Detroit Pistons for Dave DeBusschere, an all-star forward who early in his career had spent two seasons pitching in the majors with the Chicago White Sox.

With Holzman at the helm, the combination of flash, brawn and brains became a unit that meshed perfectly. In 1969–70, the Knicks won their first five games before losing to the Warriors on October 23. The Knicks then rattled off 18 straight wins, not losing again until November 28. It was a 23–1 start en route to a 60–22 season as the Knicks won the Eastern Division.

Reed led the team in scoring (21.7) and rebounding (13.9), but the Knicks' trademark was teamwork—sharing the ball and moving without it on offense while cracking down on defense.

The Knicks edged the Baltimore Bullets and cruised past the Milwaukee Bucks and rising star Abdul-Jabbar in the 1970 playoffs, setting up a championship matchup with the Los Angeles Lakers. It was a series with enough star power to make any network executive swoon. The Knicks offered the powerful Reed, the stylish and smooth Frazier and the erudite Bradley against the Lakers' trio of Jerry West, Chamberlain and Elgin Baylor.

The series lived up to its starry cast. After the teams split the first two games, the Knicks took a 102–100 lead with 3 seconds to go in Game 3 on DeBusschere's jumper. West then took the inbounds pass, dribbled three times and heaved a shot from 60 feet that hit nothing but net. Scardino's reaction to the West basket? "Horror, but it was a great shot, no doubt about it."

In the era before the three-point shot, West's basket only tied the game, and the Knicks won in overtime. The teams split the next two games, but Reed injured his leg in Game 5. Without Reed, the Knicks were dismantled in Game 6, 135–113, as the Lakers gained all the momentum, with Chamberlain (45) and West (33) combining for 78 points.

Donald Scardino attends a New York Knicks game against the Detroit Pistons at Madison Square Garden in March 2016. He's been following the Knicks since the 1960s (courtesy Donald Scardino).

Back in the Garden for Game 7, Reed hobbled onto the court with the other four Knicks starters, seizing back the momentum lost in Game 6. "The place erupted," Scardino said. "Then he hits his first two shots. You couldn't write a better script. It was tremendous."

Reed didn't score again, but Frazier took control from there, scoring 36 points and hitting all 12 of his foul shots. The Knicks won, 113–99, to capture their first NBA title.

For Scardino and other Knicks fans, that team still holds a special place in their hearts. "They knew each other's moves. They knew where to find each other on the court," Scardino said. "Everybody had a role. They all did it perfectly. To this day, I don't think I've seen a team play like that."

The Lakers got revenge in 1972, beating the Knicks, 4–1, to win the championship, and the two teams met again in 1973, the third time in four years they battled for the NBA title. Flashy guard Earl "The Pearl" Monroe, acquired in a 1971 trade, was now in the starting lineup with Bradley, Reed, Frazier and DeBusschere. Key bench players were Phil Jackson, an active forward who would later gain greater fame as a coach, and Jerry Lucas, an effective scoring threat.

This series lacked the drama of the 1970 showdown. The Lakers won Game 1 at home, 115–112, but the Knicks breezed to victory, sweeping the next four and winning the clinching Game 5 in Los Angeles, 102–93. Monroe led the offense with 23 points, and as often was the case with these Knicks teams, four other players scored in double figures.

Those championship teams, the only two in franchise history, have even caught the attention of younger fans such as Madhok. "Even though the championships came a dozen or so years before I was even born, I adore that team, both as an aesthetic product and a philosophical idea," he said.

The tone for those championship teams was set by Frazier. With a wardrobe that ranged from wide-brimmed hats to fur coats to loud, double-breasted suits, he was nicknamed "Clyde" because his style and cool evoked Warren Beatty from the 1967 film *Bonnie and Clyde* about real-life criminals Bonnie Parker and Clyde Barrow. As cool as his sense of style was, it was Frazier's calm demeanor on the court that captured fans. He was a floor leader for the offense and a disruptive force on defense, often knocking a ball away from the dribbler and bursting ahead for a breakaway layup.

"Walt Frazier is still my favorite Knick ever based on grainy highlights from the '70s alone," Madhok said.

Frazier remains a lasting presence, handling color commentary on the MSG Network broadcasts of Knicks games.

"Clyde is a huge personality in New York," said Aristud, who works in software development. "He will always talk about how he played with the team. It's definitely insightful. You get a real feel for how that team played."

The team that worked so well together—and that championship era—didn't last much longer. DeBusschere and Reed retired a year after the second title. Bradley played through 1977. The official end of the glory days came in October 1977, when Frazier was dealt to Cleveland, giving Knicks fans the traumatic image of their one-time backcourt leader finishing his career in a Cavaliers uniform. Two years later came the shocking words in the newspaper's transactions list: Frazier had been waived by the Cavaliers.

By 1978–79, the Knicks had fallen to 31–51. A new era of flash began in 1982 after the Knicks traded with the Warriors for Bernard King, a Brooklyn native who was a high-scoring, all-star forward. King was a showman, scoring 60 points against the New Jersey Nets in a 1984 Christmas Day game. In the 1984 playoffs, he averaged 42.6 points per game as the Knicks beat the Detroit Pistons in five games. In the next round, he had games of 43 and 44 points, but the Knicks fell to the Boston Celtics.

"Every time he touched the ball, you thought no one could stop him," Scardino said. "You thought maybe he could get us there [to a championship]. Obviously, that never happened."

It was symbolic of how the 1980s went for the Knicks—some flashes of brilliance but no sustained glory to recapture the magic of the early 1970s. There was a moment of joy in the middle of the decade, though. The Knicks finished 24–58 in the 1984–85 season and were fortunate to win the draft lottery, giving them the top pick in the draft. Sitting there waiting for them was Patrick Ewing, a 7-foot center who had led the Georgetown Hoyas to the NCAA national championship the previous year.

"Everybody is like, 'That's it.' We thought, 'Here come the titles,'" Scardino said.

Ewing's arrival didn't pay immediate dividends as the Knicks struggled through his first few seasons. But by 1989 they finished 52–30 and became a regular presence in the postseason.

The Knicks got to the Eastern Conference finals in 1993 against the two-time defending champion Chicago Bulls. After the Knicks won the first two games in New York and lost the next two in Chicago, Game 5 in the Garden came down to the final seconds. The Bulls led, 95–94, when Ewing passed to Charles Smith near the basket. Smith went up four times. Each time the Bulls knocked the ball away or blocked the shot.

"You're watching that and you say, 'He's going to make one of those.' Was he fouled? Who knows? The refs aren't going to call fouls at that point," Scardino said.

It was a crushing loss for the Knicks, who could have gained control of the series with a win. Instead, they went to Chicago and lost Game 6, 96–88. Ewing scored 25.8 points per game, but Jordan was the series star, averaging 32.2 points for the Bulls, who would go on to win their third straight title.

In the next season, Ewing averaged 24.5 points and 11.2 rebounds per game to lead the Knicks back to the NBA Finals for the first time in 21 years. He got scoring help from guard John Starks (19 points per game) and rebounding assistance from rugged Charles Oakley (11.8 per game).

The Knicks met the Houston Rockets to create a matchup of two of the league's best big men, Ewing and the Rockets' Hakeem Olajuwon. The series had a couple of odd twists. The national broadcast of Game 5 was interrupted as networks switched to coverage of Los Angeles police chasing O.J. Simpson in a white Bronco.

In Game 7, Starks, who had been an offensive force all season, lost all sense of a shooting touch, going 2 for 18. It was the main factor in a sluggish Knicks offense that led to a 90–84 defeat. Ewing had a solid series, but Olajuwon was named the series' most valuable player for his spectacular all-around play, averaging 26.9 points, 9.1 rebounds, 3.6 assists, 3.9 blocks and 1.6 steals.

For the next four years, the Knicks got knocked out of the playoffs in the Eastern Conference semifinals, including a 1995 series against the Indiana Pacers that ended with Ewing missing a contested, game-tying layup at the buzzer. It was a symbolic play for the Knicks of the '90s—so close but never able to make the one big play; never able to get the one crucial playoff win.

In 1999, the Knicks squeaked into the playoffs as the eighth-seeded team in the East. Ewing was still around, leading the team in scoring (17.3) with major help from Latrell Sprewell (16.4) and Allan Houston (16.3).

A 14-year-old in India at the time, Madhok started following the NBA during this season. He had noticed the sport a few years earlier, thanks to the movies. "I loved 'Space Jam' with [Michael] Jordan, which made basketball and the NBA even more likable." But now friends at school were talking basketball, and they introduced him to trading cards and

SLAM magazine. He also was watching the occasional live broadcasts of NBA games in India.

The Knicks met the top-seeded Miami Heat in the first round. In the defensive slugfest that was the decisive Game 5, the Knicks trailed, 77–76, with four seconds left. Houston took the inbounds pass and drove to the right side of the foul line. He launched a running jump shot that bounced off the front rim, hit the backboard and went in. The Knicks were just the second eighth-seeded team in league history to win a playoff series.

The Knicks then swept the Atlanta Hawks and beat the Pacers to return to the Finals against the San Antonio Spurs. All of this hooked Madhok. "I loved that they were a gritty, fearless side that was able to upset several bigger teams on their way to the Finals. I remember emulating Allan Houston's baseline turnaround fadeaways."

The Spurs had the twin towers of Tim Duncan and David Robinson, who combined to average 44 points and almost 26 rebounds a game in the series. It proved too much for the Knicks, who played without an injured Ewing and fell, 4–1.

"It was mostly a disappointment," Madhok said. "The Duncan-Robinson Spurs were better in every way, and I knew I had become a Knicks fan so quickly because of how sad I felt after the Knicks lost that series."

Ewing played one more season in New York before finishing his career with a year each in Seattle and Orlando. "I loved Ewing," Aristud said. "It was sad to not see him get a ring."

After Ewing's departure, the Knicks missed the playoffs eight of nine seasons from 2001 to 2010. "I had to suffer daily mocking from my friends," Madhok said. "The team was a laughingstock, and their goof-ups had become predictably awful. I truly felt following a team like that was self-torture, but I managed to take it in stride and stay loyal."

A three-team trade in February 2011 that brought Carmelo Anthony to New York from the Denver Nuggets helped alter the fortunes of the Knicks, who made the playoffs three years in a row.

The 2011–12 season included a burst of energy from a second-year guard from Harvard, Jeremy Lin, who was a rarity in the NBA—a player of Chinese and Taiwanese descent. For weeks, he ignited the Knicks' offense, hitting game-winning shots and capturing a ton of attention. Everyone was talking about "Lin-sanity."

"He was everything we hadn't seen before. New Yorkers love that stuff," Aristud said.

Growing up in India, Karan Madhok became a fan of the New York Knicks during the 1999 playoffs (photograph by Nina Diaz).

Even though those three straight playoff appearances were followed by losing seasons, including the horrid 17–65 record in 2014–15, Aristud was happy about the return of Anthony, a fellow New York City native. "You have to love those players," he said. "They show a lot of heart. They want to be here."

For Aristud, his love of the Knicks includes the joy of watching players such as Anthony and getting to see games in the Garden. But he also appreciates the Knicks' front office and its charitable work and community involvement. "That's one of the reasons I'll always be a die-hard fan," he said.

Madhok finds similar joy, even in the down times: "I just always believed that it was cowardly to jump bandwagons based on convenience or form. Once you choose a team, they are your team forever, good or bad. It becomes a part of your identity and your own life story. The bad times suck, but they make the good times, like Lin-sanity, so much more special."

Very Superstitious

Fans Do All They Can

OK, it's the bottom of the ninth and your team is down by a run. Or the clock shows 14 seconds left and your squad has the puck/ball with a chance to tie.

What the heck is a fan supposed to do? Dig out the most reliable ritual you have to bring your team luck, that's what.

Many sports fans, while reasonably sane in other walks of life, will turn to their own concoction of voodoo, magic, superstition and tradition to help their favorite team garner a big victory.

When cheering on his San Diego Padres, Barry Benintende takes his hat off during the seventh-inning stretch and places it on the cup holder near his seat.

"If I don't do that, I'm convinced not only will we lose, but the earth will open up and swallow me whole." There's plenty more to his game-day superstitions. He and his daughter once took the San Diego trolley's orange line to a Padres game. They arrived late, and the Padres lost that day, 9–0. Since then, the green line is the only one they take to games.

He also won't tie his shoes on game days. So, the night before heading to the ballpark, he takes his shoes off while still tied and then slips into them on the day of the game.

"I know superstitions don't have any effect, but what if they do?" he said.

Mike Dmowski, Jr., and his fellow Buffalo Bills–loving pals pack into a camper to travel to Bills home games. The crew starts the season with a time-honored ceremony.

"As soon as we set up, I hold a camper prayer," Dmowski said. "We go to the back of the trailer, everyone with a beer and a shot, and I say a few words to bring optimism to the season."

The beverages are consumed, but a beer and a shot are left on the trailer hitch. "In essence, it's the trailer's, because it is part of our crew," Dmowski said.

Jeremy Reisman will maintain a Sunday routine if it leads his Detroit Lions to victory.

"I'll listen to the Beatles on Sunday morning one week," he said. "If the Lions win that game, I'll do the same next Sunday. If not, onto the next artist. Same thing with breakfast choices."

Fashion, of course, is a key part of game-day rituals. Fans wear the same jersey or pair of socks—sometimes unwashed—to keep a winning streak going.

New York Knicks fan Karan Madhok takes the appearance thing a step further: "Whenever the Knicks make the playoffs, I grow a playoff beard for as long as they are able to survive. My facial hair grows relatively quickly—gift/curse of being Indian—but those beards haven't had too many weeks of growing in recent years because of the Knicks' playoff shortcomings."

When the Milwaukee Brewers are playing, Butch Foeckler has a list of rituals to maintain. "When the Brewers are on a roll, I won't leave my spot to eat or use the bathroom. If the opposing team starts to rally, I'll do just the opposite. If things get way out of hand, I'll give my wife the remote and go for a walk. I've also tried turning the TV off and putting the radio on to try to change the momentum of the game. As you know, sometimes we just have to grin and bear it."

For Jennifer Rogers, there's a list to be checked off before every Toronto Maple Leafs or Toronto Blue Jays game.

1. Dogs must have hockey or baseball jerseys on;
2. 12-foot homemade flag needs to be put into the garden;
3. Hockey/baseball light on the front porch has to be turned on;
4. Must be wearing team colors.

Dave King has made the switch from fan of the Phoenix Suns to someone who covers the team for the website www.brightsideofthesun.com.

"I used to get so nervous and high-strung watching games that my hands would be clammy and my stomach would be growling at the end of the game. And there was little sleep after a loss," he said.

"It got to the point I had to DVR the games and watch it 30 minutes behind, while keeping up with the live score on my phone, so I always knew what was coming. Awful way to watch, but the only way to get a good night's sleep.

"That all changed when I started covering games as a media member. It's a lot easier to turn off the emotions on press row and watch and report on the game from a detached, objective point of view. Being in media, expected to be professional and objective, has really helped add years to my life."

King also mentioned another ritual from his past: "My daughter once made a Build-A-Bear with a Suns uniform. I used to put it out on the couch during games for good luck. I stopped doing that when I joined the media. Since then the Suns haven't made the playoffs. Hmmm."

For years, Lance Verderame and his son, Matt, would watch Kansas City Chiefs games with their mixed-breed dog, Black Jack. "When we'd get excited, he'd get excited," Lance said. After Black Jack died, they would bring out the dog's picture and set it in the room before kickoff.

"It was as much for fun as for superstition," Lance said.

Buffalo Bills fan Bill Rotach turns to his Bills voodoo doll when times are tough. "I hold it and aim it at the TV when the other team is about to score or kick a field goal and throw curses at them."

Vicki Kremer, a longtime season-ticket holder for the Atlanta Hawks, didn't have any superstitions before 2014–15. In that season, she and a friend went into a game late, and the Hawks won.

It turned into a marvelous season, with the Hawks winning 60 games. Kremer wasn't messing with fate. She kept going into the arena after the game started. "We'd be there an hour early, but we'd purposely go in late," she said.

She also wore a pair of "lucky" Hawks socks to a couple of games. The Hawks lost both times. "I threw them away," she said.

Al Yellon is a man of ritual when it comes to his Chicago Cubs. "I buy a drink at the 7–11 at a specific time. I walk to my seat in a specific way, always put my stuff down in the same place."

So, does any of this work for these fans?

"Of course it's all nonsense, but when you go through so much suffering, you have to try to do something to make it stop—other than stop watching football, of course," Reisman said.

There's some sanity to this madness, though, according to Dr. Eric A. Zillmer, a neuropsychology professor and athletic director at Drexel University who has written extensively about sports psychology.

"The high-identity sports fans—the guys who wear a jersey and put cream on their face—they actually feel they have some control over the outcome," Zillmer said.

Some fans internalize the failure. When a player on their team strikes out, it is as if the fan has struck out. Fans may know this behavior makes little sense, but it's hard to stop.

"They are very invested in their beliefs—as irrational as they are—but that's part of sports," Zillmer said.

He recently traveled to Olympia in Greece, site of the original Olympics. The rituals we attach to sports date back to those early days. Part of the aura of the early Olympics was to honor the gods by celebrating youth and strength, Zillmer said.

Those traditions live on in the rituals of today. A game doesn't start until the national anthem is played and the players are introduced to the crowd. Zillmer said the structure of a game, right down to halftime or the seventh-inning stretch, can be like church, just without the group prayers, although more than a few fans have been known to ask for help in the ninth inning of a tight game.

"We want the structure. It gives us a sense of peace," Zillmer said.

While many fans are wildly superstitious, others dismiss it as malarkey. Well, then again, they aren't entirely dismissive.

Andrew Feinstein said he has no superstitions he turns to while rooting during the season for his Denver Nuggets. But when the day of the NBA draft arrives, "I will wear my lucky Nuggets socks, which are not very lucky," he said.

Jason Walker, an Atlanta Hawks supporter, said, "When you're bad that long, whatever you were trying wasn't working. It's neurotic enough to root for a team that hasn't won a championship. To assign blame to yourself? Get out the straitjacket."

Another Denver Nuggets fan, Kevin Thurston, said he grew up with a friend who was "insanely superstitious. I grew up seeing a lot of those things not working. I'm a little too scientifically inclined to believe in superstition."

But, he added, "At the same time, I catch myself yelling at the TV."

Index

Numbers in *bold italics* refer to pages with photographs.